DISCOVERING
ARABIAN
DECO

"Within the beginning of the discovery of oil, there was an extensive transformation of the city and the built environment. Buildings in the International Style, which was prevailing at that time, were mostly dominant. However, during my research and exploration around the country, I came to notice a unique style of architecture very much influenced by the Deco movement, and because it also had elements of the region, I called it 'Arabian Deco,' a very unique style that I hope will be documented and become part of our early modern history in architecture."

Ibrahim Mohamed Jaidah

IBRAHIM MOHAMED JAIDAH
DISCOVERING ARABIAN DECO
EARLY MODERN ARCHITECTURE IN QATAR

RIZZOLI
NEW YORK

New York · Paris · London · Milan

I would like to dedicate this book

*To our rulers, who upon the discovery of oil placed
education, health, and infrastructure as a priority
for the people's well-being, which is a legacy that
continues.*

*To our early merchants, who participated in building
the early modern Qatar.*

*To the current and future generations of locals,
who are tasked with the custodianship and further
exploration of our history and heritage.*

To my dear Mother, who continues to help me dream.

To the great team, who helped put this book together.

The first oil shipment from Qatar in the mid-twentieth century marked the beginning of a big change in the history of urban development in Doha. The steady increase in oil revenues had a great economic impact, which contributed to changing the architectural and urban history of the city from pre-oil to post-oil. This new source of wealth resulted in a significant growth in all aspects of the city, including increase in population, economy, trade, urban development, services, and establishing a new government. This growth and change reshaped the city of Doha through three decades (1950–1980) with continuous effort, development, and planning. The city still has some of the buildings with architectural features that tell the story of each decade. Some of these buildings are in their original state; sadly, others were demolished for new development, and thankfully a number of them were preserved or renovated.

I was from that generation who had the privilege to witness the transformation of the city and the development boom. I still remember the noise of construction around our house in Al Jasrah, where I spent my childhood in the 1960s and 1970s. The construction sites attracted my curiosity with the new materials and tools to a point that they started to become my playground. I was amazed by the vast changes taking place all over the city and everything newly constructed became a landmark to me. My interest in architecture grew with time, and with it came the passion for photography, where I photographed many buildings in Doha. Experiencing the gradual change gave me insight into the urban and architectural features for each decade. All of this inspired me to appreciate the uniqueness of the past and present and to become an architect. I acquired AEB, which is the first local consultancy in Qatar, to continue my passion in architecture. The AEB project archive and my personal photo collection are present in these pages.

This book takes the reader on an architectural journey through three decades of urban development from the time of the oil discovery. It unlocks the hidden architectural changes in each decade, from urban transition in the 1950s, urban necessity in the 1960s, and urban modernity in the 1970s. Each decade went through different political, economic, and social events that contributed to shaping the city's expansion, urban form, and architecture. It also unveils an important architectural movement that appeared in the 1960s, the Arabian Deco, which became a signature architectural style in Qatar at that time. This book should serve as a reference for students, researchers, and practitioners interested in the architecture and history of the city. The most iconic buildings in the development of the city are portrayed with commentary provoking nostalgia in the older readers and wonder in the younger generation, as many of these buildings have been demolished.

Ibrahim Mohamed Jaidah

Author
Ibrahim Mohamed Jaidah
  Group CEO and Chief Architect
  Arab Engineering Bureau

Editor, Key Researcher & Content Management
  Dr. Haitham Al Abri

Research Assistance
  Nada H. Fouad

Book Coordinator
  Amina Niksic

Graphic Design, Visuals, Maps and Drawings Reproduction
  Nada Luai Abbara
  Abderazak Chouiki
  Jade Fontanilla Hilario
  Yasmin Shaikhi
  Mah E Kamil Faisal
  Youssef Aly
  Aysha Nawrin

Sketches
  Macario Cammanong

3D Building Modeling
  Ahmad Fairuz Hod

Photographs
  Ibrahim Mohamed Jaidah Private Collection
  Abdullatif Mohamed Jaidah
  Bouthayna Al-Muftah

Projects
  AEB Archive

Agencies Photo Credits
pp. 26–27 © Pankaj & Insy Shah / Getty Images
pp. 18–19, 30–31 © ac productions / Blend Images LLC / Getty Images
pp. 58–59, 108–09 © Alexey Sergeev
p. 99 © M. Torres / Travel-Images.com / Getty Images

TABLE OF CONTENTS

CHAPTER

The pre-oil period represents the foundation of how the city of Doha emerged and, over time, grew to become the core of its development today.

PRE-OIL ARCHITECTURE

Introduction

The publication of *The History of Qatari Architecture 1800–1950* in 2009 was the first attempt by the author to shed light on vernacular architecture (pre-oil architecture) in Qatar. The book introduced the essence of Qatari architecture and the urban development of its cities. It also showcased some building typologies that referred to the pre-1950s (pre-oil period). This was followed by a detailed documentation of selected building typologies with emphasis on their architectural characteristics and significance. The book is considered a key source to unlock the door to the pre-oil architectural period.

The early modern architecture resulted from continuous growth and redevelopment from the pre-oil to the post-oil periods. The pre-oil period represents the foundation of how the city of Doha emerged and, over time, grew to become the core of its development today. Many internal and external factors will be discussed in the following pages reflecting their impact on the city's architecture and urban fabric. The impact has led the city on a morphological journey from formation to transformation, to transition, and to development. The best way to understand the architecture of the pre-oil period in the Doha area is to start from the early pearling settlements.

Early Settlements

The harsh climate and scarce resources of fresh underground water resulted in limited if not rare agricultural fields, which pushed the people toward depending on the sea for their livelihood. This resulted in the spread of human settlements in Qatar along the coastline. The central location of Qatar as a peninsula facing the Arabian Gulf, generated the opportunity for these coastline settlements to become centers for maritime activities such as pearling and trade. Other economic activities like herding and farming were present, but pearling was the main source of wealth. Pearling was a seasonal practice where some nomadic tribes would come from inland during this season to carry out pearling and trade, and to pasture their flocks.

The history of Qatari settlements is ambiguous, but it seems that pearling settlements had existed on the coastline at least since the beginning of the eighteenth century. However, the archaeological excavation by Peterson in 2010 in North Qatar indicates that the Al Ruwaida settlement dates back to as early as the sixteenth century. According to Ottoman documents, there were two settlements in the northern part of Qatar at Furaiha, in the late seventeenth century. Carsten Niebuhr mentioned five pearling settlements in his map in 1765. These settlements are: "Gattar," "Adsjär," "Huäle" (Huwailah), "Iusofie" (Ras Yusufiyya) and "Faräha" (Furaiha). To avoid any misunderstanding between the peninsula and the settlement name, "Gattar" probably refers to Al Bida' (Doha). There is some debate about Niebuhr's "Iusofie" (Ras Yusufiyya), where Colebrooke described it as being deserted in 1820, while Lorimer mentioned that it was only abandoned in 1766 after its inhabitants moved to Zubara.

The arrival of the British navy surveyors in the 1820s added more names to the coastal settlements such as Zobara (Zubarah), Khoor Hassam (Khor Hassan), Limel (Jumail), Foreihel (Furaiha), Ul Yusvee (Al Yusufiyya, deserted), Phoerol (Fuwairit, deserted), Howeleh (Huwailah), and Guttur, or Ul Buddee (Doha). In 1829, Brucks added to these Wakra, Al Khor, Ruwais, Jumail, and Rubaiya. It was not possible to estimate the size and population of these settlements at that time until Lorimer's *Gazetteer* in 1908. Brucks asserted that the population in Doha was 400 men (with a family size of five this would have been 2,000 people), increasing to 1,200 men during the pearling season.

← Early pearling settlements 1700–1820.

THE SPREAD OF PEARLING SETTLEMENTS 1700 - 1820

KEY
● Towns/Pearling centers in 1700
● Towns/Pearling centers in 1820
1 Zubara
2 Furaihah
3 Khor Hassan
4 Ruwaidah
5 Yusufiyyah
6 Jumail
7 Fuwairit
8 Huwailah
9 Bida'/Doha

The eighteenth century witnessed the dawn and increase of settlement formations that spread along the coastline of the Qatar Peninsula. Several factors contributed to the creation of these settlements during the eighteenth century until the beginning of the nineteenth century. These factors include (a) settled and migrant tribes, (b) the pearling trade, and (c) constant tribal disputes. Examples of these pearling settlements are Al Zubarah, Al Huwailah, Fuwairit and Al Bida'. These resulted in the spread of settlements and later to migratory movements within the peninsula to the southeast that culminated in the creation of new settlements such as Al Bida' (the original site of Doha) and Al Wakra (Al Jaber, 1977).

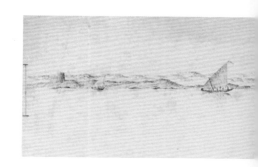

Beginning of Doha

The description, based on maps, cartographers', mariners', and diplomats' reports, indicates that Doha's existence is referred to in the early nineteenth century. The first and oldest settlement to be mentioned was Al Bida', as described by the British sea captain David Seton in 1802. Al Bida', a coastal neighborhood well within the confines of modern Doha, was its commercial rival in 1862. The English explorer William Gifford Palgrave spent several weeks in Qatar's coastal settlements, providing detailed descriptions of urban form and social construction. According to him, it was the sea not the desert that oriented village life in "Bedaa'." As far as architecture was concerned:

↓ Original map of Al Bida' on the left and Doha on the right in 1823, by Lieutenants J. M. Guy and G. B. Brucks.
The map shows the Bida' fort (later the Amiri Diwan) in the center of Bida'.

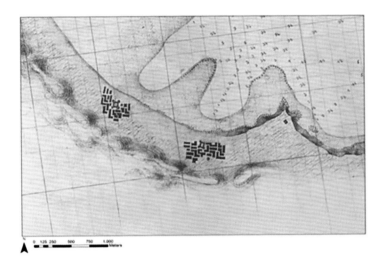

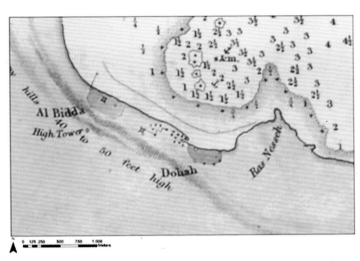

↗ Original map of Al Bida' on the left and Doha on the right in 1860, by Constable and Stiffe in 1862, *Inset Bidd'a Harbor*.
The map shows the Bida' settlements walled with the fort (Amiri Diwan) in the center.

↘ Original sketch drawn from the sea of the two settlements of Al Bida' on the right and Doha on the left in 1823, by Lieutenants J. M. Guy and G. B. Brucks. It shows Al Bida' structurally dominated by the fort (Amiri Diwan) in the center.

Little care is taken to ornament their land houses, the abodes of their wives and children at most, and the unsightly strong boxes of their gathered treasures.

(Palgrave 1866, 230)

By 1823, Doha had been founded about one and a half kilometers east of Al Bida', where both appeared as separate settlements, as shown on a map by Lieutenant Guy and Lieutenant Brucks for the East India Company in that same year. Later a spread of habitation named "Doheh Seghireh" or later "Duwayḥa" (Little Doha) appeared between Al Bida' and Doha on a map by Constable and Stiffe in 1860. The map shows both settlements of Al Bida' and Doha fortified

View from the Anchorage

with walls and concentrations of buildings around two forts, presumably the fort in Al Bida' and the original fort in Doha. According to Lorimer in 1908, from the end of the nineteenth century to the early twentieth century growth had been witnessed in the settlements, resulting in them becoming one single, large town collectively known as Doha.

A few hundred meters to the north of the coastline, Palgrave describes the settlement of Doha:

> Dowhah, a village to the north of Bedaa', and of about half its size—is situated—in a small deep bay, where the cliffs behind—give it a somewhat picturesque appearance. But the houses of Dowhah are even lower or meaner than at Bedaa', and the market-place is narrower and dirtier. Two castles overtop the place: one stands on the neighbouring cliff, the other within the town itself.
>
> (Palgrave 1866, 237)

The beauty of the architecture of Al Bida' and Doha, on the

A decade later, the French merchant, seaman, and consular agent Hyacinthe Chapuis gives a far more sanguine description of life in the Doha settlement:

> The bank of the Gulf swarms with people. Fishermen unload their catches. It is truly beautiful—People bustle about—chat—squabble but laugh a lot—I walk quickly through the side streets; I pass two partially covered markets—Veiled women slip away before my eyes; merely dark silhouettes—Some of them carry water drawn from the town's only water well on their head—The townspeople are not rich, but they seem happy.
>
> The city, hardly vast, is cut off from the outside world. Its population is estimated at approximately 10,000 inhabitants—Houses made of coral stone and brick adorned in *moucharabieh* [*mashrabiya*], but also modest houses made of dried mud and huts constructed from palm tree branches. These huts, that can have two levels, are very common. Several mosques: their tiny minarets have a simple construction, but elegance does not escape them. Very few trees. Massive dryness. It is the city of the famous Sheikh of Katar, Sheikh Yassim ben Mohammed be Thani [Jassim bin Mohammed Al-Thani], son of the late Sheikh Mohammed ben Thani]. My goal is to meet this prince who, it seems, has an excellent reputation.
>
> (quoted in Beguin-Billecocq 2003, 98)

In Palgrave's nineteenth-century description, every settlement had its own "collector-in-chief" who collected revenues and settled disputes. He describes the form–function relationship between a typical village and political instability:

> The villages of Katar are each and all carefully walled in, while the towns beyond
> are lined with towers, and here and there a castle 'huge and square'—these cas-
> tles are in reality by no means superfluous, for Katar has wealth in plenty, and
> there are robbers against whom that wealth must be guarded.
>
> (Palgrave 1866, 231–34)

The name of Doha or Ad Doha means a circular shape, which refers to the shape of the bay that lies to the east of the city. The local inhabitants used to call Doha 'Dohat Qatar' mainly to distinguish this settlement from other parts of the peninsula that apparently had the same name (Al-Kuwari, 1987). In ad-dition, other meanings for the word Doha do exist in Arabic. For example, the name refers to a big tree or a big house (Al-Kuwari, 1994).

edge of the bay, was described by many travelers and tradesmen

There are several factors, which may have contributed to the creation of Doha. Among these, the geopolitical standpoint may represent an important factor. Doha's favorable location away from the continuous source of conflicts on one hand, and territorial land claims on the other hand. Such a location at the midpoint of the eastern coast puts it in easy reach of other settlements in the country.

Furthermore, its deep water was an important factor in its early development as a major port settlement characterized by thriving fishing and pearl diving activities of which pearling was the most significant trading commodity. Also, the circular shape of Doha Bay made it a haven for the fishing and pearling ves-sels taking refuge from the gusty north wind. Finally, the availability of nearby water wells and relatively fertile soil made it a prime location for a permanent settlement (Al-Kuwari, 1987; Al-Kuwari, 1992; Al Jaber, 1977).

In 1918, a French artist and naval officer gave a colorful description of Do-ha's humble origins:

> From the sea, Doha provides an amazing panorama of ochre-colored sculpture.
> A caramel-colored city with its houses cloaked in bronze sand, in tawny stone,
> and in copper adobe. In the harbor, a patched-up sail whips against a heavily
> loaded Arab sailboat, or dhow—

← The route of the natural-outlet water channels through Doha from inland to the seashore.

On land—I push my way through the labyrinth of this strange, chocolate-colored, austere city's tiny back streets. A marked simplicity adorns these houses resembling clothes trunks. They have only one level—A few rare white houses, two stories high—belong to noted figures of the Moresque city—The architecture is laced with latticework, arches, and towers—Several mosques aim their small minarets at the sky, displaying the marks of Islam: the crescent moon encircling a star. Here and there, a bunch of scraggly palm trees and spiny bushes with stunted little branches can be seen.

(Charles Dominique Fouqueray, in Beguin-Billecocq 2003, 151–52)

Landform

Doha is located along the lowlands on the eastern coastline of Qatar, where three to four major *wadis* (streambeds) flow into the Doha Bay. It is also clear that Doha experienced higher rainfall in the past than it does at present, which resulted in repeated floods in urbanized lowlands. The extent of the *wadis* can be traced all the way to higher land in the hinterlands.

Aerial photographs show the *wadi* route from the hinterland and discharging water through the *souq* (marketplace) during the winter rainfall season; they also show the main access route through the *souq* to Doha Bay. Historically, it was a common practice that *wadi* channels were used as routes or passages in settlements all around the world. The only disadvantages, however, were the challenges for those using the route during the rainy season. This resulted in Doha suffering from significant flooding during winter rains.

The main natural drainage channel for winter rainwater falling to the south of Doha is known as Wadi al-Sail, which can be identified on aerial photos. Wadi al-Sail flows through the center of Doha and can be seen as a white line through the *souq*. There was a dam close to the intersection of Wadi al-Sail and the Salwa road to control the stream of water that flowed periodically through the *souq* toward its outlet into the Doha Bay. The dam sometimes protected the *souq* from floods, but water still filled parts of the road during heavy winter rains that transcended the capacity of Doha's drainage system. This created a very muddy road that certainly reduced the *souq's* livability for many people during these periods.

Economy

The livelihood of the people in Qatar during the pre-oil time depended on three main economic activities: pasturing and herding, limited cultivation, and sea activities. The most prosperous for them was always linked to the sea, with pearling, fishing, and trading for commodities being the main sources of wealth. During the pearling season, from May to August, the merchants provided the opportunity for part-time diving and fishing jobs for the nomads that came from inland. The proximity of the *souq* to the coastline gave them the benefit of being able to trade and sell their animals and local products

→ Pearl divers working on a boat during the pearling season.

in the market. These local products included the sale of fertilizer and cloth made from goat's hair, as well as camel and horse breeding. The relationship between the merchants in the city and the seasonal visiting nomads was always of an investment nature on the merchant's side, where they provided the necessary capital (advanced payments) for pearl divers as a form of mutual investment. Investors would then take a large share of the pearls and sell them to middlemen or directly sell them in India. This economic reciprocal structure prevailed until the collapse of the pearling industry in the 1930s. After the pearling season ended, the nomads migrated to other settlements for trade or would travel back to the inlands and continue earning their livelihood with pasturing, herding, and cultivation.

Building Materials

The inherited construction knowledge and the availability of local materials and natural resources contributed to the growth and development of the pre-oil settlements in Doha. The traditional Qatari houses were built out of local, available, and inexpensive materials using traditional methods passed down through generations. The construction of a new dwelling started by appointing a master builder (*al banaa* or *tendail*). The construction would proceed with the *al banaa* giving instructions to the builders, who were mostly from the family or local community. The construction utilized local materials and often reused more valuable materials, such as wooden beams, windows, doorframes, and doors from older buildings. The walls of traditional buildings were constructed from locally sourced limestone. This stone was quarried near the outskirts of the settlement in order to keep up with the increased demand for building materials as the settlement expanded.

↑ Building ruins that show the traditional construction material used in Qatar.

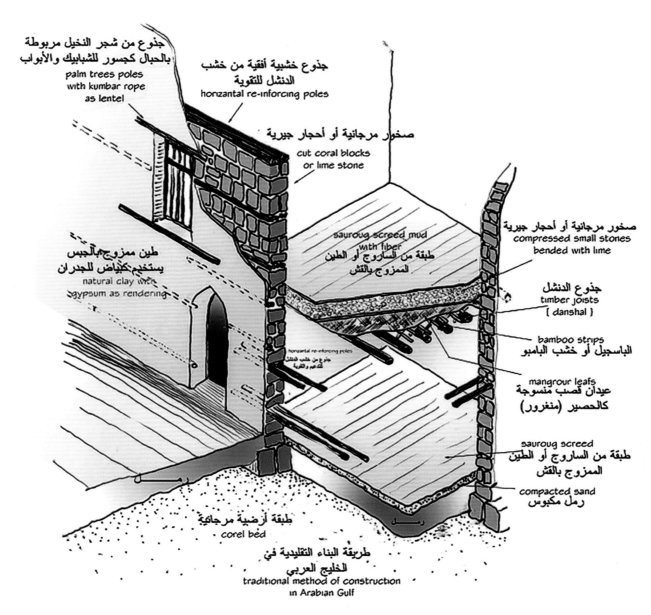

جذوع من شجر النخيل مربوطة
بالحبال كجسور للشبابيك والأبواب
palm trees poles
with kumbar rope
as lentel

جذوع خشبية أفقية من خشب
الدنشل للتقوية
honzantal re-inforcing poles

صخور مرجانية أو أحجار جيرية
cut coral blocks
or lime stone

طين ممزوج بالجبس
يستخدم كبياض للجدران
natural clay with
gypsum as rendering

sauroug screed mud
with fiber
طبقة من الساروج أو الطين
الممزوج بالقش

صخور مرجانية أو أحجار جيرية
compressed small stones
bended with lime

جذوع الدنشل
timber joists
(danshal)

bamboo strips
الباسجيل أو خشب البامبو

mangrour leafs
عيدان قصب منسوجة
كالحصير (منغرور)

sauroug screed
طبقة من الساروج أو الطين
الممزوج بالقش

compacted sand
رمل مكبوس

رمل

طبقة أرضية مرجانية
corel bed

طريقة البناء التقليدية في
الخليج العربي
traditional method of construction
in Arabian Gulf

↗ Sectional perspective showing the different layers of construction materials reflecting the traditional construction method.

Unbaked mudbrick was also used by builders to construct the walls in traditional buildings. The clay for the mudbrick mixture was sourced from the ground depression areas where it combined with rainwater. The mudbrick was made from a mixture of mud and straw and was known as *libn*. The wall thickness ranged between 0.40 meter and 0.60 meter and was formed by two parallel rows of larger facing stones and a packed core of mud, gravel, and smaller stones. Walls were plastered with a layer of locally mixed, clay-rich mud or gypsum-based render, which was expensive and less common. The rainwater on the roof was drained through wooden waterspouts that required constant maintenance. Several types of plaster (*juss*) were used as wall render, where masons normally applied three layers of plaster. The first contained mud used to even out the wall, the second consisted of gypsum and created a smooth finish, the third created a fine decorative finish and contained lime or gypsum.

The lintels of the doors and windows as well as the lintels of the colonnaded veranda (*liwan*) were built using mangrove poles bound with jute rope. Geometric designs decorated the upper corners of the colonnade. The roofs were built using rafters of mangrove beams (*danshal*) laid directly on top of the walls and which commonly protruded beyond the exterior walls on either side. The *danshal* beams were imported from East Africa and had a length that dictated the dimensions of the rooms of the house—usually 2.5 m to 3 m. The beams were overlaid with a layer of split bamboo, woven reed, and a palm mat (*manghrour*). The top layer of the roof was made waterproof with the addition of several layers of well-tamped-down earth.

Urban Growth

The growth of the early al Bida' (Doha) settlement depended on the natural setting and geographical features. Doha was formed along the lowland side of the east coast where several *wadis* flow through the city to the bay. Historical records indicate that Doha experienced heavy rainfall during the

↓ A map sketch of Qatar drawn in detail in 1937 (left) and enlarged part of the map (right) with "Al Doha" underlined in blue crayon and "DOHAH" added in a later hand with coordinates inserted in pencil and an annotation:
"All these villages now form the town of Dohah the capital of QATAR."
This is the first map that mentions Qal'at Al Askar within Doha, which indicates the significance of the fort at that time.

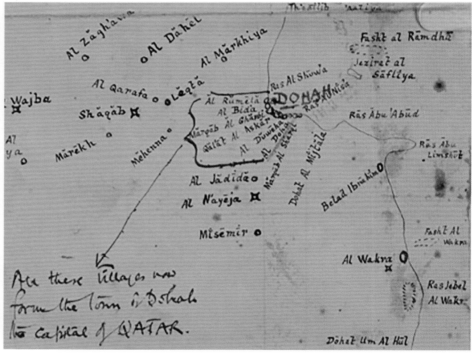

winter seasons, which resulted in *wadi* overflow floods that overlapped with the street network of the settlement. This explains why all types of buildings were not built along these natural flow lines to allow for water discharge. This relationship of the natural flow network between land and water was a key factor in shaping the city. The Doha market, located at the center of the settlement stretched along the main wadi stream (wadi As Sail) connecting the

First Occupied (Year)	Residential Areas (Farij)
At the foundation year	Doha & Al Bida'
Before 1950s	Al Bin Ali (currently Al Hitmi and Old Al Khelaifat), Al Salata, Eastern Al Murqab (now the New Markets Zone), Ad Doha comprising the main market area, Western Murqab, Al Rumailah (East), Al Asmakh, Al Najadah, Mushireb and Turkish Fort
1950s	Fareeq Abdul Aziz, New Al Ghanim, Al Doha Al Jadidah, Al Rumailah (West), Umm Guwailina, Al Mansoura, Old Airport (Zone 45), Neaja East
1960s	Najma, Mansoura, Al Muntazah, Bin Dirham, Wadi Al Sail (West), Al Sadd, Bin Mahmoud, New Al Murqab / Al Nasr, Bin Omran, New Salata, Khalifa Towns (North & South), Has Abu Aboud, Al Murour, Doha International Airport (East), Al Hilal (West), Al Hilal (East)
1970s & 1980s	Kulaib, Old Airport (Zone 47), New Al Khelaifat, Al Markhiya, Wadi Al Sail (East), Wadi Al Sail (West), Al Dohail, New Districts of Doha (Zones 60-69)

➜ Table 1. The district expansion with the city's growth through different decades.

Doha coastline to the inlands. The central location of the market and its connection to all the main roads and the harbor gave it a socioeconomic significance. The south edge of the *souq* was marked by the Al Koot fort, while the north edge was connected to the harbor. The harbor consisted of: shipyards, open markets, shops, *majlis*, mosques, and the Palace. Therefore, the harbor was considered the town center and hub where most of the activities took place. The historical maps and aerial photos also reveal that social relations were based on tribal affiliation, which had a great impact on the urban form. This is evident in the urban pattern, where members of one tribe, regardless of their economic status, resided in one area (*farij*) of the city.

The use of historical maps and textual sources contributed to mapping the development of Doha and the location and names of its districts (*firjan*) between 1823 and 1956. Over time, Doha (collective districts of al Bida' and Doha) started to expand with new districts around it. Historical records by both Lorimer in 1908 and Burchardt in 1906 indicate that Salata existed by the middle of the first decade of the twentieth century. Lorimer also mentioned in his list Rumayla (northwest of Bida'), Marqab Al Gharbi, Qalaat Al Askar, and Duwayha (between Bida' and Doha), Marqab Al Sharqi, Salata, and Al Bin Ali (later Hitmi). By the mid-twentieth century mappers also defined as Ahl Al Najd the inland side of the old Doha district. The remaining districts were indicated in the first 1952 survey map of Doha carried out by Hunting Survey Ltd.

These districts were present in a 1937 aerial photo, which indicates that they were established between 1908 and 1937, and are al-Ḥalah (joined Salata to old Doha), a southern spread comprising Barahat Al Jufayri, Ahmed Bajiz, and Amadahia (Al Madahiya), and a southwestern addition named after Mohamed bin Jasim. The three districts of Mushayrib, Najada, and Al Asmakh, although considered today part of old Doha, were founded after the 1950s. The districts changed over time: some remained the same, others got new names, changed boundaries, extended, split, or were merged into other districts. The districts or *firjan* were associated especially with kinship groups (tribes or other groups related by blood or geographical origin), which resulted in giving the districts their names. A district or *farij* would be established by a courtyard house, a mosque, and a *majlis* for the tribe leader, who would have the largest two-story house with some decorated details. Table-1 on the previous page shows the increase and changes in districts over time.

The historical development of Doha shares some common characteristics and structural principles of Arab and Islamic cities, which can be summarized as follows:

The separation between the economic activity zone and residential zone is clearly shown in Doha by the central *souq* (now known as Souq Waqif). This *souq* generated most of the town's day-to-day commercial activities. It included permanent shops, arcades, and a few permanent stalls on the seashore and the edges of the *souq*, as well as an adjoining open space used as a livestock market. The central *souq* zone encompassed areas beyond the well-known covered alleys and waterfront warehouses. It also included western parts of Al Ahmed, eastern parts of Al Jasrah, and the edge of Barahat Al Jufayri. Almost all economic activity took place in this area, and many of the merchants lived nearby in Al Jasrah.

The Arabic neighborhood or district was a key element in forming the urban pattern of the city, where the social, environmental, economic, and political influences contributed to shaping it. The landform and natural water outlet channels (*wadis*) in Doha contributed to defining an organic urban form for the districts. These districts or *firjan* were diverse, physically self-contained in terms of (in)accessibility and separation from neighboring districts, as well as being socially self-contained, particularly in terms of the provision of mosques and public spaces. The continuous migration of trade groups into Doha also contributed to defining some of the names of the districts. The internal logic of the residential neighborhood in Doha revolved largely around its network of local roads and public spaces, its *sikkas* and *barahas*. The urban plan of the district shows that each district had a low-access inner area of changing size and density, implying that each maintained its own structure of containment that contributed to the solidarity of the community and the closeness of its inhabitants.

The fortification of Doha was a key factor in shaping its urban pattern, due to the number of attacks and the amount of destruction it underwent. The British shelled Doha in 1821, 1828, and 1841, and there was a combined attack by Abu Dhabi and Bahrain in 1867. Hence, it was normal for the settlement to be walled with a central fort that served also as the sheikh's residence. The wall protected the people from raiders from inland, so it was important to bring the people and herds back within the wall before nightfall. The first map of Bida' and Doha (Guy and Brucks, 1823) indicates the cluster of buildings around two forts, the Al Bida' fort and the fort in Doha. The 1860 map description by Constable and Stiffe shows separate town walls around both Bida' and Doha, which had not yet quite grown together; the wall around Doha had at least five towers along it. There was another large tower in western Doha, which is visible in Guy and Brucks's 1823 map. The map also shows a new fort built in about 1850 between Doha and al Bida'. Later it be-

↑ The Turkish fort (Amiri Diwan) with Doha in the background. Photo taken by Burchardt during his visit to Doha in 1904.

came the base of the Turkish garrison and the inhabitants of Doha referred to it as the Qalaat Al Askar (soldiers' fort). The Al Thani ruler, Sheikh Abdullah bin Jassim, moved his base from the Old Palace in Hitmi to the Turkish fort—after the Turkish withdrawal in 1915—and rebuilt it as the Amiri Diwan. There were two more square fortifications, one next to Souq Waqif (Al Koot fort, possibly built in 1925), and the other in Rumailah, about 1.7 kilometers northwest of the Amiri Diwan, where the outline of a ruined fort can be seen in the 1950s aerial photos (probably the so-called "White fort"). Other defensive structures were present in the form of small round lookout towers and a defensive breastwork shown on Constable's and Stiffe's map and on a 1915 sketch of the Qalaat Al Askar. The locations and presence of the different fortifications in Doha indicate the continuous multiple threats the city was facing, the importance of defending the central coastal area, and the influence of visible fortification to reflect a stronghold against enemies. The remains of these fortifications showed an important political and administrative power. Some of these forts were converted and used as a residence for the ruling family or as a palace for the rulers.

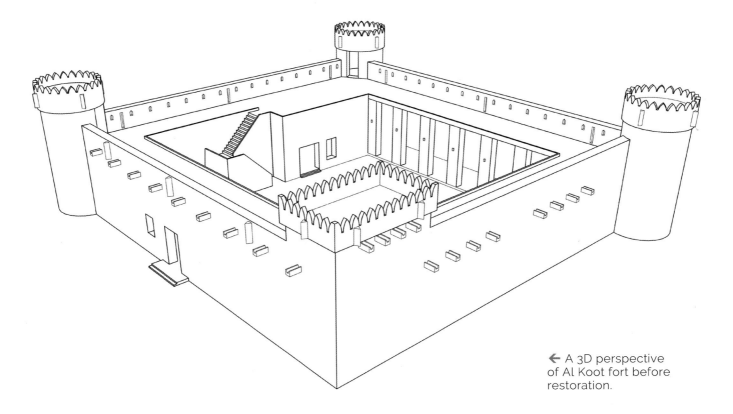

← A 3D perspective of Al Koot fort before restoration.

Fortified Buildings

The importance of Doha's fortification illustrated in historical maps and its influence in shaping the city has been mentioned in the previous section. However, the significance of their architecture can be presented in two examples, Al Koot fort and Qalaat Al Askar/Amiri Diwan. Al Koot fort, built in 1925, is located near Souq Waqif and in proximity to the Amiri Diwan and the Diwan Mosque. Its original purpose was to protect the town of Doha, but over the years it has served as a prison and nowadays as a museum. The fort is square in shape, with walls rising to five meters high and one meter thick. Round towers exist on three of the four corners, with a rectangular room on top of the fourth corner. The round turrets, roof room, and exterior walls are all decorated with pointed parapets. The upper levels of the towers are fitted with protected openings and machicolations for defensive purposes.

The first floor consists of sixteen rooms, two sides of which contain *liwans*. A gateway marks the central entrance, where large double wooden doors lead to the central courtyard that contains a well. The walls are made from stone, with additional reinforcement of the towers at their junction with the ground. The roofs are made with heavy, wooden beams covered by *danshal* and *mangh-rour*, possibly topped with a layer of rocks and mud plaster, leading wooden waterspouts along the outer walls.

↗ A sketch of Qalaat Al Askar as it appeared in 1934 in an aerial image.

↑ Aerial image showing the Amiri Diwan in 1934 (see p. 61).

Initially, the Amiri Diwan was known as Al Bida' fort, which was originally a fortress built and fortified by watchtowers in the eighteenth century. During the Ottoman presence (1871–1915), the fortress was known as the Military fort (Qalaat Al Askar). After the departure of the Ottomans in 1915, Sheikh Abdullah bin Jassim, the Ruler of Qatar at the time, restored the fort to later become the official workplace and office of Qatar's rulers, and to be renamed both as the Doha Palace as well as the Fort of the Sheikhs (Qalaat Al Shuyukh). In 1971, after the end of the Anglo-Qatari treaty of 1916, the title of the Ruler of the State of Qatar was changed to Amir, and the fort was renamed as the Amiri Diwan.

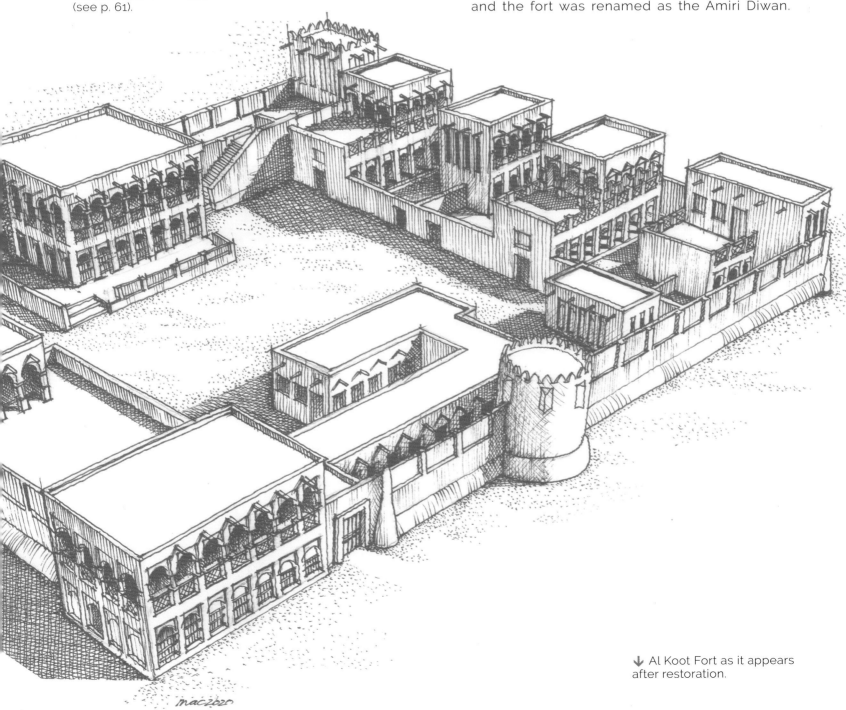

↓ Al Koot Fort as it appears after restoration.

Qalaat Al Askar has one round tower at the center of its wall facing the eastern coastline with the main gate to its left and a two-story rectangular room in the left-hand corner. The two corners of the opposite wall are anchored by square-shaped towers facing inland. The structures in Qalaat Al Askar are aligned internally along the four sides of the wall, creating a central courtyard with two wells. The round and square-shaped towers are topped with castellations indicating their function as defensive structures. Most of the window openings of the structures face east and south toward the coastline to catch the breeze and overlook the surrounding activities. A ceremonial two-story building was added later, attached to the south corner of the east wall with a U-shaped flight of stairs leading to the center of the terrace on the second floor. Additionally, there were two identical one-floor, U-shaped structures added to part of the extension with a ceremonial building.

Religious Buildings

Al Qubib Mosque

Jama' Al Meera is the first manifestation of a multi-domed mosque that was built at the same time as the Al Zubarah fort and its walls in 1740. It was a concept imitating the Ottoman multidomed mosques. Sheikh Jassim bin Mohammed Al Thani was impressed when he saw the mosque for the first time during his visit to Zubarah in 1878. The moment Sheikh Jassim arrived back in Doha, he hired Ibrahim Al Humaili, a popular master builder, to reproduce a larger scale of Jama' Al Meera in the heart of the settlement. The mosque was officially named Sheikh Mohammed bin Jassim Mosque but known among locals as Al Qubib Mosque. The inner prayer area was in four rows of *riwaq* (open porch) with pointed arches resting on cylindrical columns. The roof was covered with half-circular domes sitting on square bases constructed using stone and plaster. The courtyard was defined on two sides by pointed arches of the *iwan* (vaulted hall) along the side wall and connected by the wall that consists of the minaret and ablution area.

↑ A sketch of how Al Qubib Mosque appeared originally.

The nature of a multidomed mosque with four covered aisles and an open courtyard layout introduced a new architectural trend and planning for mosques in Qatar. Al Qubib Mosque witnessed a lot of demolition, reconstruction, and renovation in the second half of the twentieth century. It was first renovated in the late 1950s by adding extensive decorations to it.

↓ Sheikh Mohammed bin Jassim Mosque, also known among locals as Al Qubib Mosque.

Bin Obaid Mosque

In 1935, Bin Obaid Mosque was built half a kilometer away from the Museum and the sea in Old Salata, at a time when Doha was 1.5 square kilometers in size. This indicates how the mosque was positioned away from the city center at that time. The mosque consisted of two main parts, the prayer hall and the courtyard. It had two main access doors in the north and south walls leading to the courtyard. The courtyard was defined on the western side by the arcade *iwan* and on the other three sides by the boundary wall. The minaret stands at the southeastern corner with a height of no more than five meters. The *iwan* is about three meters in depth with an arcade of ten square arches and eleven columns. The windows on the north and south facade are topped with gypsum decorations.

↘ Sketches of the old Bin Obaid Mosque.

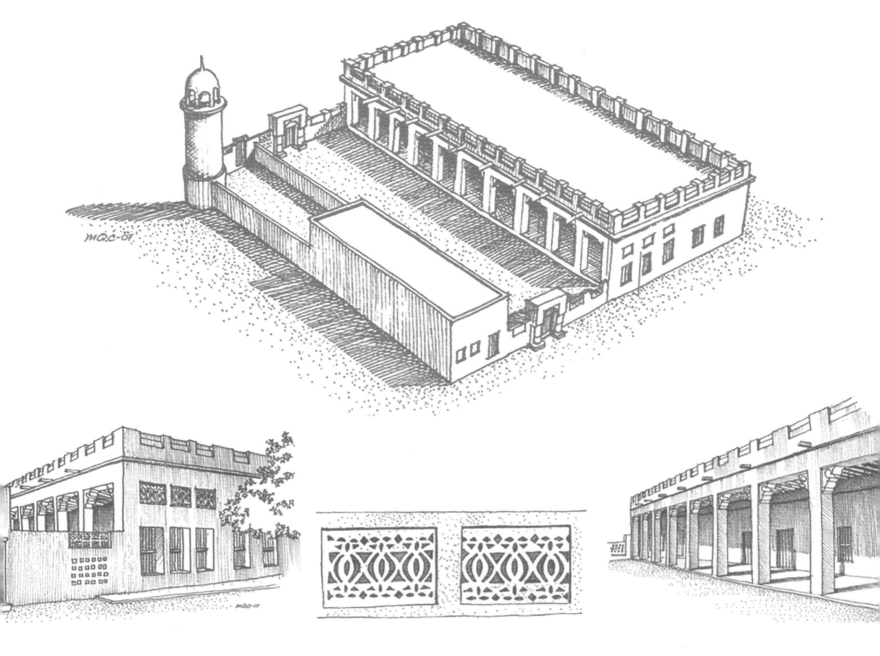

The prayer hall has a depth of three meters with four windows on the north and south walls, two on each side. The *qibla* wall has three windows on each side of the *mihrab*. The *mihrab* is semicircular in plan and roofed with a pointed dome structure decorated with a gypsum crescent. The *mihrab* wall has three openings that provide ventilation and natural light.

Residential Buildings

Nasser Bin Ahmed Obeidan House

This house belongs to the Obeidan family, built in 1940 and considered one of the oldest in Doha, located half a kilometer away from the Corniche. Nasser Bin Ahmed Obeidan House is a large building, rectangular in shape. At the southeastern end of the plot, a large portion has been sectioned off and a new building occupies the space, leaving a clear, square court measuring approximately nineteen meters on each side. The main building consists of two major sections; one runs along the entire length of the northern boundary of the plot and contains the main entrance. The

↑ A sketch of Nasser Bin Ahmed Obeidan House.

second section is an L-shaped building that runs along part of the southern and western walls. The L-shaped building consists of four rectangular rooms, similar in size. Outside the rooms, thirteen decorative octagonal columns border an *iwan*. A staircase occupying the central corner of the L-shape provides access to the roof.

The other section of the house, running along the northern wall, consists of a narrow rectangle that houses seven rooms, a staircase, and the main entrance gate. Some rooms are fitted with vertical recesses that run along the height of the wall, while other recesses are divided into two. This part has an L-shaped staircase leading to the roof area 4.3 meters above the courtyard level. The ceiling of this house has been totally changed. The original ceiling consisting of *danshal* wood beams overlain with *basgill* and *manghrour* no longer exists. On the northeastern corner of the plot, the main gate was the only gate in Qatar decorated with a muqarnas feature, a three-dimensional honeycomb pattern that is specific to Islamic architecture.

Sheikh Hamad Bin Abdullah House

Sheikh Hamad Bin Abdullah House is located very near the Corniche in a complex that includes the Amiri Diwan and the Diwan Mosque. It was built in 1930 and underwent a major renovation at the time of the survey and many areas have been completed. A feature of this house was the extensive use of gypsum decorations both inside and outside, the mark of a home of an important family.

The house is built around a central courtyard with both upper and ground-level floors. There are two entrances to this courtyard, one in the western wall and one in the southern wall.

↓ A sketch of Sheikh Hamad Bin Abdullah House.

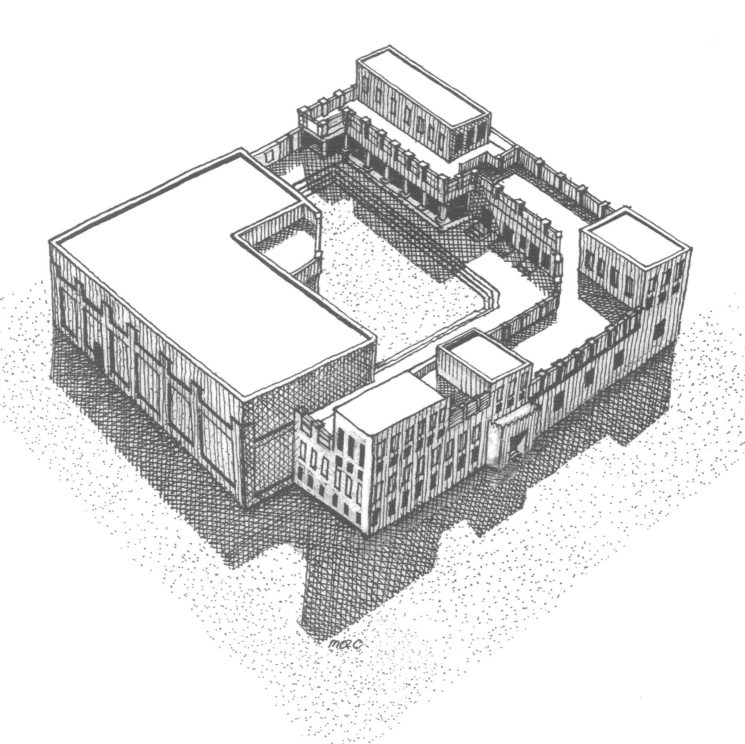

The entrance on the west side has a large wooden gate that has been restored with a *khokha*. The entrance in the western wall gives access to the lobby of the building, which was probably the *majlis* in earlier times. The second gate in the southern wall is less ornate and probably served as a secondary entrance for staff or as a private entrance. The buildings around the courtyard all have an arched arcade with octagonal columns on square bases and with square capitals decorated with gypsum inlays. The courtyard and house do not appear to have been altered, with the latter totally constructed from the traditional materials of limestone, mud, and gypsum plaster, albeit recently restored.

↖↓ Sketches of the ornamented wooden gate on the western elevation of Sheikh Hamad Bin Abdullah House.

Internally, the rooms have been adapted for use as offices and are well restored and renovated. The original roof construction consists of *danshal* wood beams overlain with *basgill* and *manghrour*. The many elaborate gypsum details and coloring are a features of this property. Upstairs, there appears to be a winter *majlis*, which is still under restoration.

Conclusion

The traditional Qatari architecture (pre-oil) was influenced by geographic, cultural, social, political, and economic logic in terms of its physical fabric and layout. Vernacular Qatari architecture can easily be adapted to meet the requirements of modern functionality and high living standards while maintaining congruence with its natural, social, and cultural environments. It evolved organically along with its squares, streets, and styles of accommodation, and was affected by economic and climatic conditions in addition to social customs. In the traditional model, the mosque was usually situated in the city center and the minarets were high enough to provide a landmark for arriving travelers. The *souq* near the coastline in the city center defined the main streets and the physical layout of the neighborhoods—based on the values of extended family and privacy—together forming the underlying structure of the urban form. The historical development of Doha shares common characteristics and structural principles of Arab and Islamic cities. This is reflected in the separation between the economic-activity zone and the residential zone, clearly manifested in Doha by the central *souq*. This *souq* generated most of the town's day-to-day commercial activities. The landform and natural water outflow channels (*wadis*) in Doha contributed to defining an organic urban form for the districts.

CHAPTER 2

The beginning of oil revenues in the 1950s was the dawn of urban development, which started with primary needs, services, education, health, and central administration.

BEGINNING OF OIL

Introduction

The first three decades of the twentieth century did not witness any changes in the urban pattern and architecture of the traditional settlement of Doha. However, the early 1930s came with shattering economic developments that affected the pearling industry in the Gulf. First, the worldwide economy was struck by the great economic depression in 1929, which lasted until the 1930s. This was followed by another blow in 1933, when the Japanese developed the cultured pearl, which dealt a crippling blow to the Gulf pearl industry from which it never recovered. The population of Qatar at this time dropped steeply due to extreme living conditions and migration away from the peninsula in search of jobs. Moreover, the outbreak of World War II, which lasted from 1939 to 1945, aggravated the economic situation even more. The final blow to the pearl industry came with India's independence in 1947, where their new national government prohibited the import of luxury items like pearls.

→ The first production test in 1939.

Driven by the economic and geopolitical conditions, especially the American interest in the Gulf, the British government began negotiations with the Sheikh of Qatar Abdullah bin Jasim Al Thani on oil concession, and an agreement was signed in 1935. The oil exploration started in the Dukhan area in the same year, and the first drilling took place in the same area in 1938. By 1939, the first oil discovery was made and a telegram from the political agent in Bahrain to that one resident in Kuwait confirms that: "Petroleum Development Qatar have had slight show of oil in their test well near Zekrit. Drilling continues."

However, the impact of World War II postponed the first oil exports for a decade. In 1942, the three appraisal wells were sealed with cement, and the company's staff had to leave: prosperity was to be delayed. All these worldwide factors contributed to the decline of the pearl industry, hence the ending of Doha's pre-oil urban history and the beginning of oil development. It was not until December 1949 that the first shipment of crude oil left the shores of Qatar from Umm Said on the S.S. *President Manny*.

The beginning of both oil wealth and urban development was slow, due to three possible reasons to do with (a) transition of economy, (b) amount of oil exploited and its revenues, and (c) the system of governance. First, the transition from the pearl to oil economy meant producing a new division of labor, and the invention of new methods for distributing wealth. Second, the pace of development was directly related to the growth in oil revenues and the amount of oil exploited. For example, the first oil revenue in 1950 was one million US dollars, which then increased to thirty-five million US dollars in 1955, and reached seventy million US dollars by the mid-1960s. Finally, there was the absence of an official authority or a system of governance to take responsibility for the city's planning and development. Therefore, the power of decision-making was operated through direct, personal orders of the ruler.

The dawn of development was marked with the beginning of oil revenues. This was in addition to bringing in a group of British experts in engineering, administration, and utilities, who worked as executive managers for all government offices. The experts included a police commander, head of government engineers, and administration managers for water, electricity, mechanics, health, postal service, and telephone utilities. This indicated the transition to and beginning of government projects and utilities that would change the life in Qatar to its prosperity.

↑ Oil rig in Dukhan in 1956.

Primary Needs

One of the main priorities of the administration, after the establishment of the oil operations and available funds for development, was to provide the primary needs of water and electricity. Given the scarce availability of underground water, the consultant contracted by the government recommended constructing a desalination plant. A small plant was built in 1951, with its output reserved

← The desalination plant and electric power station.

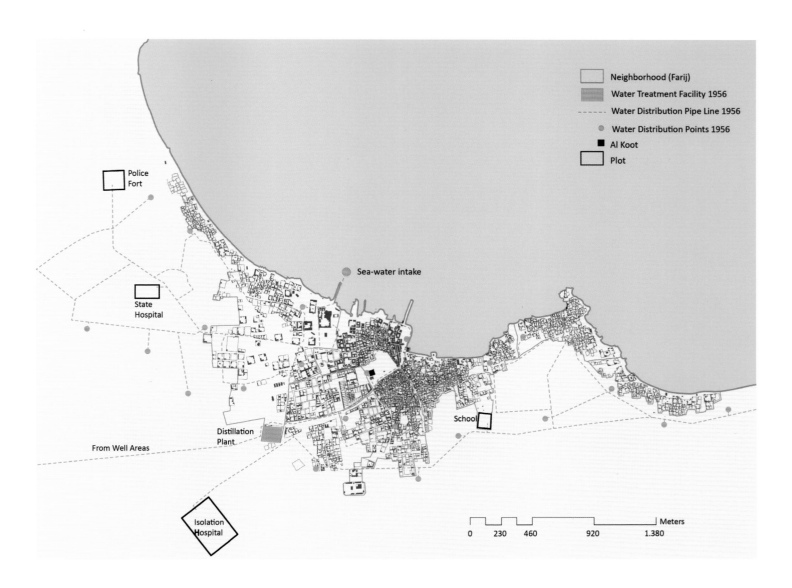

Legend:

- Neighborhood (Farij)
- Water Treatment Facility 1956
- Water Distribution Pipe Line 1956
- Water Distribution Points 1956
- Al Koot
- Plot

Police Fort

State Hospital

Sea-water intake

Distillation Plant

From Well Areas

School

Isolation Hospital

Meters
0   230   460   920   1.380

↑ The water-distribution network through the city from the desalination plant.

for the use of the oil company. It was determined that the new water supply would be a mixture of desalinated water and saline groundwater, to ensure a steady supply of water and reduce the burden on the new desalination plant.

The desalination plant was constructed away from the coast, next to the newly built power plant in Kahraba street, near Musheireb, in 1957. This location was chosen due to the large space required for the new desalination plant and the existing structures along the coastline. The intake pipe for the plant was established in Doha Harbor, near the Ruler's Palace, and extended along Wadi Musheireb through Souq Waqif (known locally as Al Kharees) while the overflow was released near the Customs jetty.

The water-supply pipe network was not connected directly to houses in Doha. Instead, several public distribution sites were established throughout the city, with the intention that no houses should be more than 300 yards from the water supply. By 1954, the desalination plant and water supply network were operational, and the growing demand for water necessitated the construction of a second desalination plant five years later.

Services

The 1950s gave a true sense of development, which began to be felt by the people with the road construction throughout the city. An aerial image from 1952 shows the new road constructed in the city center around the Amiri Diwan to Al Rayyan. The remarkable progress of road construction continued from the mid-1950s to the end of the decade, where it connects Doha to many areas outside the city center toward the inlands including Dukhan and Al Wakra. The asphalt road network started to redefine the city's urban pattern, where the larger roads started from the city center and gradually diminished in size as they radiated into the residential areas. The radial organic and concentric fabric of the city contributed to gradually introducing the ring roads with the expansion of the city.

→ An aerial image from 1952 shows the new road constructed in the city center around the Amiri Diwan to Al Rayyan.

Doha, being a coastal city famous for its maritime activities with newly constructed roads leading to the coastline, contributed to giving a share of the development to the waterfront. This was achieved through building a new dock extending to reach deep waters, creating a deeper harbor by 1956, in addition to sea landfill to accommodate more activities related to the newly built dock.

The airport, which was a landing strip, had been marked out by the Royal Air Force in 1932 by dropping bags of chalk from the air, was abandoned. Instead, the oil company's landing grounds in Qatar were used.

↖ The construction of the first asphalt road in 1952 in Doha, in front of Amiri Diwan Building.

← The airport in Doha in 1955, the customs building and radio tower on the left.

↑ Construction of the new dock extending to reach deep waters.

They had been built at Dukhan, Oom Said, and Doha. In 1950 the Gulf Aviation Company (the forerunner to Gulf Air, which was owned in equal shares by Qatar, Bahrain, the UAE, and Oman) established a regular air service between Bahrain and Doha. It initially used the old Royal Air Force landing strip but abandoned it the following year as it was no longer serviceable. They used the oil company landing ground in Doha instead. The Government of Qatar took over this airfield in 1952 and built the necessary facilities on it. Civil Aviation was then under the control of Her Majesty's Government. The first purpose-built airport was constructed in 1963, the runway measured 2,481 meters in 1968 and was extended to 4,572 meters in 1972. In 1979 it was upgraded to accommodate the Concorde.

Schools

The first primary school in the pre-oil period was established in 1948 in a rented building, known as Al Eslah Al Hmadia. Later, at the beginning of the 1950s, a new school was under construction on a plot measuring 90 m x 110 m, located one hundred meters from the southwest corner of Doha. The building was of a rectangular form with aligned classrooms connected by a terrace. The walls were made of coral stone topped by a ceiling layered with *danshal* wood, *manghrour* matt, mud, and sand. Steel beams were added to the dividing walls to support the ceiling load, due to the length extending up to 5.5 meters, which marks the beginning of introducing new construction materials and methods to the old ones. The form and style of this building marked a new architectural phase in Doha. It became the first primary school for boys and opened in 1952.

The first school for girls in the 1950s was established by Amna Mahmood Al Jaidah in her house in Al Jasrah. By 1955, the name had changed to Amna Mahmood, and then later changed to Girls' Primary School. Amna's house could no longer host the increasing number of girls enrolled. In the first year, there were sixty girls, then the number increased to 111, which led the Ministry of Ma'arif (Education) to rent a bigger building named Doha Girls' School in Fareej Al Karrani, in south Musheirb Street. The number of girls enrolled continued to increase, which led the Ministry of Ma'arif to establish another school in the east named Al Khansa. Later in 1978, the Al Khansa school moved to the first primary school for boys after it was refurbished. The refurbishment transformed the school from rectangular to U-shaped with a new additional floor on top of the ground-level floor. The main entrance is defined by the larger projection of both the stairs and the elevation of the entrance.

→ The first primary school for boys after an increase in enrollment due to economic development in Doha; first floor (top), second floor (middle), and sectional perspective (bottom).

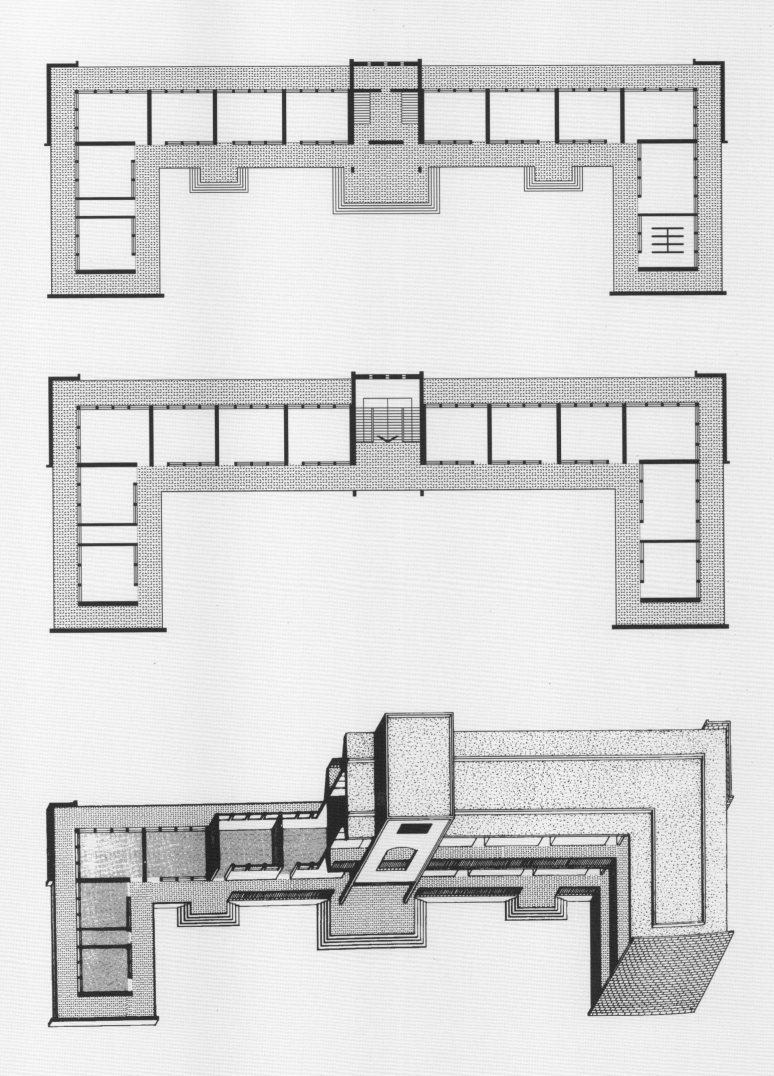

The construction of the secondary school in Fareej Al Raffa in 1956 is considered one of the largest education projects of that time. The project was designed to be constructed in three phases, first school building in phase one, second school building and a football field (Doha Stadium) in phase two, and amphitheatre for the football field in phase three. The longitudinal plot was 95 meters long and was subdivided into three plots, the middle for phase one, the eastern plot for phase two, and the western one for phase three. The construction of phase one consisted of four buildings:

The classroom building is aligned on an east-west axis, where its long walls face north and south to provide natural ventilation and avoid the direct sunlight from the east and west. The building is on two floors, consisting of eleven

classrooms, two workshops, and a staircase. The administration building is on the northern side opposite the classrooms, which is on one floor level divided into sections with a gap in between during the construction stage. This building can be reached through the school yard, which separates it from the classroom building. There are two shading structures on both sides of the school yard and a multi-purpose room, 10 m x 22 m in size, located on the south of the plot, which can be reached by an access in the middle of the classroom building on the ground-floor level. A storage building of seventy square meters, is located between the multi-purpose room and the eastern wall of the football field. The walls are built in concrete, while the roof is made of corrugated, galvanized iron, supported by a single-layer, grid-space frame made of wood and steel. The projection of the roof contributes to shading the walls, in this way preventing direct sunlight and reducing the heat.

← The vertical and horizontal concrete sun breakers in the school elevation, which showed climate consideration in the design.

In 1957, a new school was under construction on a small plot of 53 m x 70 m in Fareej Abdul Aziz in central Doha. The construction was completed and opened as the Al Wsat School in 1958, when students were transferred to it from a rented building. The school was renamed after opening for a short period as Khalid bin Al Walid Primary School for Boys. Later, in 1961, it became a school for girls and was renamed to Doha Girls' Primary School. The two-floor school building has an interesting (mirrored H) form, with long, parallel wings on the east-west axis. The north and south wings each consist of eight classrooms

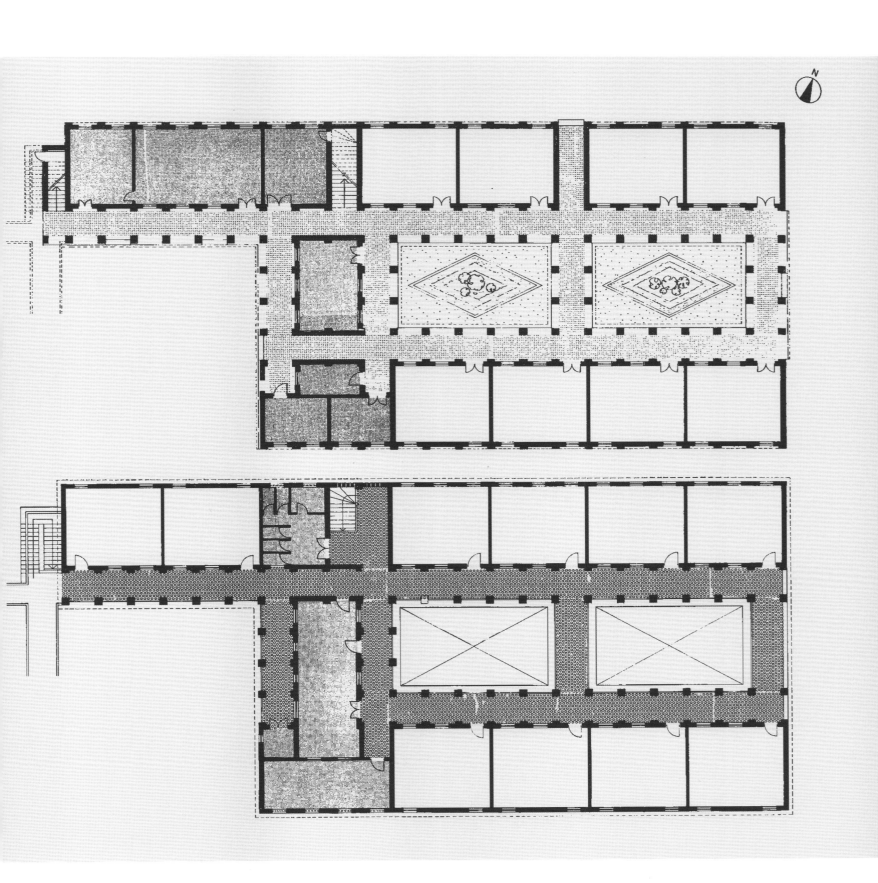

↑ Doha Girls' Primary School with its mirrored H-shaped concept, first floor (top), and second floor (bottom).

(four classes per floor) connected by a hallway. The two wings are separated by a 6.5-meter-wide courtyard and are connected by the west wing, which consists of the administration office, teachers' room, a clinic, and storage. The courtyard is centrally divided by a hallway bridge connecting both floors of the north and south wings. Due to the limitation of the size of the school plot, the Ministry had to acquire a plot opposite the school to the south, separated by a street. In the early 1960s, a concrete bridge was constructed above the street to connect the school building to the football field. By 1963, a new two-floor wing was added on the southwestern side connected by a hallway to the north wing and the concrete bridge.

In the same year that the school opened, another school with the same design was opened in Al Bida', and students from Al Bida' Primary School for Boys moved to it from a rented building. Later it became a school for girls and was renamed Um Al Muminin Primary School for Girls. Both schools (Al Wsta and Al Bida') were constructed in concrete and designed to have the windows facing north and south to avoid direct sunlight from the east and west, in addition to gaining more natural ventilation coming from the north throughout the year. Wooden horizontal sunshades were placed on the top space between the columns in the hallways of the second floor to reduce direct sunlight. The proportions of the courtyard suit the school size perfectly, providing a micro,

comfortable, outdoor space for multipurpose activities. The school design proved that it could accommodate small plots not exceeding the dimensions of 70 m x 80 m. This was the first school to have its football field not only on another plot but also connected by an overhead, concrete bridge.

Arabian Gulf School and Abu Baker Al Sidiq School for Boys both have the same design carried out by the Ministry of Public Works in mid-1959. Arabian Gulf School is in Um Ghuwailah and opened in 1960, while Abu Baker Al Sidiq School is located in Fareej Salata and opened in 1961. The school was constructed in two phases: phase one consisted of a two-floor rectangular building cantered by a 15 m x 18 m courtyard. Each floor consists of six classrooms and one workshop connected by a hallway defining the perimeter of the courtyard. Phase two was constructed between 1963 and 1966 and it consisted of three classrooms and a gymnasium measuring 11 m x 21 m. The double-height gymnasium could be accessed directly from the first floor and from an overlooking walkway on the second floor, which can be used to watch sports activities. Most of the openings in the school are facing north and south to protect from direct sunlight in addition to having sunshades. Wooden horizontal sunshades are also implemented and placed at the top between the columns

← Um Al Muminin Primary School for Girls with the same design as Doha Girls' Primary School with blue horizontal screens fixed at the top between the columns to reduce direct sunlight.

→ The closed design concept floor plans (top) carried out by the Ministry of Public Works and a sectional perspective (bottom), for both Arabian Gulf School and Abu Baker Al Sidiq School for Boys.

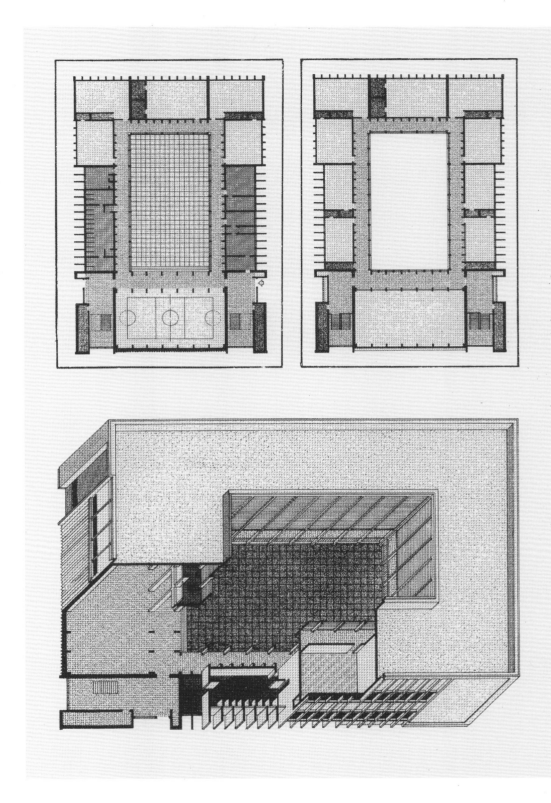

in the hallways of the second floor to reduce direct sunlight. A double layered roof was used, topped with corrugated, galvanized iron to reflect sunlight, while the lower layer is in concrete, with a gap between the two layers for ventilation. The roof projection also contributed to interrupting direct sunlight on the elevation of the building. The external wall of the gymnasium is a double wall: the inner wall is twenty-three centimeters thick, and the outer wall is forty-five centimeters thick.

The construction of the first hospital in 1945 reflects the

Hospitals

The first hospital in Qatar was under construction in 1945, funded by Sheikh Ab-dullah bin Jassim Al Thani in partnership with the American Mission. It opened in 1947 with a capacity for about twelve inpatients, and by early 1948 was al-ready being visited by around seventy-five outpatients per day. There was only one doctor for the hospital, from India, Dr. George, who was hired together with Indian nurses, and the American Mission agreed to send one Mission doctor at a time, on rotation. It became known among the locals as the "one-doc-tor hospital" or Doha Hospital, and was later known as Mustashfa Al Jasrah. In 1948, the American Mission sent Dr. Mary Allison there to work. The hospital was located approximately two hundred meters east of the Amiri Diwan along the coastline. It was a two-floor building with a central courtyard surrounded by a colonnaded hallway, which led to the various rooms.

Dr. Gotting described the hospital in 1953:

The hospital had 15 in-patient beds, a rudimentary casualty room and one small-er room which served as an operating theatre. It was situated on the seashore

↑ First hospital in Qatar while under construction in 1945, funded by Sheikh Abdullah bin Jassim Al Thani in partnership with the American Mission.

in Farig al Jasrah. It is interesting to describe the actual facilities in the theatre as much work was done under primitive conditions. The theatre light was one 6-foot neon tube, all the available surgical appliances were accommodated in one small glass-fronted cupboard. Sterilisation of dressings and instruments was done by boiling them in a pan on a Kerosene Primus stove (Gotting, 1955).

A Medical Services Department was first established in 1951 as a government agency, responsible for free medical care. Health was regarded as a major priority as infant mortality was very high, and that first hospital could not cope. The American Mission in Doha was losing its medical staff due to retirement and death. As a result, the Mission stopped assigning medical doctors to the

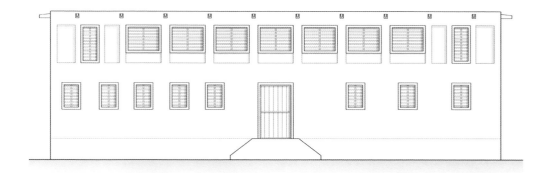

importance of the quality of life as a priority at that time

↗ Front elevation of the first hospital in Qatar.

↓ A 1952 aerial view showing both Al Jasrah Hospital, on the left, and the first hospital, on the right, with its new annex extension.

hospital and in February 1952 handed over the administration of the hospital to the Government of Qatar.

Although limited in services and capacity, the establishment of this hospital marked the beginning of health care in Qatar and it continued to operate as Government State Hospital throughout the early 1950s. Later, permission was given to expand the existing facilities by building annexes to accommodate four additional wards, giving sixty extra beds, a kitchen, laundry, pharmacy, laboratory, x-ray department, physiotherapy unit, and operating theatres. The work was done by the Civil and Government Public Works Department and was completed at record speed by 1955. Staff was recruited from Armenia, India, Pakistan, and Egypt. New State Hospital was opened in 1957 and Al Jasrah Hospital was converted to cater for maternity services, chronic diseases, psychiatry, and tuberculosis, with Dr. Gotting in charge.

By 1952, a new two-floor building had been constructed a few meters east from Mustashfa Al Jasrah.

← Front view of the
Al Jasrah Hospital.

There is no historical record of its function at that time, but in the 1970s it was operating as a psychiatric hospital. Based on aerial photos, the building had a rectangular form raised on an approximately one-meter-high platform. The steps in the center of the northern elevation led to a loggia leading to the main entrance door. The elevation had two separate staircases leading to the upper floor. The window openings were a simple rectangular form with a steel grid. The parapet followed the same column spacing from the first and second floors with a square, concrete breeze wall in between. In the 1970s, the first Doha Hospital became a hospital for infectious and chronic diseases, and then provided care for psychiatric and orthopedic patients in the 1970s. It was subsequently demolished as the sea front was redeveloped.

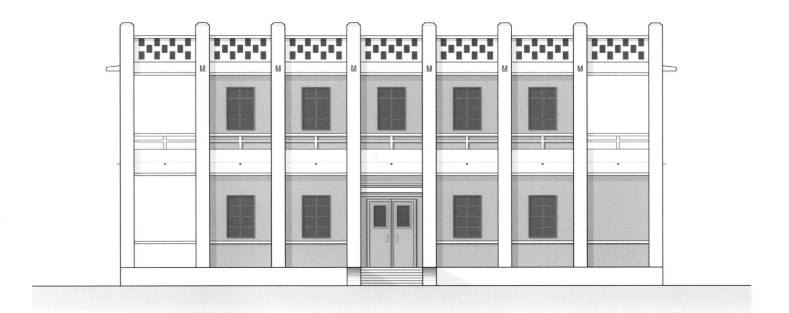

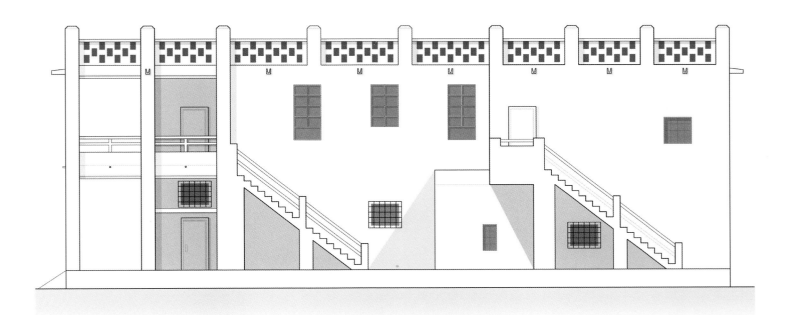

↑ Front (top) and partial side elevation (above) of Al Jasrah Hospital.

Al Rumailah Hospital

The Ruler of Qatar, Sheikh Ali bin Abdullah bin Jasim Al Thani, gave instructions for the building of a new State Hospital in 1952. The hospital project was part of the program being planned for the development of the country that aimed at raising the standard of living for everyone.

In 1952, a design competition for a new state hospital in Al Rumailah was held by RIBA (Royal Institute of British Architects). The competition was widely advertised and aroused interest around the world. Three hundred thirty-five architects entered the competition from as far away as Aden, Australia, Ceylon, Ethiopia, Hong Kong, India, Kuwait, Singapore, South Africa, Sweden, and the United Kingdom. Seventy-four designs were finally submitted and judged

in September 1953. Mr. Alexander S. Gray, the competition assessor, awarded first place to the design prepared by John R. Harris and Jill Rowe for design and supervision. After the Ruler inspected the plans on September 26, 1953, and held discussions with the Government, minor amendments were made to the competition drawings. These revisions and the final siting of the hospital were approved by the Government on December 17, 1953.

The site of the State Hospital was chosen eight hundred meters to the west of what was then Doha, at Rumailah, and named Al Rumailah Hospital in 1972. The site had a good view north to the sea and consisted of eleven senior staff houses, four self-contained apartments, twelve apartments for senior nurses, an apartment for the head nurse with a dining room for senior nurses, and fifty-six nurses' quarters in addition to residential dining blocks and servants' quarters. The residential accommodation was on the western side of the site.

The design of the hospital had the following principles: to keep all main blocks to two stories; to reduce the need for lifts for running the hospital in an emergency; to keep male and female wards totally separate—male wards were on the first floor and female wards were on the second floor; and to create a separate isolation block. In addition, the wards were all to be facing north, to face the sea and catch the prevailing breeze; the verandas of the single-bed wards faced east or west so as to be pleasantly lit; the need for cross ventilation was to be met in case the air-conditioning should fail; the building was to

↑ Aerial view of Al Rumailah Hospital when first completed in 1957.

→ A 1966 aerial view of Al Rumailah Hospital showing the mosque in the central courtyard.

be framed to a standard grid to give flexibility to changing requirements within the building; the kitchen and servants' areas were planned on the southwest of the leeward side of the hospital; some roofs were to be paved for the use of patients and staff, with stairs to the roofs to serve the dual purpose of access and fire escape; the frame and foundations were designed in the case of two of the one-story blocks to receive second-floor extensions at a later date, so as to form two additional complete ward units; the air-conditioning was designed to accommodate further extensions when required; the roofs and the second floors were constructed with prestressed concrete; the flat roofs for use of patients and staff were insulated by lightweight concrete and sand in addition to the surfacing of precast, white concrete tiles; and the external cavity walls were insulated. Copper-lined teak rainwater chutes discharged rainwater from the roofs over the canopies; the steel windows were side hung to form a scoop for the breeze and were fitted with locks with a master key for locking while the air-conditioning was activated; the external walls were designed with concrete vertical fins and canopies with teak and pine subsidiary sunbreakers; light to the medical and surgical single-bed wards was controlled by aluminum sunbreakers with the possibility to alter the pitch from within the building; the external wall surfaces were to be kept light in color. All the bathrooms faced away from the east.

There was a mosque in the main central courtyard, a separate suite for the use of the ruler and his family at the end of the single-bed wing, and an of-

→ Al Rumailah Hospital, annex elevations showing the vertical and horizontal concrete sun breakers.

← Photo of a partial front elevation of Al Rumailah Hospital.

fice for the Minister of Health, which later became the offices for the Preventive Health Department. Many other alterations took place over the years. The hospital opened in 1957 and went through several expansions and renovations in the following years but kept its status as Doha's oldest remaining hospital and still operates today. This 130-bed hospital was a major departure from the primitive health care available in the 1940s.

The building was especially praised for its integration of modern technology, including air-conditioning. This hospital also had the resources to provide

→ A section showing the vertical and horizontal concrete sun breakers.

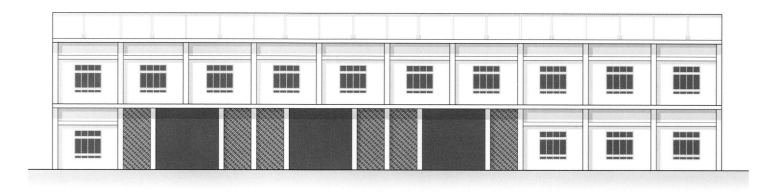

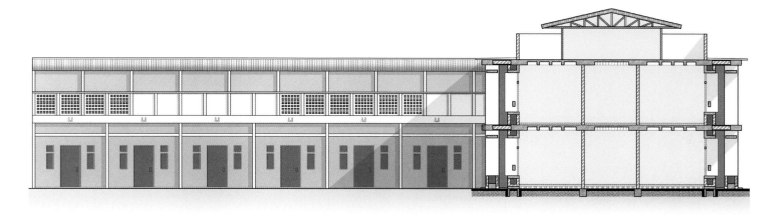

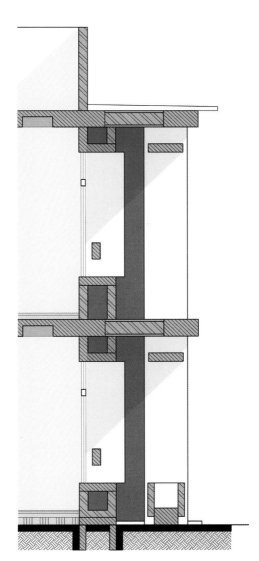

traveling medical care to the remote areas of Qatar. The establishment of this hospital brought medical facilities and help, unique for that time, to this area of the world. It attracted a vast amount of publicity at the time and won first prize at the Berlin Trade Fair. It was the first large, framed building to be constructed in Doha.

An Australian medical team came to Qatar to study the problems of rehabilitation, geriatrics, and extended care within the existing services of the State of Qatar. In close collaboration with the Doha office of John R. Harris Architects, the State's Ministry of Public Health, and the Ministry of Public Works, it was recommended that Rumailah Hospital be redeveloped into a sophisticated rehabilitation complex, with the same high standards as the Hamad and Women's hospitals, opened in 1982 and 1987 respectively.

Among the changes made over the years were: a staff room obtained by putting up a partition in the entrance hall and a telephone exchange built in the front of the hospital. In 1967 a new outpatients' clinic, known as the Polyclinic, was built in the grounds of the hospital with specialty clinics for surgery, medicine, pediatrics, dermatology, ophthalmology, and otolaryngology. A special burns unit was built as was a purpose-built intensive care unit, next to the operating theater suite. A coronary care unit was built in 1979. The improvement of public health began with the establishment of the Public Health Department by the Qatari Government in 1954.

Central Administration Buildings

Clock Tower

In 1956, a new civic center was created to the west of the old one. The Grand Mosque and the Amiri Diwan were built around a ceremonial square that became a very distinctive feature of Doha. A Clock Tower landmark was constructed on a small promontory, an important focus point for one of the first new developments built with the proceeds of the increasing oil revenue. Hugh Hale, the State Engineer at that time, helped design the clock outside the Diwan. The mechanisms were bought by Jassim Darwish and it had to have a special foundation to support it. The impressive Clock Tower, which is one of Doha's best-known landmarks, was constructed by CAT and Darwish. This photograph shows the Clock Tower under construction before the surrounding vaulted canopy was built. In the same photo, the entrance to the Amiri Diwan and its car park can be seen at the corner. In its completion, the pair of structures forming on plan represent a star—the Clock Tower—and crescent moon—the vaulted canopy.

← The Clock Tower during construction in 1956 (left) and an aerial view (right).

The Clock Tower was built to complete a modern architectural ensemble intended to represent Qatar's independence as well as indicate a clear break with Doha's traditional building style. With the construction of the first road along the north side of the *souq*, several merchants constructed the first modern offices in Doha. This area has now been cleared but, at that time, it represented the strong link that existed between the merchants and ruling families. The main mosque (*masjid*), which represented the secular and religious faces of the new Doha, went through several changes but the older entrance porch has been retained, and its design resembles the Clock Tower. The Clock Tower is a significant public work of art that benefits the urban development and regeneration of the city.

→ A front elevation showing the architectural details of the Clock Tower after completion.

↓ The Clock Tower today.

British Consulate

The British Political Agency Building formed a part of the visual urban enclosure of the area in front of the Sheikhs' Mosque and Sheikh Abdullah's complex to the west and northwest respectively. The building was used to house the British Political Agency in Doha and occupied a site on the eastern side of the area, facing west where the site of the Clock Tower was soon to be located, and past that, to Sheikh Abdullah's complex to its northwest and with Sheikh Hamad's Council (*majlis*) and the Sheikhs' Mosque immediately to its southwest.

The photograph below was taken in the early 1950s, perhaps in 1952, and looks approximately northeast and east respectively. The second one shows

the building as it appeared in 1963. The architecture has echoes of Sheikh Abdullah's residence at Fareej Salata in its construction as well as its plan form of central rooms with surrounding veranda. Note the small features in the junction between beam and columns, adopted from the local design of Qatari vernacular. In 1972, little had changed on the facade other than its then being used by the Qatari Government.

↖ The British Political Agency Building as it appeared in 1952 (left) and after restoration in 1963 (right).

Amiri Diwan

In the early 1920s, Sheikh Abdullah bin Jasim Al Thani resided with his sons at Bida', described by the historian Sayf Marzuq Al Shimlan in 1952:

→ A 1934 aerial image showing the Ruler's Palace, known today as the Amiri Diwan.

> The fort is located at the western side of Doha and along the coast, a large structure constructed over the ruins of the barracks where the Ottoman soldiers resided when Qatar was under the hegemony of the [Ottoman] State.

↓ Aerial image showing the Ruler's Palace in 1952.

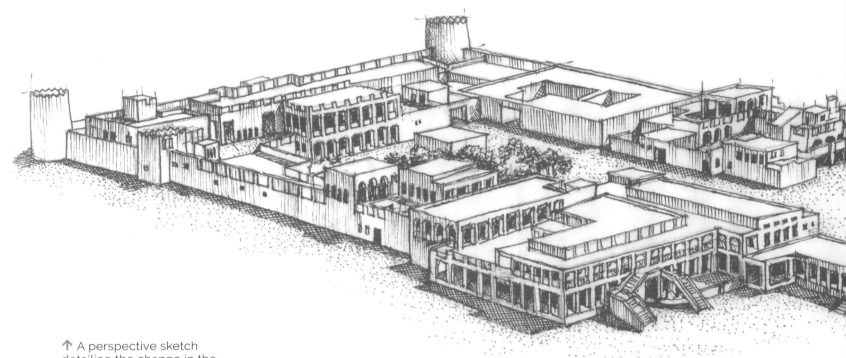

↑ A perspective sketch detailing the change in the Ruler's Palace in 1959.

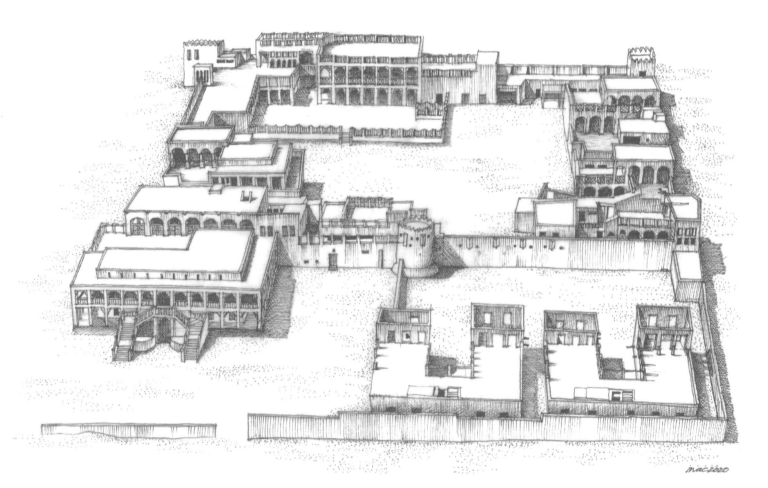

↑ A perspective sketch detailing the ceremonial building and offices added on the northern side of the Ruler's Palace in 1952.

The fort is located on a dais and has two doors. A large door to the south and a second door to the east overlooking the gulf. Along the south wall is a long *dakkah* [built-in raised bench/seating] where the Ruler of Qatar sits in the Summer afternoons. As soon as he is seated the *dakkah* fills up with people. Adjacent to this, to the east along the coast, is a large Majlis built in the modern style, for HH the Amir. Close by is the staff with the official Qatari dark red flag. Over the Fort's eastern gate is a small flagpole where the flag is raised when the Amir is inside and pulled down when he leaves the fort (Al Shimlan, 1952).

In 1952, a ceremonial two-story building was added attached later to the south corner of the east wall, with a U-shaped flight of stairs leading to the center of the terrace on the second floor. Furthermore, two identical single-story, U-shaped structures were built as part of the extension of the ceremonial building. Later, in 1959, the U-shaped structures were demolished but the extended boundary wall remained.

→ Aerial image showing Al Marmar Palace after construction.

Al Marmar Palace

The construction of the "Marmar" or Guest Palace took place between 1956 and 1959, and was carried out by Darwish Engineering and its partner, CAT. It was constructed in Rumailah opposite the State Hospital and a mile to the west of the Amiri Diwan. The scale of the building and complex after completion was outstanding at that time compared with the residential developments around it. There are two gates identical in design within its boundary wall with a large, pointed arch (two centers) supported by a Tuscan coupled column, one gate on the eastern wall, and the main one on the southern wall. After the main gate, there is a welcoming view of a landscaped roundabout with a fountain in the center; the path around it leads to a gentle, symmetrical, curved ramp to the drop-off point by the main entrance door.

The main elevation facing south was breathtaking with its symmetry and grand arch entrance typical of gates, with an extension of a wide veranda of ten pointed arches on each side. Balustrades on the veranda were kept low

and there was a wide staircase connecting the path around the fountain to the building. The design was unique for the time with a reflection of Indian subcontinent touch in its facade. The veranda arches were covered by diamond-mesh lath to give the south facade a degree of solar protection.

The south elevation indicates the simple layout inside the building, consisting of a basement level for parking and service facilities, a ground level for reception lounges and delegation guest rooms with their facilities and services, and an upper floor with royal guest suites with their facilities and services. The central grand corridor from the main entrance through the first floor leads to an exit door to the main porch, which has an amazing view of the back garden and of the sea. The main porch leads to a grand staircase, which descends to the garden.

The roof of the structure, together with the walls being capped with green, and glazed roof tiles on the entrance building, reflects the architectural appearance of the Guest Palace. There are two roundels on the face of the structure, each incorporating religious calligraphy, and over the doors is the customary *bismillah*, or religious exhortation. The garden at the back, facing north, has a decorative pool toward the center designed to replicate the character of the seven-barrel vaults of the clock tower.

↑ Al Marmar Palace (top) and front elevation (above).

→ Al Marmar Palace during construction (top) and the *liwan* from the front elevation (bottom).

Dar Al Hukumah

Dar Al Hukumah was designed by the same architect, John R. Harris, who won the design competition for the State Hospital in Rumailah. The beginning of the construction of Dar Al Hukumah coincided with the construction of the Clock Tower in 1956 by Darwish Engineering and was completed in 1957. The building is located on the shoreline facing north, next to the first hospital and approximately 250 meters east of the Amiri Diwan. This building was used as a central Ministry for All Government Affairs. It consisted of two buildings, the one-floor, U-shaped building in front, facing the coastline raised on a high-level platform, and the four-floor building behind it. The building reflected some elements of the Qatari vernacular: the window shape and the courtyard concept.

↙ Dar Al Hukumah while it was under construction in 1956 (left) and an aerial view in 1959 (right).

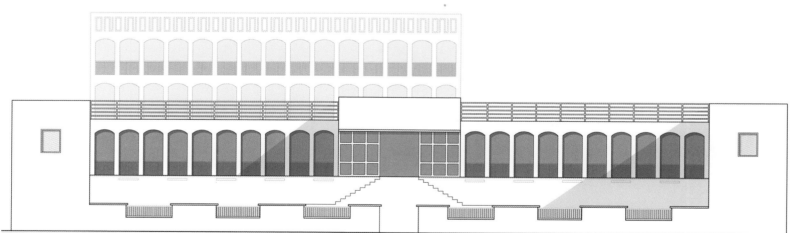

Urban and Architectural Features

The need for banking first rose from the exploration and export of oil in 1949 and was serviced, until Qatar's independence, by a mixture of foreign and Arab banks. Until 1954, the Eastern Bank Ltd (now Standard Chartered Bank) was the only bank operating in Qatar. With a need for more banks several began operations in Qatar in the 1950s: the British Bank of

↑ Front elevation of Dar Al Hukumah after construction completion.

the Middle East opened in 1953 (acquired by HSBC), the Othman Bank (formerly Grindlays Bank, acquired by Standard Chartered and currently IBQ), and the Arab Bank, followed by the Lebanese Bank (now Al Mashrek Bank) in 1960.

Al Usmani Bank, built in 1957, is one of the early banks established after the oil boom in the 1950s, which indicates the increase in the financial sector at that time. It is a three-floor building with a modern veranda facade reflecting the sense of a financial building.

The increase in the financial sector was also associated with the hospitality sector in the form of small hotels. The 1950s saw the establishment of the Gulf Hotel, which was a simple two-floor building with a veranda facade. At street level there was a series of shops indicating it was located within a *souq* area,

↘ The British Bank of the Middle East opened in 1953.

↓ Al Usmani Bank built in 1957.

↓ Front and side elevation of Al Usmani Bank.

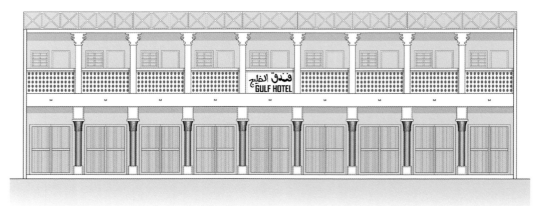

← Front elevation of Gulf Hotel in the early 1950s.

← The famous Bismillah Hotel located within Souq Waqif.

→ Oasis Hotel when first opened in 1954, aerial view (top), a back view (middle), and front elevation (bottom).

while the second floor was the hotel. Bismillah Hotel is another example located within Souq Waqif with a similar function to that of the Gulf Hotel but with a more vernacular element to it. The combination of commercial and hospitality services in one building indicates the increase in trade and commercial activities with overseas connections. Oasis Hotel was the first to be constructed as a luxury hotel in 1954. The two-floor, U-shaped building facing the beach introduced the sense of modern architecture at that time. The entrance facade had a distinguished architectural character with a horizontal concrete pergola with a fake large window behind it and topped with a wavy parapet and a large projecting tower-like mass on both sides. The rooms extended on both sides, accessed from a semi-open corridor on the south with a metal grid screen to interrupt direct sunlight. The rooms had balconies facing north toward the sea.

The *souqs* in Old Doha were among the first facilities to be built in the 1950s: the area lay adjacent to the sea with some buildings directly on the shoreline, close to the port area for the easy unloading of goods. All the trade took place

here and Souq Al Baker formed part of the daily routine at the time. It is located in the Al Ahmed area around Al Ahmed Street that encompasses Souq Al Ahmed, Souq Al Toyour, Al Ahmed Plaza, Al Ahmed Mosque, and Bism Allah Hotel. Originally this section was Kharis (wetland and shoreline) separated from the original old *souq* by Wadi (river) Mishrieb. It was totally newly made and has no authenticity but it created a pedestrian promenade by covering the river that divided the whole area into two.

↙ Aerial view of Souq Al Baker in 1956.

↓ Souq Al Baker as it appears today.

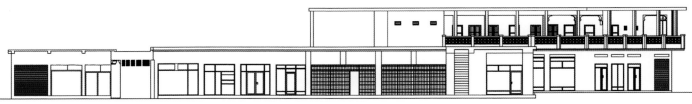

↑ Front elevation of Souq Al Baker.

Souq Al Baker is one of the few traditional markets remaining in Doha. The building was as it stands today—modern, with two stories. The upper floor has been added relatively recently. The original market was a single-story structure with two rows of shops and a covered walkway between them.

Unfortunately, little of the original building remains, as Souq Al Baker has recently been rebuilt. The modern structure, however, still serves as an active market, with many jewelry and multipurpose shops. The upstairs area has been converted into accommodation, with many small rooms. This occupies approximately a quarter of the roof area, leaving the rest open. Stairs on the east side of the *sikka* lead to an open hallway and the upstairs rooms. The hallway then gives access to the open part of the roof.

The Grand Mosque with the Amiri Diwan and the Clock Tower formed part of a ceremonial square to reflect the beginning of a new prosperous state for future development. The first redevelopment on the mosque was carried out in 1957, when a new minaret, prayer area, *mihrab*, and gate were constructed. This was done at the same time as the Clock Tower was built, giving inspiration for the Grand Mosque gate. In 1963, the Grand Mosque was under

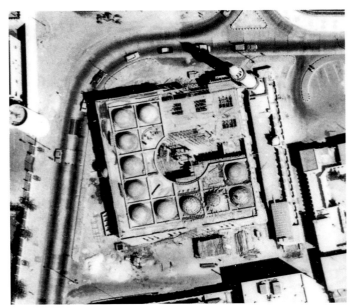

↑ Aerial view of the Grand Mosque next to the Amiri Diwan in 1959 (top).

Aerial view of Al Shuyukh Mosque under construction, 1963 (above).

↗ Al Shuyukh Mosque after the completion of its construction.

construction as part of a new redevelopment plan and renamed as Al Shuyukh Mosque, which has a distinguished central dome that covers a significant part of the prayer hall.

Doha was full of mosques. The most popular and important were the Sheikh's Mosque alongside the Fort, the al-Ahmad Mosque and the Jassem [al-Qubaib] Mosque—which was unique in its architecture and quite the most beautiful mosque to be found anywhere in Qatar.

(Othman, 1984)

Modern Construction Materials

Modern construction materials in the 1950s introduced an interesting architecture combined with the vernacular Qatari style. This combination was due to two main factors: (a) the master builder (*al banaa*) was constructing new buildings using his traditional methods with new materials; (b) some of the new materials were applied on existing vernacular buildings. The new buildings by the *al banaa* had the Qatari character with the use of new materials

such as, square wooden beams for the ceiling projecting from the external wall, colored glass for the windows, steel bars and frame for the windows, cement plaster for the walls, and concrete for the ceiling. The existing buildings had minor interventions of new materials such as, using cement for external and internal wall plaster, using cement plaster for the roof, and connecting the building with electricity through exposed electrical conduits on the walls and ceilings. The narrow passages between the buildings were also covered with a layer of concrete to reduce dust and smoothly discharge stormwater.

↑ The use of new construction materials in old buildings.

← Cement plaster applied on the old buildings.

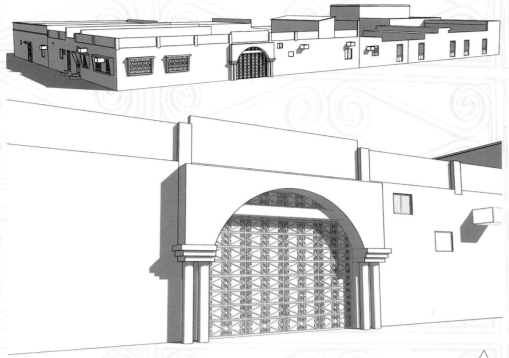

→ Two sketches of new residential block module with more than one unit, complete (top) and detail (bottom).

→ Some residential blocks would be associated with a mosque or shops.

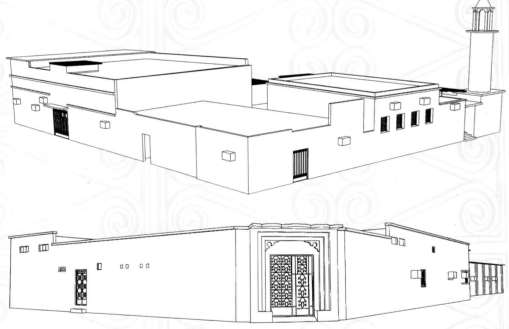

→ In some cases, they have decorative metal doors in one corner.

The newly built residential units differed from the previous individual pattern in the sense that they were constructed together within a block. The block would contain more than one residential unit and sometimes some shops were present on one side or more, with a mosque in the corner. Most of the residential blocks were one story high, and in some cases a half story was added on top. The one or two steps in front of the entrance door indicates the consideration of raising the newly built blocks. These steps led to a metal door encased with a simple concrete flange. The windows had a framed concrete projection to interrupt direct sunlight. Most of the elevations had horizontal

← Example (top) and front elevation (bottom) of grand entrance gates for residential buildings.

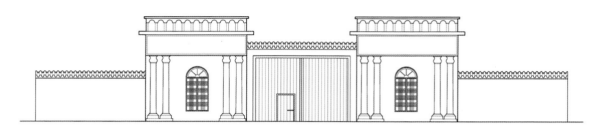

concrete ledges to block some sunlight and cast some shade on the facade. Through the main door, entry was either directly to the house or to a courtyard space leading to other rooms and facilities. The decoration on these blocks was limited to the doors and windows, and in some cases the concrete projection frame around the door. The window AC units (box-like) projecting on the facade also introduced a new element, not only new to architecture but also to how people lived. In some cases, the outdoor courtyard shade or the roofs over some rooms were made of corrugated galvanized iron.

The 1950s also witnessed the construction of grand entrance gates for residential buildings that were in the proximity of the Amiri Diwan. These gates consisted of a large two-fold wooden gate with a wicket gate formed by a concrete projection and topped with corrugated galvanized iron. On the two sides, there was usually a guard room with a Qatari-style window shaded by a concrete projection supported by a Tuscan, coupled column. The parapet is made of a concrete baluster coated in white paint. The walls extending on both sides of the gate to the room are the same color as the gate and topped with corrugated galvanized iron. The architectural details introduced on these gates symbolize the wealth and social status of the owners.

Sheikh Ali bin Abdullah Palace in Al Rayyan also introduced some modern transitions in its architecture. The main gate is represented by a semicircular arch supported by square columns on each side and topped with a small horizontal projection with a spade-shaped (or inverted heart-like shape) parapet and

→ Sheikh Ali bin Abdullah Palace gate in Al-Rayyan.

↘ Architectural details from Sheikh Ali bin Abdullah Palace, (a) the gate with a small dome on top, (b) the minaret, and (c) the spade-shape parapet.

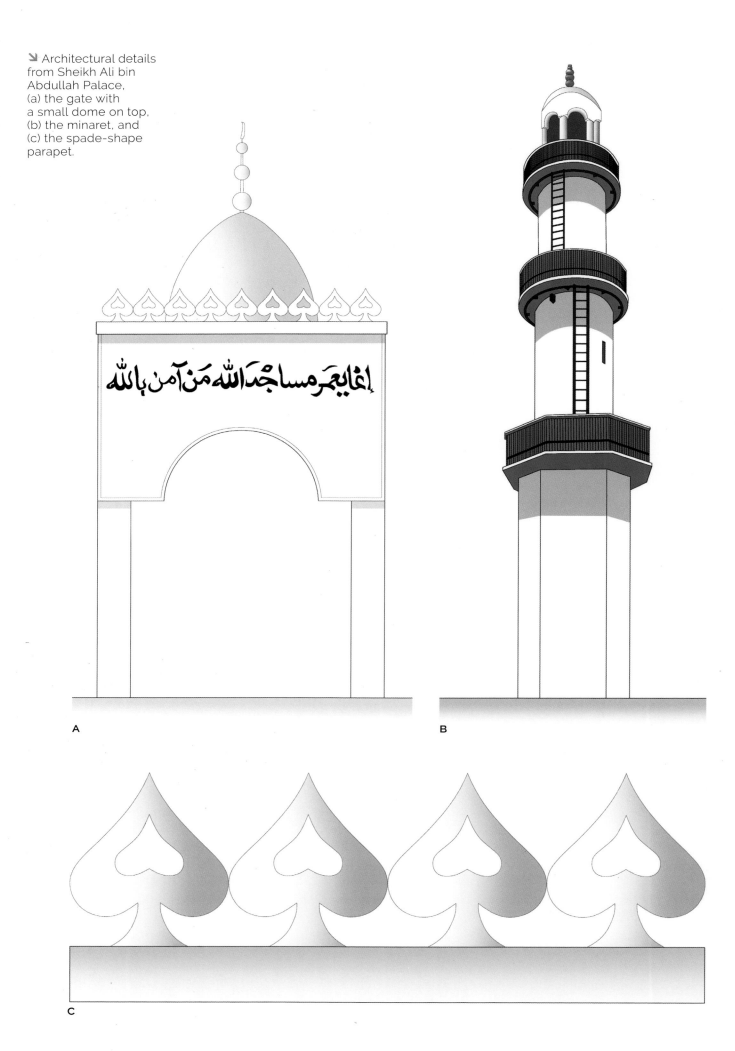

A

B

C

↑ The blue wooden door of the gate.

↗ The internal floor tiles with decorative, colored Islamic patterns.

↑ The *liwan* with blue windows.

crowned with a small dome. There is a calligraphy caption from the Holy Quran located between the arch and the parapet. Behind the arch is a large two-fold blue wooden door with a wicket gate. The gate is decorated by horizontal, blue, large metal nails. The glass window is protected by a decorative metal grill and framed by a concrete projection. Some of the internal floor tiles have decorative, colored, Islamic patterns. The courtyard is defined by a two-step-high veranda leading to an alignment of rooms overlooking the courtyard through blue grill windows with a spade shape at the top.

A

B

C

D

E

F

←↑ Examples of the four types of doors that were present in the 1950s: (a, b) Bab Al Mismari, (c, d) Bab Abu Farkha, (e) Bab Al Muqatta, and (f) Bab Al Baghdadi.

The wooden door was the most expensive element during the construction of a house because it was imported from India and Africa through foreign trade. The most common and desirable type imported and used for doors was teak wood from India due to its resistance to humidity and the fact that it was easy to carve. The height varied between 150–200 centimeters and width 100–140 centimeters, and these were normally made for wealthy families. There are four types of doors that were present in the 1950s: Bab Al Mismari, Bab Abu Farkha, Bab Al Muqatta, and Bab Al Baghdadi. Bab Al Mismari is characterized by the large projecting horizontal nails and is commonly used for large gates (*dirwazah*). Bab Abu Farkha is known for the small opening within one or both folds of the door. Bab Al Muqatta, also called Abu Manather, consists of several rectangular wooden pieces (*manather*) joined together, which appeared in buildings after Al Mismari. Bab Al Baghdadi is the most recent door type that is characterized by having a single piece of wood as a one-door fold with a decorated frame. Most of the doors had a transom for light and ventilation. These doors had a historical social significance for the owner, which explains why they were sometimes transferred from older to modern buildings.

Conclusion

The historic city of Doha went through many changes under new developments in the early 1950s, which contributed to its expansion. Two main factors contributed to the expansion: one in the center of the city, the other on the outskirts of the city. The building within the city center of a new ceremonial square that consisted of the Amiri Diwan, the Clock Tower and the Al Shuyukh Mosque, British Agency, and Dar Al Hukumah defined a new central administrative state within the city by which the new development era was launched. From there, new roads were developed to connect central Doha to other distant regions

within Qatar. The new infrastructure facilitated the network of electricity and water, contributing to redefining the city's urban fabric and accelerating the new development projects. The construction of a new dock and expansion of Souq Waqif contributed to the increase of commercial and hospitality projects. The construction of new hospital and education projects on the outskirts of the city and connecting them with new roads also encouraged the expansion of the city toward them.

↑ The new roads and automobiles that started to change how people lived in the city.

→ Aerial image from 1959 showing the changes in Doha.

CHAPTER 3

The 1960s, with the oil boom and its increase in oil revenues, is considered the decade that introduced modern urban governance and the Qatari Deco.

OIL BOOM

Introduction

A decade after the discovery of oil, Doha started to witness a major urban expansion from transition in the 1950s to urbanity in the 1960s, which is considered the decade of the introduction of modern urban governance. The 1960s brought new prospects to Qatar that contributed to a dramatic increase in oil revenues, approaching seventy million US dollars. The discovery of commercial quantities of oil offshore in 1961 and the start of production in 1964, Qatar joining the Organization of Petroleum Exporting Countries (OPEC) in 1961, and the increase in oil-field production, all contributed to the increase in Qatar's revenues during this decade. The increase in revenues contributed to increasing urban expansion, by ten times, reaching around twelve kilometers. This includes 26.3 hectares of landfill on the seafront for the expressway and public buildings, new administrative and ministerial government buildings, expansion of infrastructure facilities and utilities, public service projects, and housing and residential planning.

The process of urban development to create good conditions for Qatar in the 1960s started by setting up a centralized administration system to take control of its affairs. Such newly established government entities included several administrations and some independent ministries. These comprised the Ministry of Finance, Islamic Institute, Teacher Training Institute, Dar Al Kutub, administration of Labor and Social Affairs, administration of Education, Qatar Municipality, and the Islamic Court Building. The formation of these ministries was followed by the issue of a series of decrees and laws to govern the country's administrations and systems. This decade also marked the establishment of Qatar National Navigation and Transport Co, which was developed in parallel with the expansion of the airport and the transportation network in the city as well as the development of Doha Harbor. It also introduced new services like the post office, the telephone and telegram service, radio and television, and a new power plant.

The education sector not only constructed more schools but also started giving scholarships for students to study abroad. The first official housing policy was also established. The *Private Printing Press* started to emerge as one of the first newspapers in Qatar. The industrial and commercial sector also had

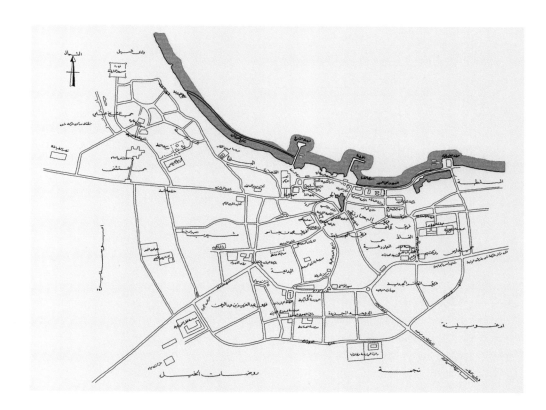

→ Map of Doha in 1963 issued by the Ministry of Ma'arif.

← Road intersections and roundabouts in central Doha in 1963.

a share of the development, where it witnessed the establishment of Qatar National Fishing Company and the construction of a new fish market, in addition to the opening of a National Cement Company and Flour Mill Company. A fair share of the development was also given to the media by establishing a Cinema and Film Distribution Company. All of these started to change not only the services and lifestyle of the people in Qatar but also transformed the city's urban form.

Expansion of Services

The construction of an asphalt road network continued throughout the 1960s, connecting the main roads together through sub-district roads. These connecting roads contributed not only to expanding the street network in the city but also to defining the urban form of the districts and creating ring roads. The street network showed new patterns of grid development in the urban planning of the city. In 1963 the Ministry of Ma'arif (Education) issued a map of the city that highlighted, and named, the new development of roads and buildings. During the 1960s, the straightness of roads was prioritized: therefore buildings were demolished for that purpose. The straightness of the road network introduced three-sided and four-sided roundabouts at the intersections as a new urban and landscape element for the city.

The new government urban housing, south of the city, contributed not only to introducing a new grid pattern to the city planning but also migration from

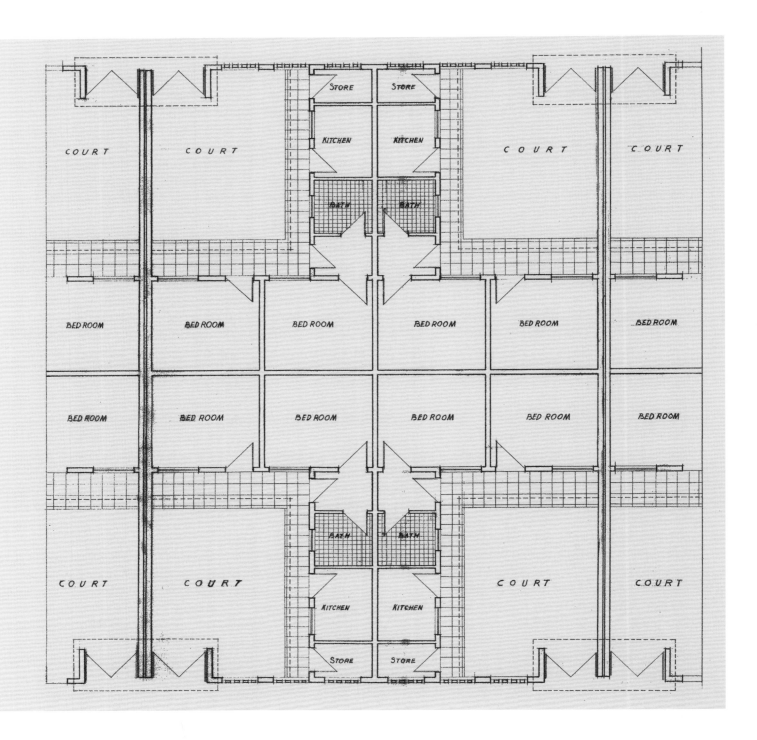

The following labels appear within the floor plan:

COURT · COURT · STORE · STORE · COURT · COURT

KITCHEN · KITCHEN

BATH · BATH

BED ROOM · BED ROOM · BED ROOM · BED ROOM · BED ROOM · BED ROOM

BED ROOM · BED ROOM · BED ROOM · BED ROOM · BED ROOM · BED ROOM

BATH · BATH

COURT · COURT · KITCHEN · KITCHEN · COURT · COURT

STORE · STORE

The expansion of the road network contributed to defining

traditional houses to new ones. They were big walled plots with an open yard to allow car parking inside and two blocks: the larger one had a *liwan* containing the rooms while the other block was for services. Additionally, public houses were developed in 1968, in grid, back-to-back plots, each with a courtyard and rooms and services aligned around it in an L-shaped form. This public housing moved the people with low incomes to live in the newly developed houses. The new urban housing gave people easier access to schools, utilities, and the main connecting roads in and out of the city.

↑ Layout of public housing, developed in 1968 in an L-shaped concept.

→ New government urban housing south of the city in the Al Montazah area in the 1960s.

→ Roundabouts with the city's new road network in the 1960s.

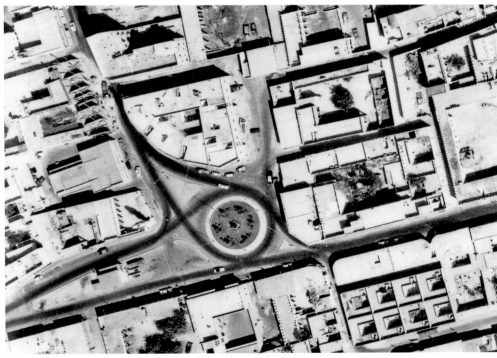

the urban form of the old and new districts and the ring roads

↓ Intersections with the city's new road network in the 1960s.

The streets also became a reference point to expand the infrastructure services and utilities, especially with the expansion of the Ras Bu Aboud desalination plant in 1962 and the power plant to accommodate the increasing demand that came with the city's urban growth. The reclamation on the coastline increased from 1.5 percent in 1952 to 4.8 percent in 1963, reaching up to 26.3 hectares, which gave the opportunity to develop a road and public buildings by the seafront. The expansion of Doha Harbor took seven years to complete starting from 1963, that resulted in a 5,632.7-meter-wide and 8.2-meter-deep channel that was created for the port.

The expansion of Doha International Airport between 1961 and 1963 with a new terminal building and control tower was one of the main milestone projects in that decade, designed by CAT consultants and constructed by Darwish Engineering. The new rectangular shaped, two-story terminal building was constructed opposite the old one with a grid concrete frame elevation topped on the third floor with a zigzag rooftop shading a terrace overlooking the runway. The three-story octagonal-shaped control tower is attached to the terminal building on one side and has a modern glass elevation on the other sides. It is crowned with a glass octagonal-shaped room for air-traffic control.

↖ Expansion of the Doha airport in 1962.

↑ New terminal building and control tower of Doha International Airport.

By 1961, a new post-office building was constructed in the reclaimed area by the shoreline, east of the Ministry of Education. The two-story rectangular-shaped building is simply designed with pointed windows with a triangle-pattern-like facade and a continuous *mashrabiya* wrapping around the second floor. Later in 1964, Qatar National Bank was established and used the post-office building as its main office.

By 1966, the Qatari telephone and telegraph service was operating from a newly constructed building located in Musherib. The three-story, rectangular-shaped building had a plain white, solid wall with a horizontal glass opening wrapped around its highest level. The second floor had rectangular windows framed with a simple concrete projection to break up direct sunlight, while the top floor was semi-open with a metal screen for ventilation and daylight. The year 1966 also marked the establishment of Qatar National Navigation and Transport Co, which

← New Doha post office that opened in 1961 (top) and the architectural features of the elevation (bottom).

→ New Doha post office, front elevation (top) and side elevation (middle).

→ Main elevation of Qatar National Navigation and Transport Company Limited in 1966 (bottom).

↓ Telephone and telegraph service building in Musherib in 1966.

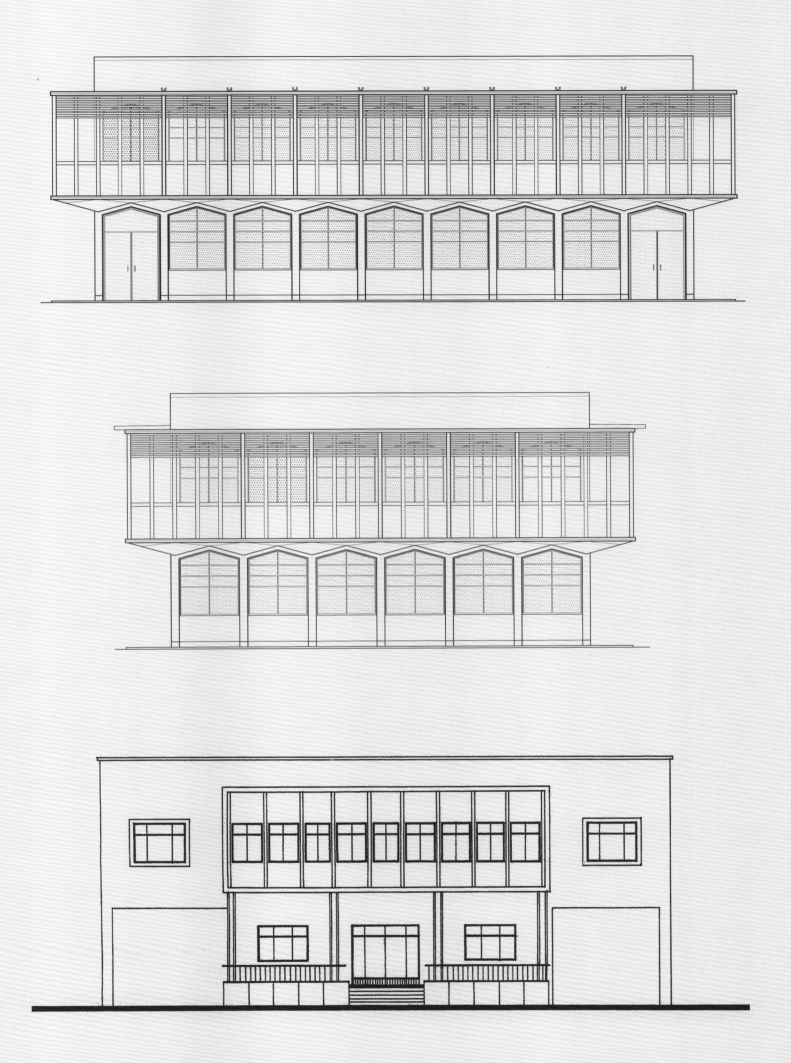

← First complex for Qatar Media Corporation, where the radio and television services are permanently located.

was a two-story symmetrical building with a small veranda by the entrance and a row of windows on the second floor. The radio and television service started temporarily broadcasting from a rented building located in Al Rumailah in 1968. Then the service moved to their new permanent building located in the current complex of the Qatar Media Corporation. The one-and-a-half-story building has a simple rectangular form with small windows grouped linearly under a concrete frame projection to break up the direct sunlight.

Abdullah Hussain Al Naima House was built in the 1960s with a symmetrical two-story, multiuse building, where the commercial front is aligned on both sides of the main entrance at the center on the ground level and the rest is residential. Despite the strong symmetrical concept of the elevation, the entrance at the center dominates the visual attraction with its vertical early-Deco pediment, which is decorated in the center with an open book

→ Front elevation of Abdullah Hussain Al Naima House.

→ Abdullah Hussain Al Naima House, which was built in the 1960s.

↓ Abdullah Hussain Al Naima House, early-Deco pediment (left) and some sense of the Qatari vernacular in the veranda and the gypsum patterns on the parapet (right).

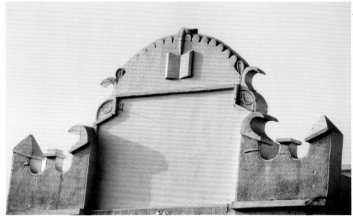

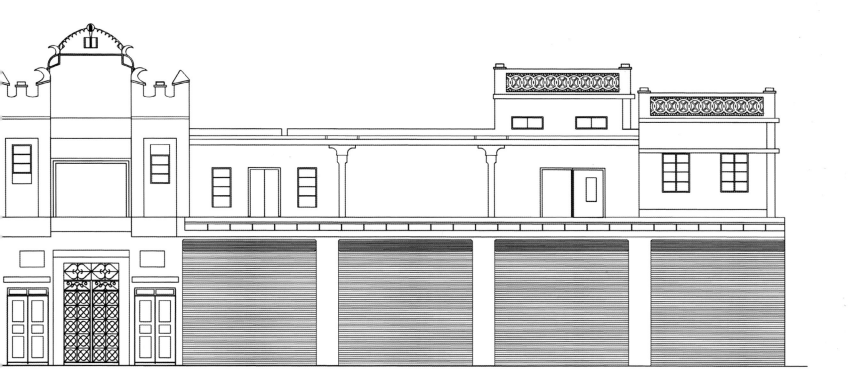

↑ Residential building in the Al Asmakh area with a similar early-Deco pediment.

↗ The elevation of the early-Deco pediment appears on a smaller scale but more colorful, with a large steel gate.

and a torch above it, while the two plain, rectangular spaces below it indicate they were for signage. The veranda on the upper floor and the gypsum patterns on the parapet give some idea of the Qatari vernacular. Abdullah Hussain Al Naima is considered the founder of the first published newspaper in Qatar. Another residential building in the Al Asmakh area also has a similar pediment to the one in Al Naima House but located in the corner on a smaller scale with more details and a larger gate.

Dar Al Kutub

Qatar had the lead in establishing the first public library in the Gulf region in 1962, it was known as Dar Al Kutub. It was established by Sheikh Ali bin Abdullah—the ruler—to merge the public library that was established in 1956 with the Al Ma'arif library that was set up in 1954 to form a national library, Dar Al Kutub. It is located at the intersection of Sharia' Al Madaris (School Street) and Sharia' Abu Aboud in the Al Ghanim neighborhood. The library consists of two buildings: the main building at the front and an L-shaped annex connected to it at the back. The main library building was on one floor with a *liwan* at its main elevation cantered by a big circular arch defining the main entrance door. The *liwan* is divided by cylindrical columns and connected at the top with circular arches. The square glass windows are topped with a circular recess like the *liwan* arches. Later, in the early 1980s, a new typical floor was added to the main library building to expand its capacity and services to the public. The main elevation of the upper floor has a metal grill of geometric patterns on its windows.

↑ Dar Al Kutub when first established in 1962.

→ Dar Al Kutub in the 1980s with the addition of a typical floor.

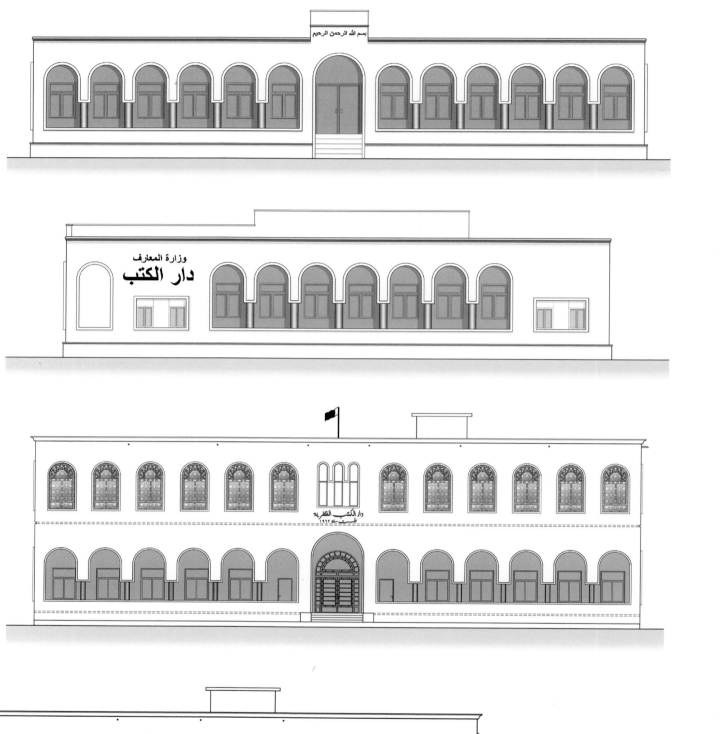

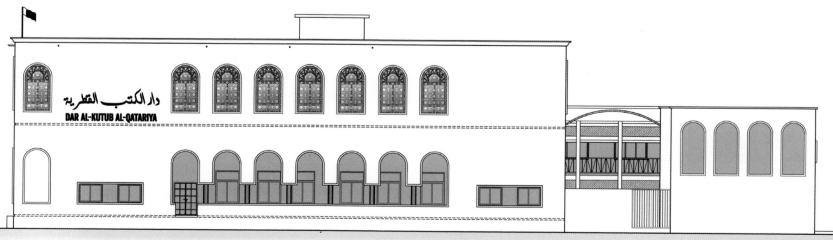

↑ Front elevation (top) and side elevation (middle) of Dar Al Kutub in 1962.

↑ Dar Al Kutub in the 1980s, front elevation (middle) and side elevation (above).

→ Dar Al Kutub today.

Schools

In the early 1960s, a new engineering department was established within the structure of the Ministry of Education. The scope of the department was to handle not only the challenges in the existing school buildings but to create a new unified design that could be flexible in its capacity, bringing a sense of the Qatari vernacular to it. The design issued by the department in mid-1961 was for a primary school for boys located west of Al Handassa Street. In 1963, the school level and name changed from Qatar Primary School for Boys to Preparatory School. The two-story school consisted of three annexes perpendicular to one another resulting in a symmetrical U-shape-like building.

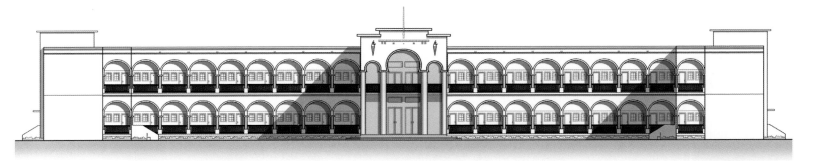

The main entrance is located in the middle of the central annex and defined by the three large, projecting, double-height, rounded horseshoe arches. The central, large arch is topped with a small decorative cantilever, while the two smaller arches on the sides are topped with a decorative torch. A veranda extends on both sides of the main entrance throughout the length of the annexes as a hallway to the classrooms and other spaces, and is overlooking the main school yard. The veranda is spaced by cylindrical columns three meters apart and connected from below by a metal railing and a circular arch at the top.

The U-shaped design carried out by the engineering department became a unified module used for seven other schools in Doha. Some modifications were made on the original design and implemented on the other schools; for example, the circular arches on the veranda were replaced with flat horizontal arches, and most were constructed on one floor, with the possibility of another floor being added later when necessary. The U-shaped school with long annexes was ideal for large plots, but

↑ Qatar Primary School for Boys, which in 1963 changed to Preparatory School.

→ Arab Gulf Primary School for Girls, first-floor plan (top) and second-floor plan (bottom).

↓ Front elevation of Arab Gulf Primary School for Girls.

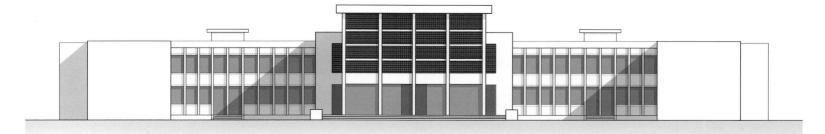

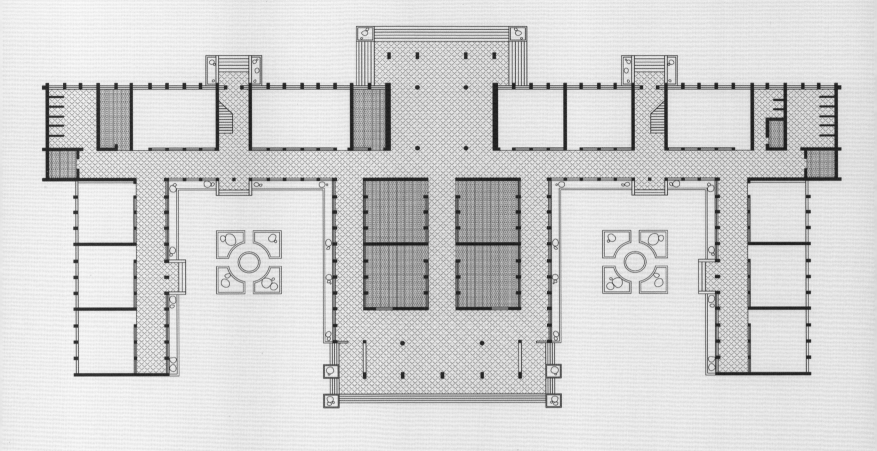
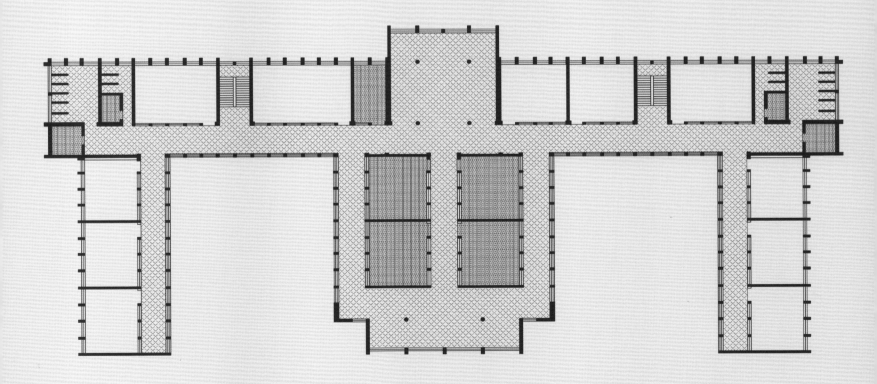

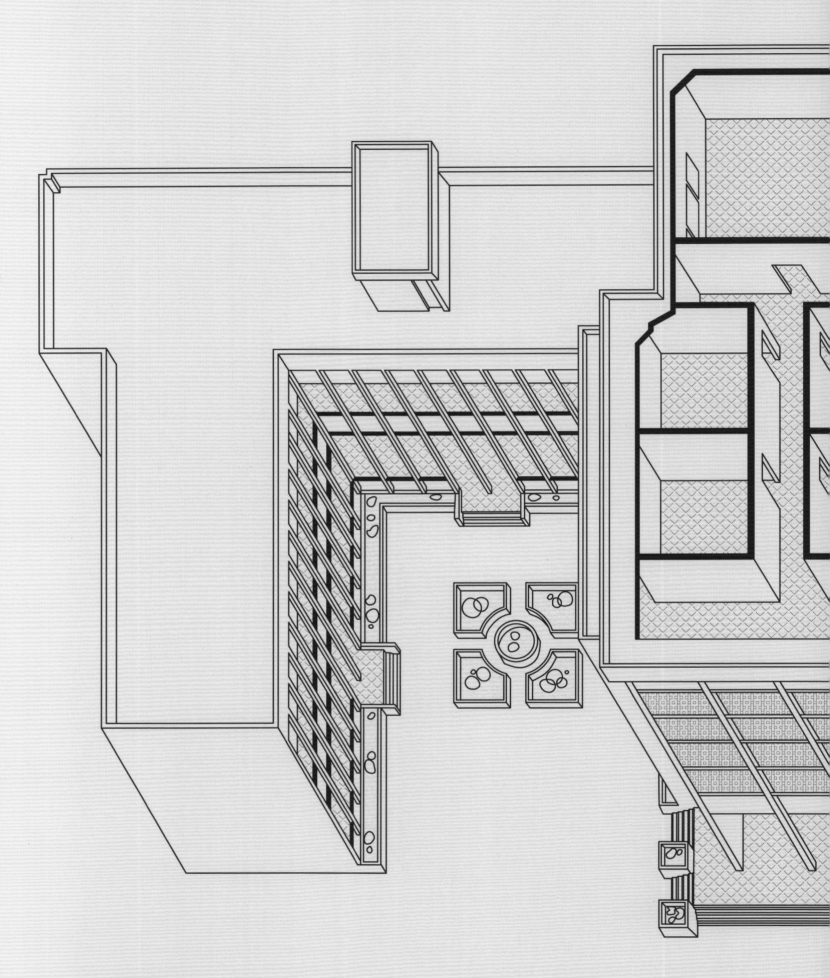

↑ Perspective of Arab Gulf
Primary School for Girls.

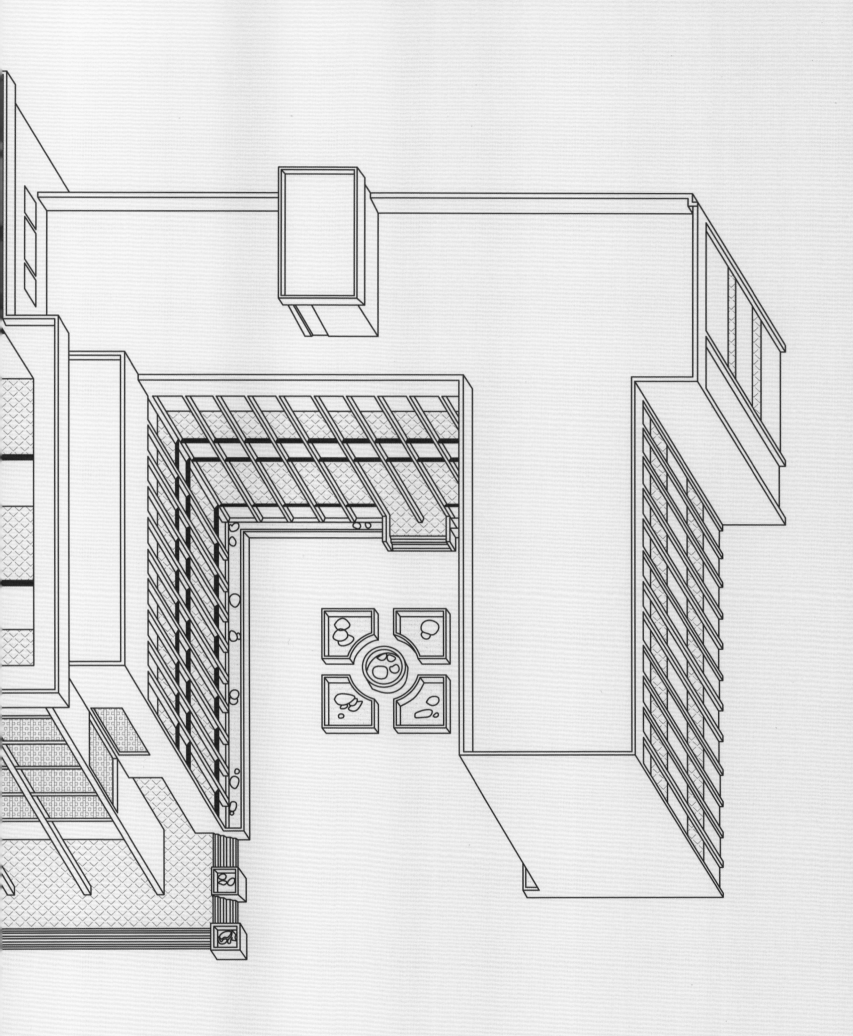

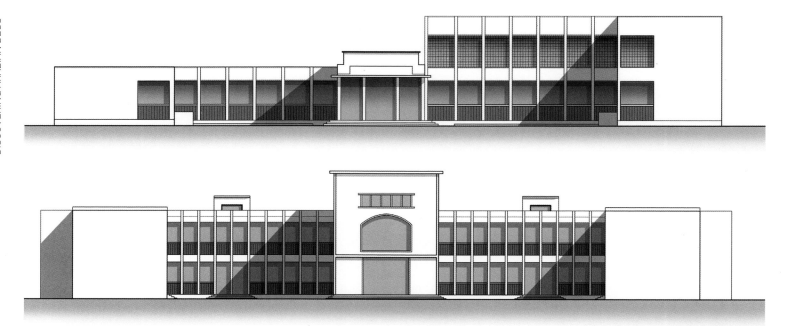

the annexes had to be shortened and a new annex added in the middle to present a new E-shaped school to accommodate the small plots. This was the case for the new Arab Gulf Primary School for Girls, where the main entrance to the middle annex was defined by its three floors, while the other annexes had two floors. The E-shaped module continued to be used for other schools, where the main difference, apart from the number of floors, was the design of the middle annex as the main entrance to the school. For example, the entrance extension in the new Al Rayyan Primary School for Girls had one floor and was defined by a portico supported by four columns, while Salah Ad Deen Primary School for Boys had three floors where the ground-level floor was open, the upper floor had a large semicircular opening, and above it was a rectangular glass opening. Other schools like the Arab Gulf Primary School for Girls and Doha Preparatory School for Boys used screen walls on the upper floors to define the entrance annex. The E-shaped school module was modified by making the columns span four meters and by enhancing the elevation with circular arches. An example of this enhanced E-shaped module is Ahmed bin Hanbal Secondary School for Boys.

↑ Front elevation of Al Rayyan Primary School for Girls (top).

Front elevation of Salah Ad Deen Primary School for Boys (above).

→ Ground-level floor (top) and upper-floor plan (bottom) of Ahmed bin Hanbal Secondary School for Boys.

↓ Front elevation of Doha Preparatory School for Boys.

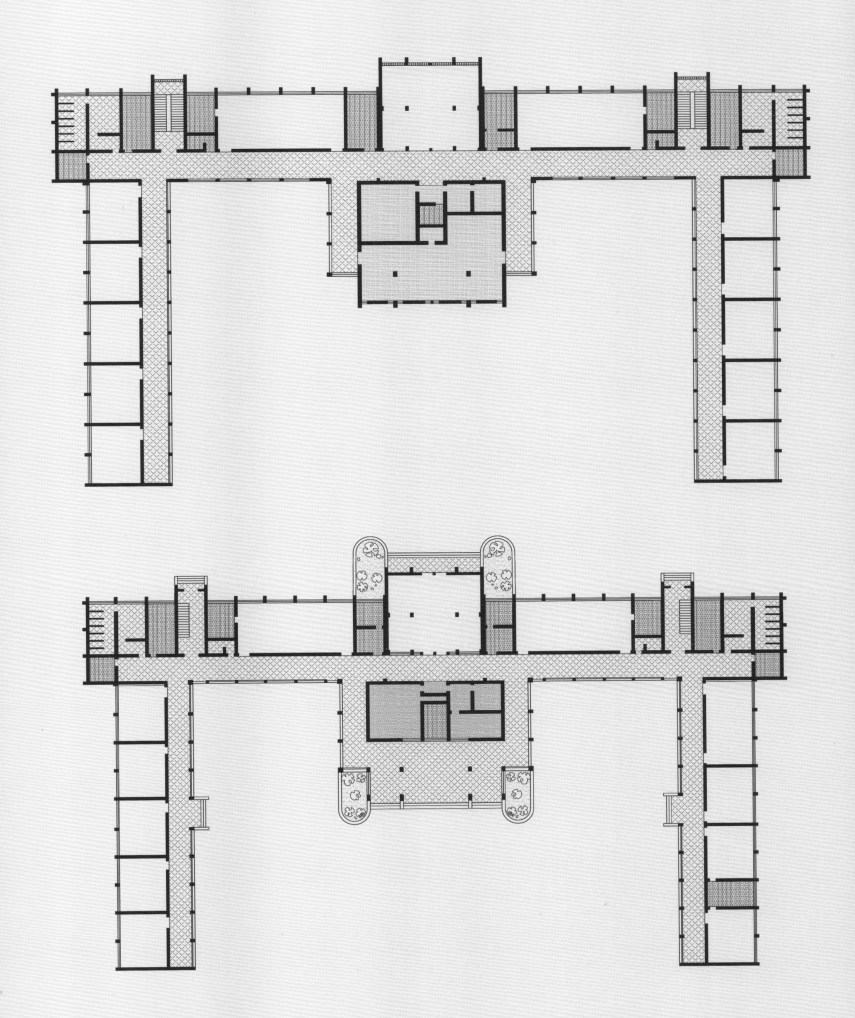

Expansion of Central Administration

The Amiri Diwan

In 1962, a modern office building for the ruler was built at the location of the old palace—the residence of the ruler and his sons remained on the site, along with the eastern tower of the fort. It became known as Doha Palace and formed part

→ The new annex after completion in the Amiri Diwan in 1962.

of a formal group of buildings, including a Clock Tower (1956) and the Grand Mosque, Masjid Al Shuyukh (1963). The new Diwan building itself increasingly became the public face of the new modern State of Qatar and a focus for the program of new development in the city. Under the supervision of the office director, a British firm was commissioned to produce a draft plan for a new building behind the existing Diwan. This plan included a grand entrance facing toward the south, and another gatehouse to the west. The landscape plan was done by a multidisciplinary studio, and included a ceremonial forecourt and the retention and restoration at its southern edge of two historical houses and a tower remaining from the old palace complex.

This building, designed by a Yugoslavian architect, is characterized by the use of a flattened, ogee-arch (onion-shaped-arch) motif, reflecting Qatar's historical trading bridge with India. This pattern extends throughout the external and internal elevations of the building, highlighting its linear quality. The building has a grand exterior porch facing east and is surrounded by a narrow colonnade.

← Aerial view showing the new annex after completion in the Amiri Diwan in 1966.

→ Another aerial view of the new Amiri Diwan annex.

↓ The main entrance of the new Amiri Diwan annex today.

The Diwan was also constructed with modern material, with a more ornamental aesthetic, and external, decorative paintwork in blue on the columns of the porch and the recesses of the arches. These designs link it to what might be regarded as Art Deco–inspired influences from abroad, while the private courtyard within reflects the enclosed patterns of traditional walled buildings in Doha.

The design and construction of the Amiri Diwan represented an important statement during the 1960s for the development of Doha. The design of the new Diwan introduced international and local initiatives to establish a new path in architectural design.

↖ An aerial view (left) of the Ministry of Labor and Social Affairs and the entrance (right).

Ministry of Labor and Social Affairs

The urban development of Doha on one hand and the newly established public and private sectors on the other, contributed to creating an attractive job market for locals and migrant laborers, which led to the establishment of a Ministry of Labor and Social Affairs in 1963. The Ministry is located south of the British Consulate and east of Masjid Al Shuyukh facing the Amiri Diwan ceremonial square. The three-story building is on a corner plot with two main elevations, one facing south and the other facing west. The southern elevation has narrow horizontal windows at the top of the wall on each floor and concrete projecting frames on the upper levels provide some shade, while the ground-level windows are shaded by a horizontal cantilever. The building is protected on the roof by a plain rooftop structure to reduce direct sunlight. The western elevation has no openings except for the ground-level floor, which is decorated with a concrete grid pattern. The waterspouts on the north and south elevations are inspired by the Qatari vernacular.

Ministry of Education

The construction of the Ministry of Education (Ministry of Ma'arif) on the reclaimed land by the seashore in a plot between the Islamic Court Building and the post office started in 1959, and began operating in the early 1960s. The two-story building is formed by two parallel wings connected in the center by a perpendicular annex forming an H-shape. The main building facade is facing

↑ Aerial view in 1962 showing the post office on the left, the Ministry of Education in the middle, and the Islamic Court Building on the right.

north to the shoreline with a colonnade projection in the center introducing the main entrance. The north facade is patterned with offset, vertical, concrete layers that cast shade on the openings. The two semi-open courtyards provide a comfortable microenvironment with landscaping. The building is reached through a gate structure with guard rooms on both sides followed by a landscaped roundabout with parking lots on both sides and a drop-off point by the main entrance. The Ministry of Education was considered the largest newly constructed, administrative government building at that time.

Islamic Court Building

The Islamic Court Building is one of the early government buildings that was constructed in 1962 on the reclaimed land by the seashore, between the vegetable market and the Ministry of Endowment. The main elevation of the rectangular two-story building faces west with a projecting screen wall defining the main entrance. The elevation has an offset vertical screen pattern of colored glass supported by columns wrapping around the main building. The colored glass was commonly used for verandas and windows. The roof is also protected from direct sunlight with a plain, shading structure with waterspouts projecting from its west side. This building is also one of the early government buildings to be walled with an entry and exit gate. Moreover, the building is surrounded by planned landscaping, driveways, and parking lots.

↑ Islamic Court Building.

Urban & Architectural Features

Showrooms

The beginning of road construction in the 1950s and its expansion as a road network in the city in the 1960s, attracted not only a new market for automobiles but also a new type of building, including showrooms. This was the case for the Al Mannai Trading Company, a showroom for automobiles that was constructed in 1967. The building is L-shaped with one and a half floors, where the ground level is divided into three parts—the offices are in the middle and the two sides are open-space showrooms—while the upper level is used for offices. The elevation has a showroom feature of mostly glass facade to allow viewing of the display of cars.

→ Al Hamad Automobiles Showroom, front elevation (top) and perspective (bottom).

↓ Front elevation (below) and first-floor plan (bottom) of the Al Mannai Trading Company Showroom.

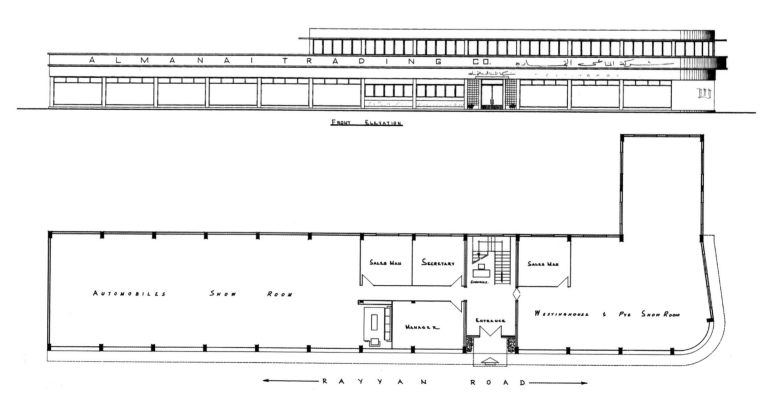

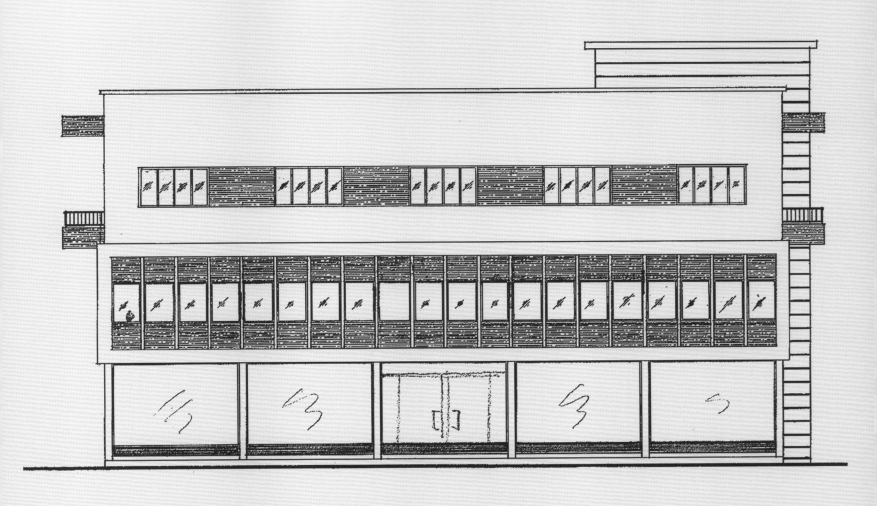
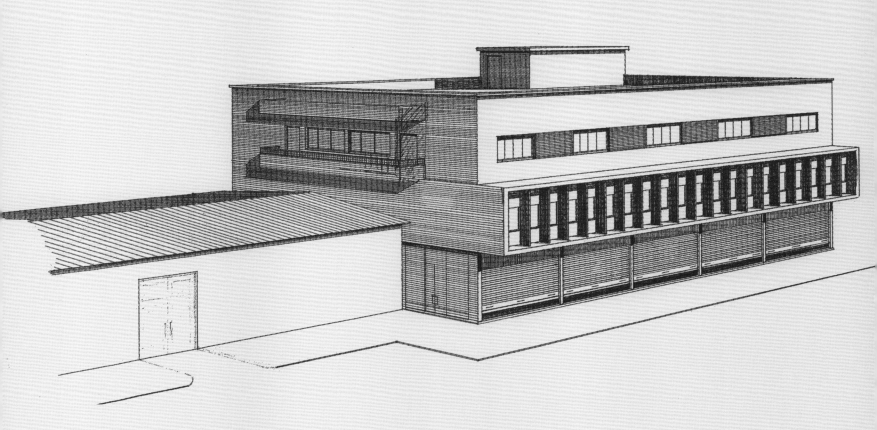

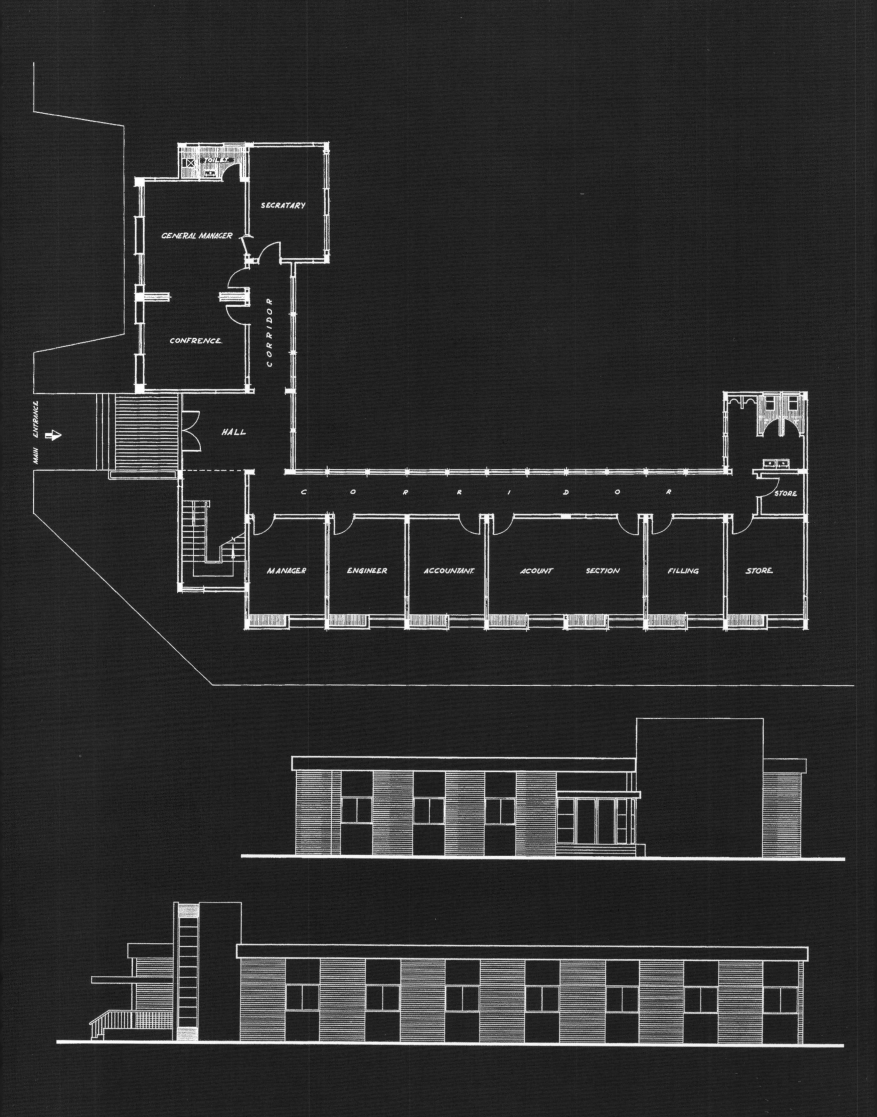

MAIN ENTRANCE

GENERAL MANAGER

SECRATARY

CONFRENCE.

CORRIDOR

HALL

CORRIDOR

MANAGER ENGINEER ACCOUNTANT. ACOUNT SECTION FILLING STORE.

STORE

Another example is the Al Hamad Automobiles Showroom established in 1968 in a multipurpose commercial building where the display is on the ground level and offices on the upper floor. The windows of the upper level are protected by vertical sunbreak projections in concrete.

Another interesting project is National Oil Distribution Company that was established in 1969. The one-floor building has a simple L-shaped layout with offices and other spaces connected by a corridor. The elevation has a series of rectangular glass windows protected by the vertical projection spacing between them.

← National Oil Distribution Company, floor plan (top), front elevation (middle), and side elevation (bottom).

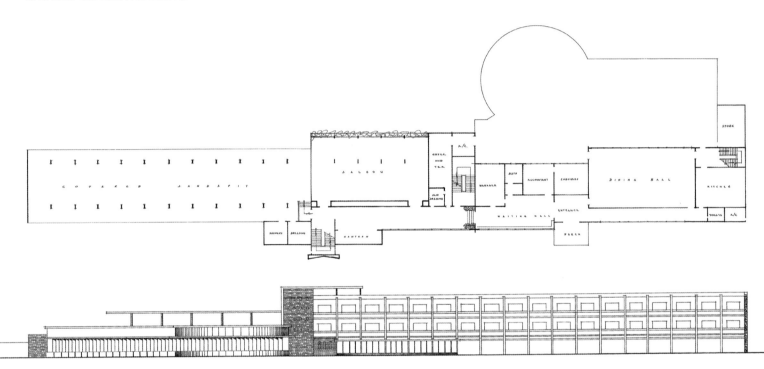

↑ First-floor plan (top) and front elevation (above) of the luxury beach hotel.

The second half of the 1960s also witnessed hospitality projects like the luxury beach hotel that was constructed in 1967. The building had a bigger and more longitudinal layout compared to previous ones to maximize its capacity and make the beach view available to all spaces. The north elevation had shaded balconies for the guest rooms and a vertical glass facade with some stone-cladded feature walls for the common facilities.

Palaces

In 1966, the Arab Engineering Bureau (AEB) was established as the first registered architectural firm in the State of Qatar. It was involved in the design and consultancy of many governmental, industrial, commercial, and residential development projects in Qatar including palaces and *majlis*. Since AEB was considered one of the first design consultants in Qatar, it received an increased demand for designing private residential palaces on large plots.

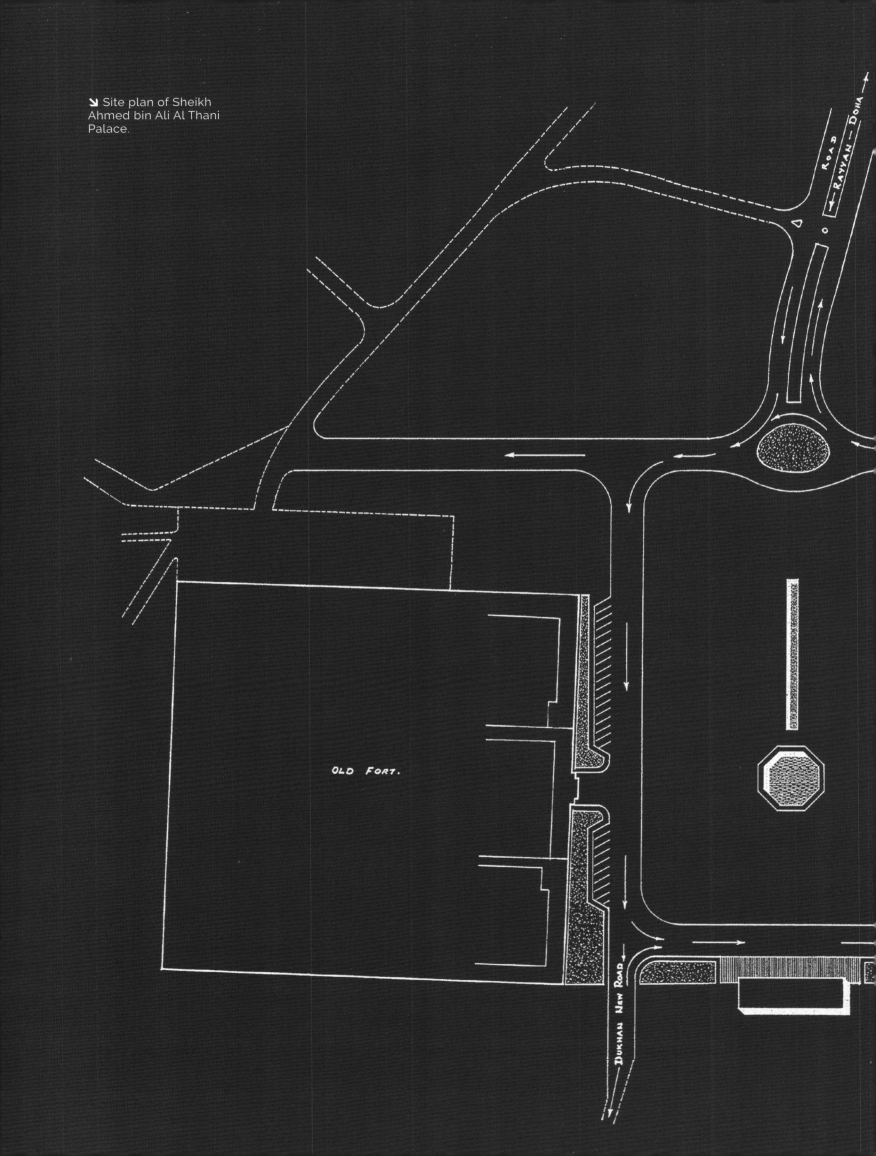

Site plan of Sheikh Ahmed bin Ali Al Thani Palace.

OLD FORT.

RAYYAN — DOHA

ROAD

DUKHAN NEW ROAD

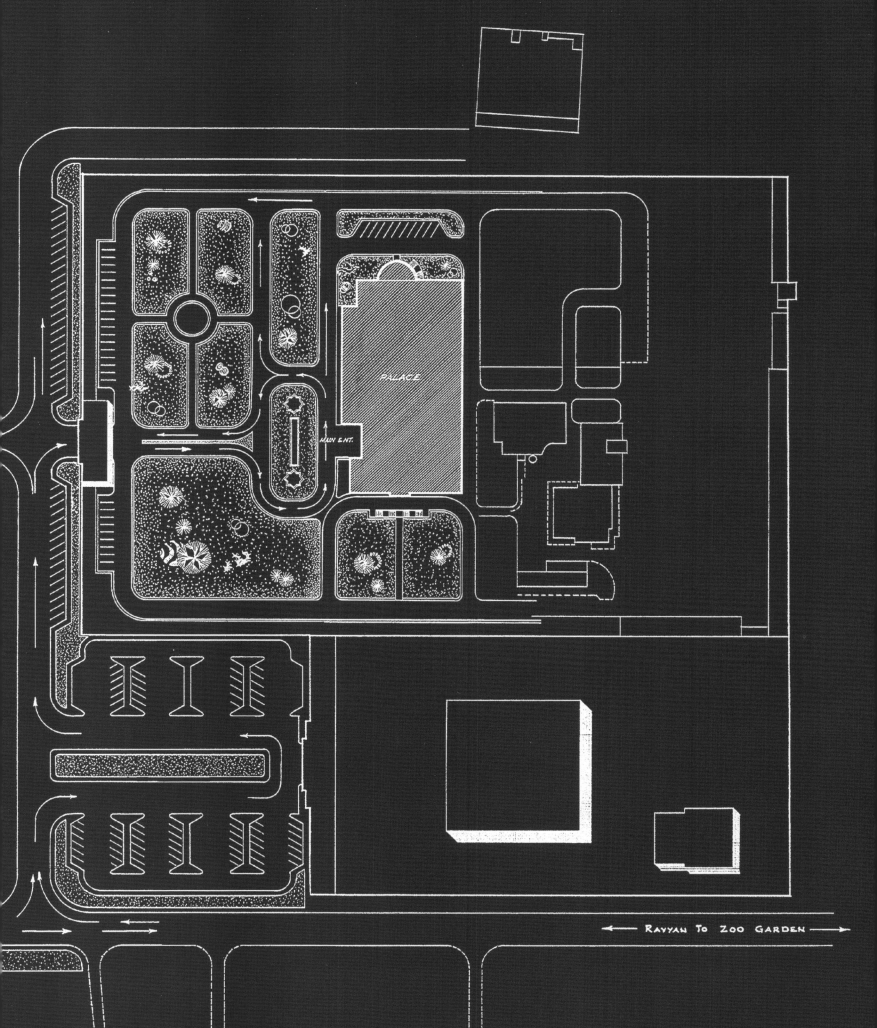

PALACE

MAIN ENT.

RAYYAN TO ZOO GARDEN

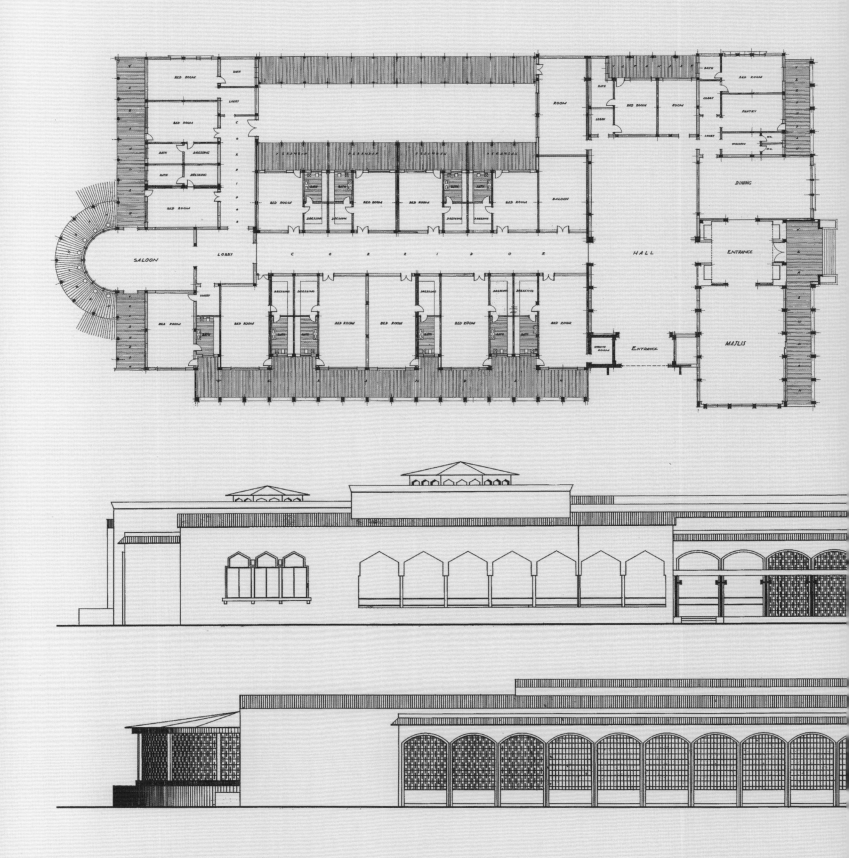

↑ Sheikh Ahmed bin Ali
Al Thani Palace, first-floor
plan (top), front elevation
(middle), and side elevation
(above).

→ Left side elevation.

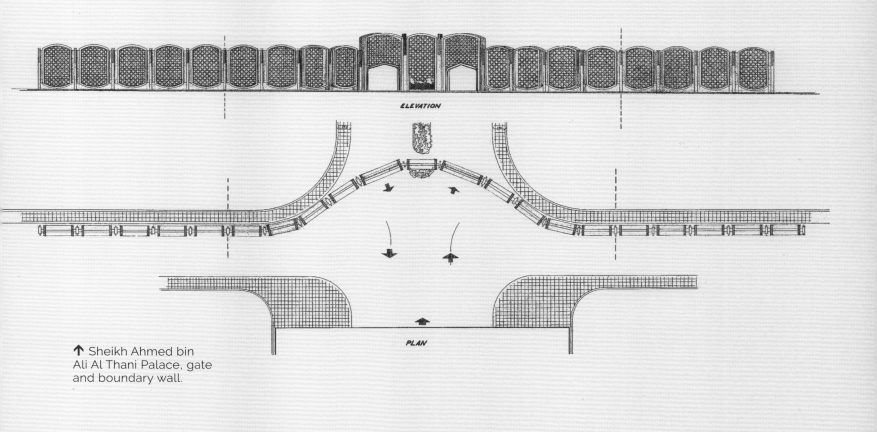

ELEVATION

PLAN

↑ Sheikh Ahmed bin
Ali Al Thani Palace, gate
and boundary wall.

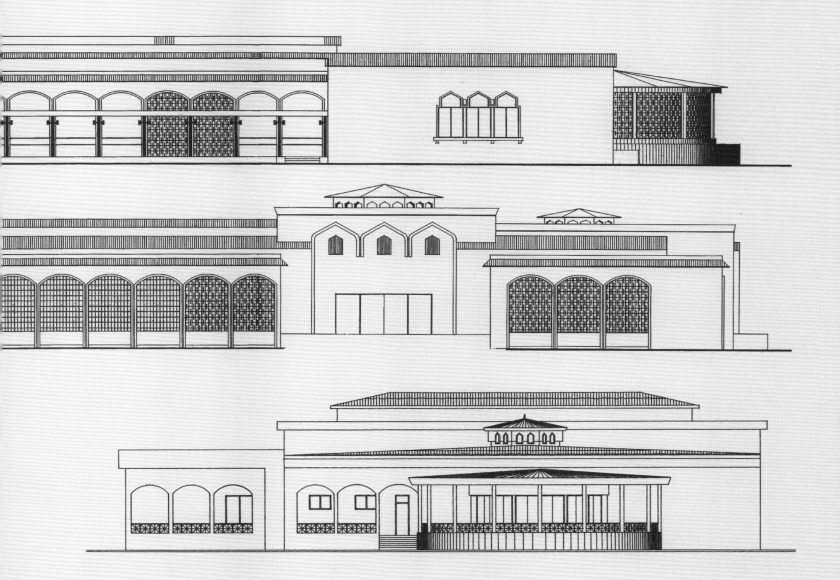

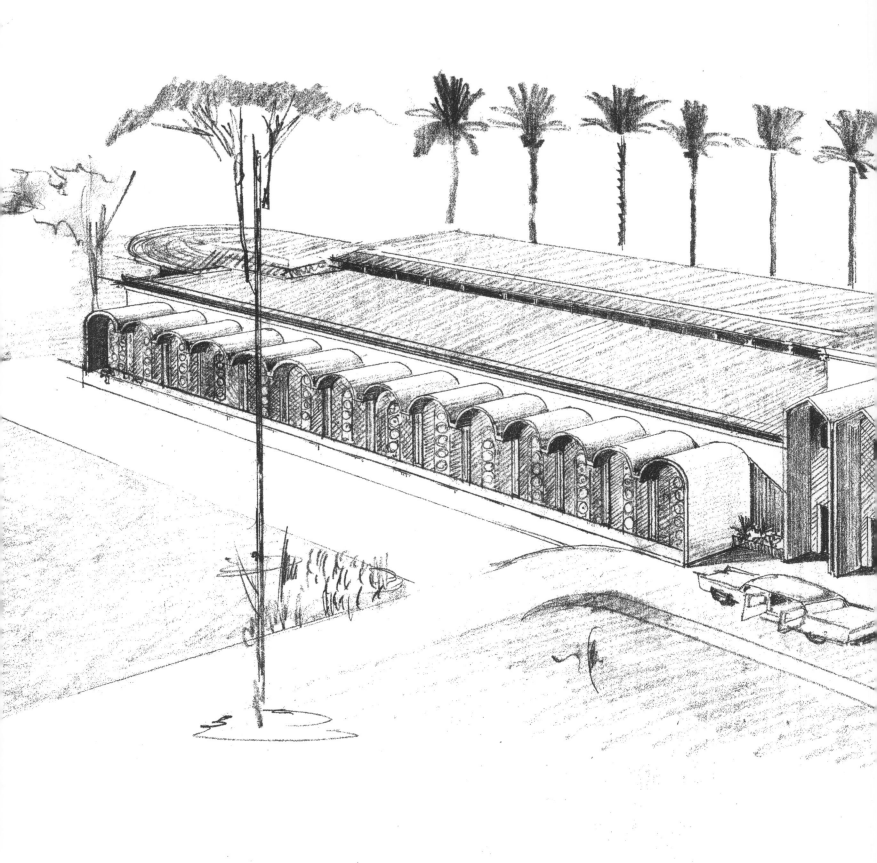

The architectural language of the designs was similar to what could be seen
in Lebanon and Egypt at that time. AEB designed two palaces for Sheikh
Ahmed bin Ali Al Thani in 1969: one is large and the other is smaller in scale.
The first grand palace is longitudinal with two entrances on the first floor,

↑ Proposed perspective
of Sheikh Ahmed bin
Ali Al Thani Palace.

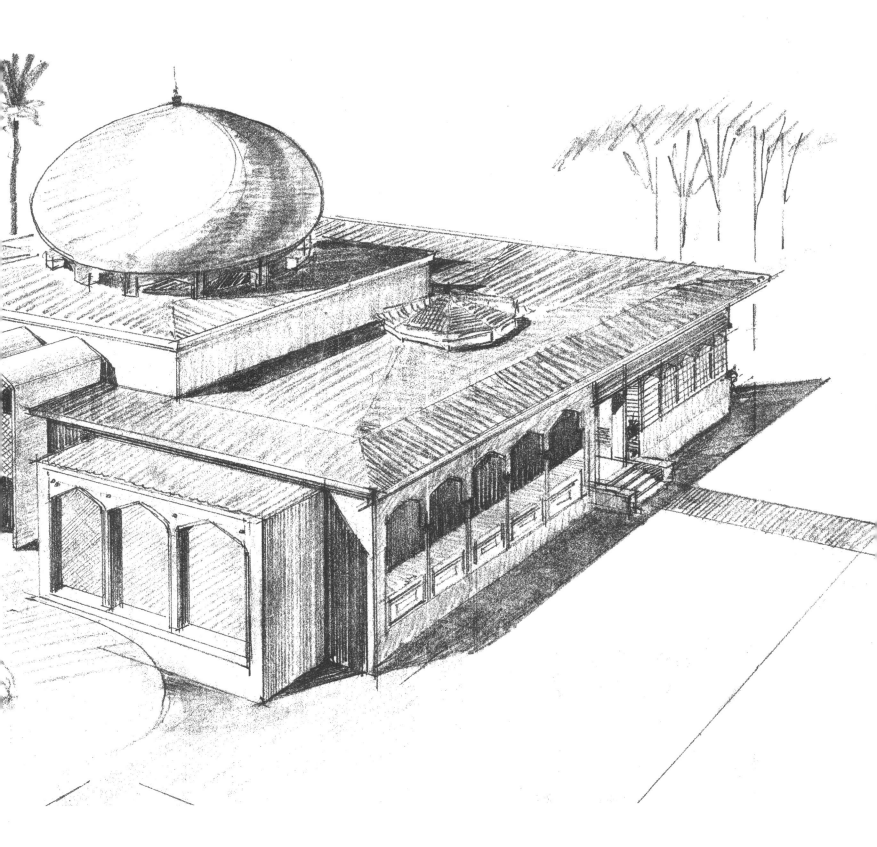

meeting in a large hall that connects to a corridor leading to other spaces along it and ending with a circular veranda. Parallel to the corridor is a long courtyard formed by a veranda on both its longer sides. The veranda on the elevation has a combination of a pointed arch like the one in Al Marmar Palace

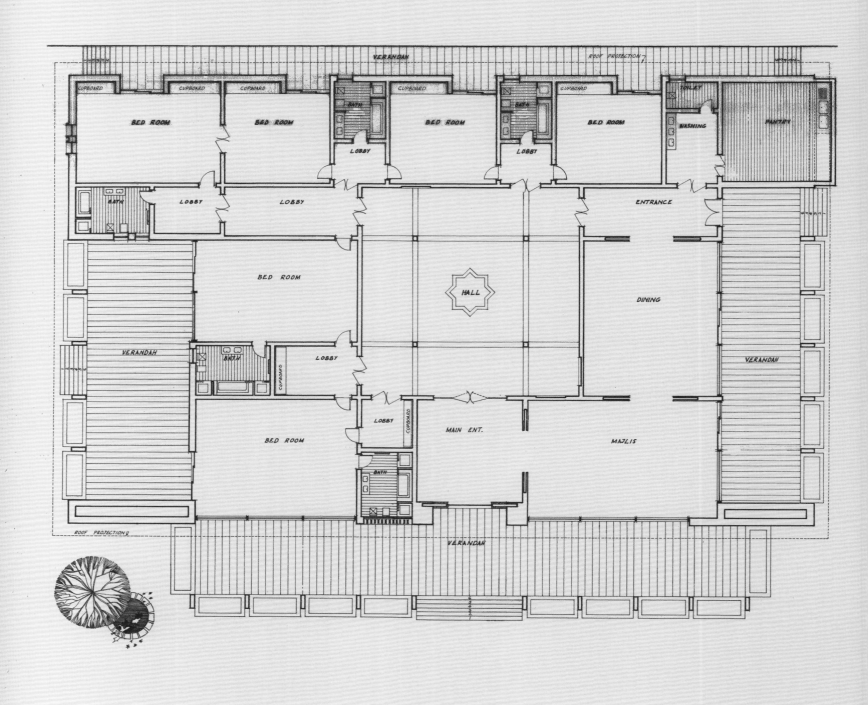

and a semicircular arch. Beyond the main boundary gate of the palace is a second seven-meter-high gated wall with a curved in-and-out access. The smaller palace also has the veranda concept on three sides with similar pointed arches to that of Al Marmar, but the most unique element beyond the pitched roof is another higher square-pitched roof with a tall spire. The elevation walls are also ornamented with ceramic, marble, and stones.

↑ First-floor plan of Sheikh Ahmed bin Ali Al Thani's other palace.

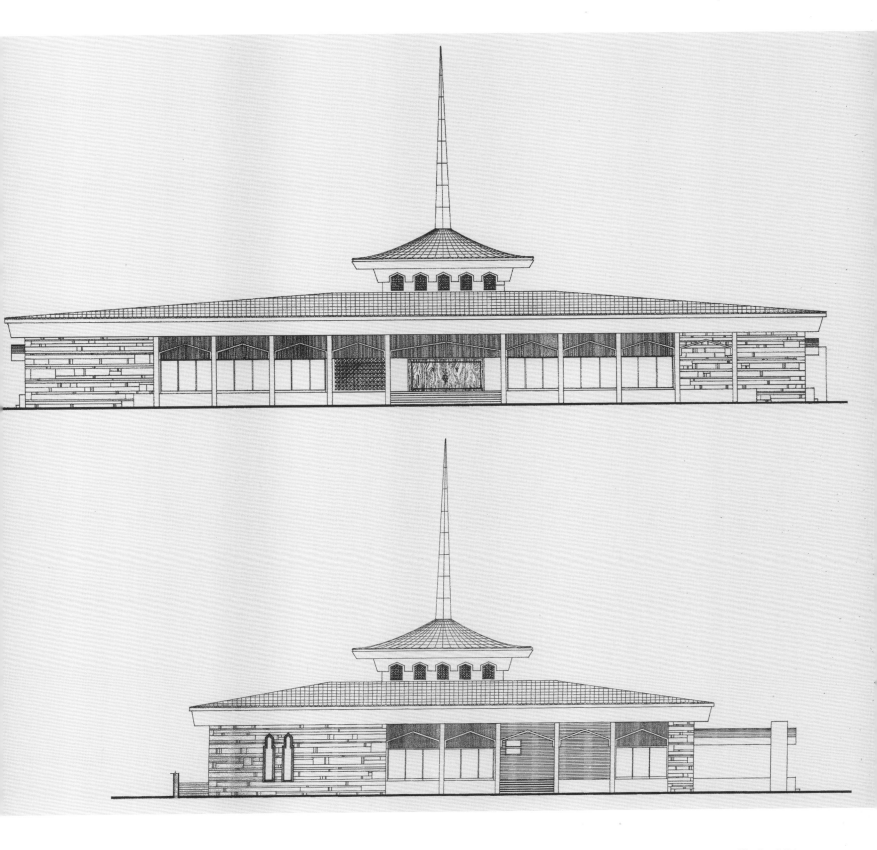

↑ Front elevation (top) and side elevation (above) of Sheikh Ahmed bin Ali Al Thani's other palace.

AEB also made three designs for another client, a palace and a *majlis* for HH Sheikh Abdul Aziz bin Ahmed Al Thani in 1967 and another *majlis* in 1969. One of the early palaces was designed in 1967 on a grand scale with a unique, novel pitched roof as well as a circular dome or veranda design, inspired by the Qatari vernacular but with an adapted, early modern look. The horizontal screen at the top of the *liwan* and the window size show the ongoing sensitivity to the environment.

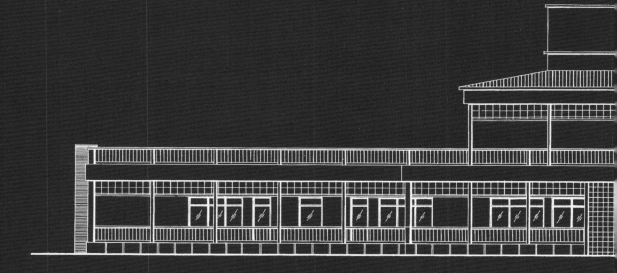

→ HH Sheikh Abdul Aziz bin Ahmed Al Thani Palace, front elevation.

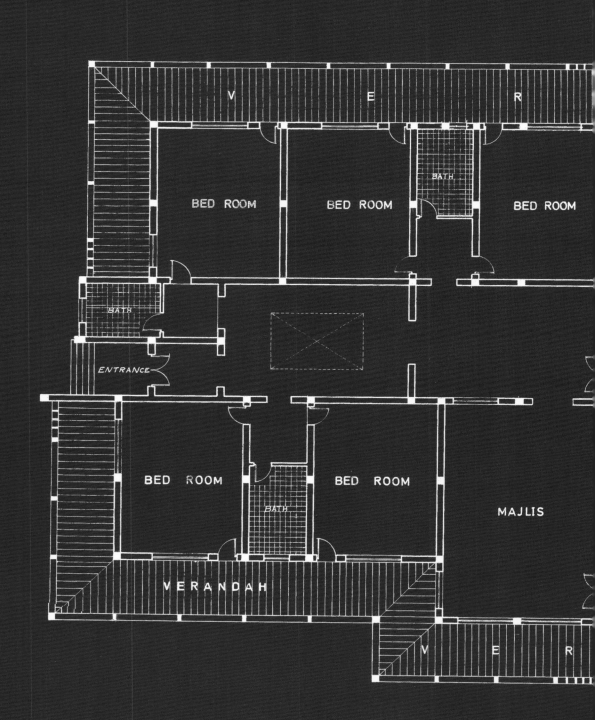

→ First-floor plan of HH Sheikh Abdul Aziz bin Ahmed Al Thani Palace.

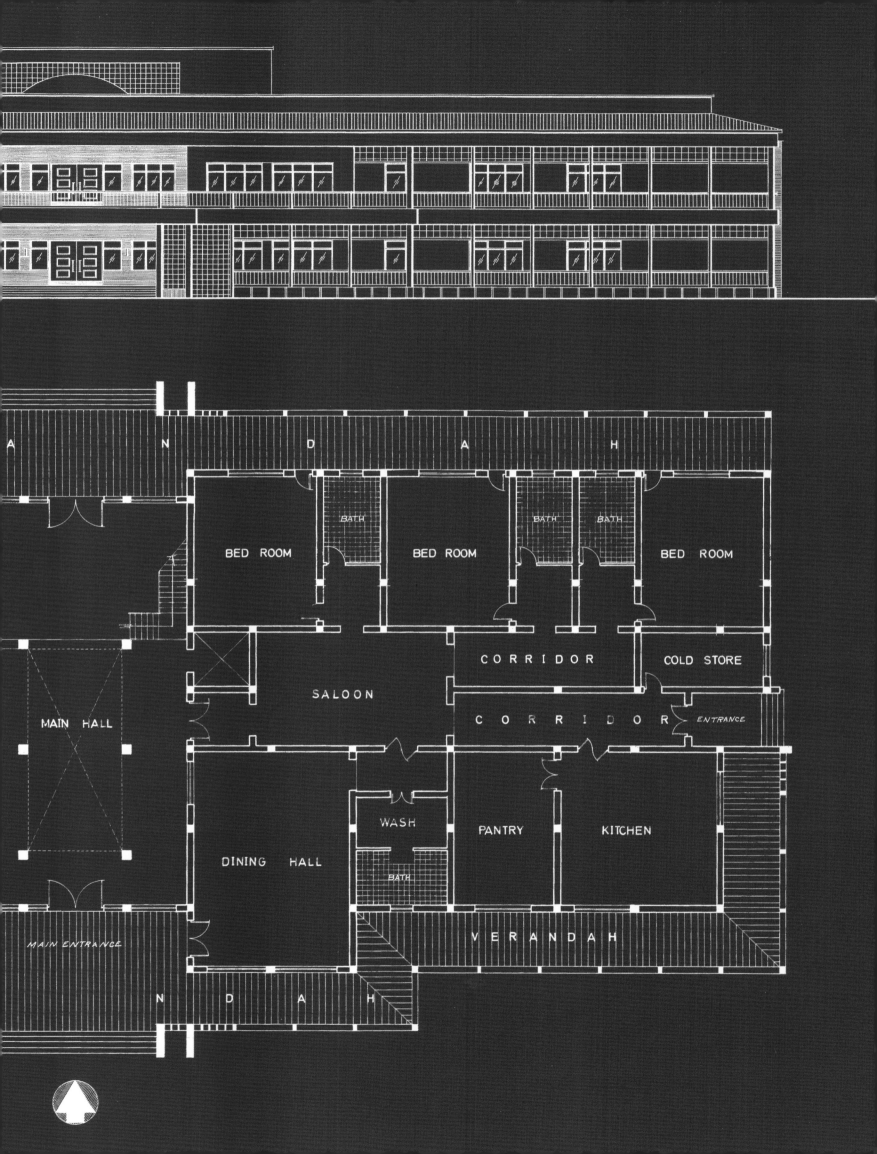

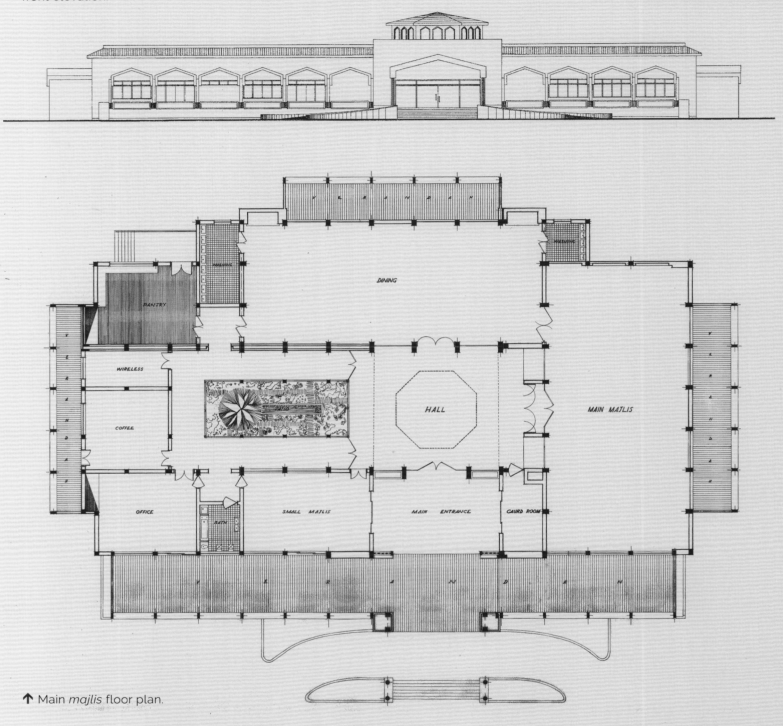

↓ HH Sheikh Abdul Aziz
bin Ahmed Al Thani Palace,
front elevation.

↑ Main *majlis* floor plan.

The *majlis* also had the *liwan* concept on every side with pointed arches like
the ones in Al Marmar with a pitched roof and an octagonal dome at the top.
The spaces inside were organized around a longitudinal central hall that connected to a small internal garden. The other *majlis* designed in 1969 for Sheikh
Abdul Aziz bin Ahmed Al Thani had the same design features as the previous
majlis but with two levels.

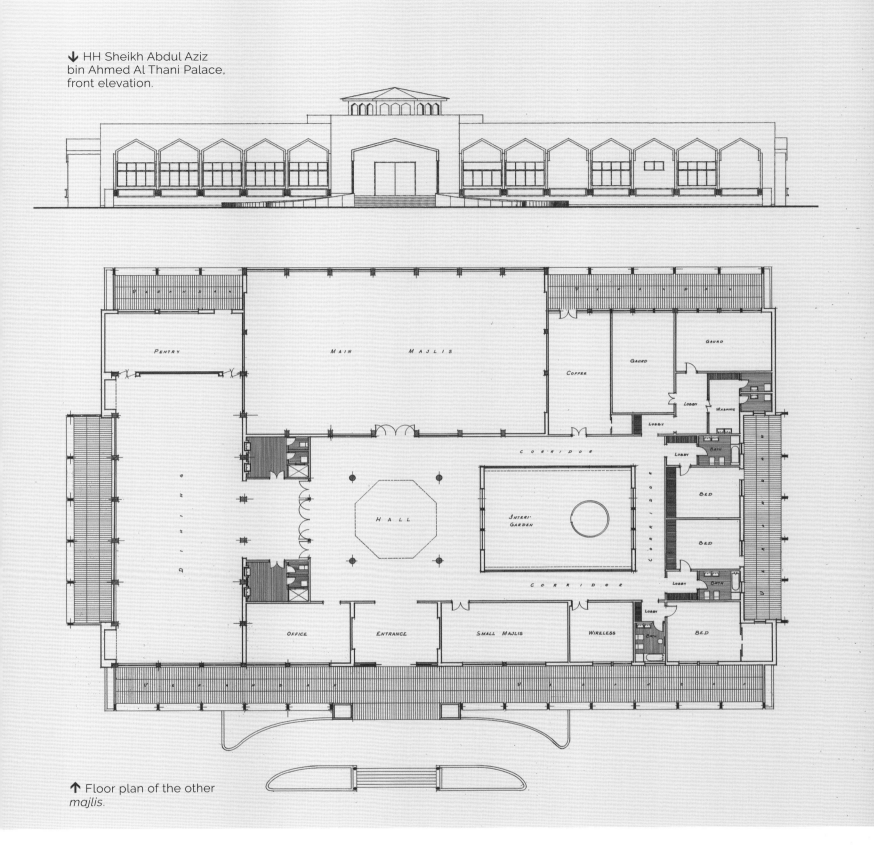

↓ HH Sheikh Abdul Aziz
bin Ahmed Al Thani Palace,
front elevation.

PENTRY

MAIN MAJLIS

COFFEE

GAURD

GAURD

LOBBY

WASHING

LOBBY

LOBBY

BATH

CORRIDOR

DINING

HALL

INTERI GARDEN

CORRIDOR

BED

BED

CORRIDOR

LOBBY

BATH

OFFICE

ENTRANCE

SMALL MAJLIS

WIRELESS

BATH

LOBBY

BED

↑ Floor plan of the other
majlis.

Two other *majlis* with their gates were designed by AEB in 1968 for another client with two different concepts. The first one for Sheikh Khalifa bin Ali Al Thani, which was designed in a similar concept to the previous ones with veranda and semicircular dome with a central hall leading to all spaces through a corridor. The other *majlis* was designed in an orthodox way, where all the spaces extend in an L-shaped concept and are accessed externally through a veranda.

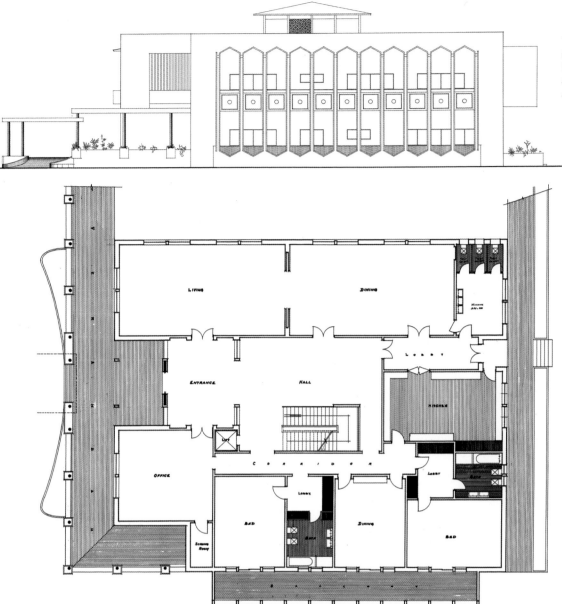

← ↙ Side elevation and ground-floor plan of the main *majlis* of HH Sheikh Abdul Aziz bin Ahmed Al Thani Palace.

The gate was designed in an interesting zigzag form with a flower bed defining the entrance gate. AEB also designed another type of residential building in 1968, known as a vacation home for Sheikh Ali bin Abdullah Al Thani for weekends or holidays. The building proposed had a wooden cabin concept with a pitched roof.

↓ Front elevation of the *majlis* of HH Sheikh Khalifa bin Ali Al Thani Palace.

The construction of palaces on large plots became a trend

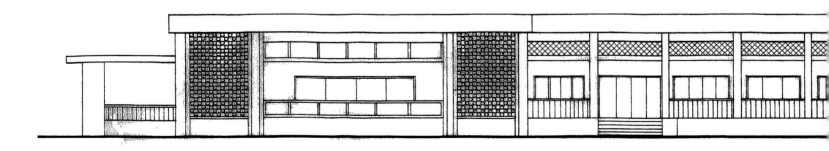

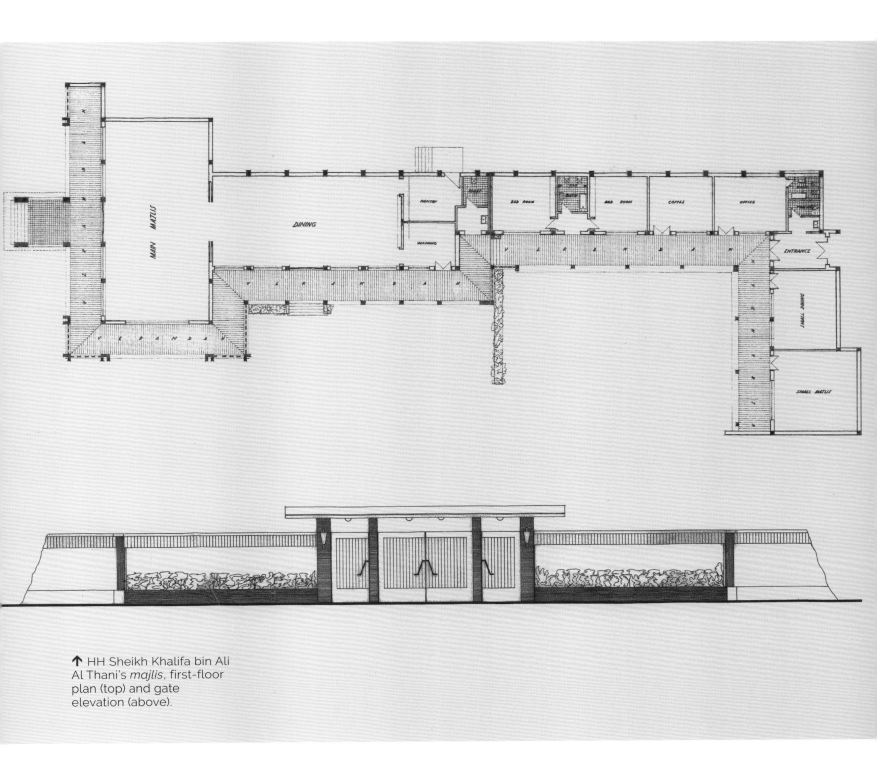

↑ HH Sheikh Khalifa bin Ali Al Thani's *majlis*, first-floor plan (top) and gate elevation (above).

in Doha in the 1960s; most of them were designed by AEB

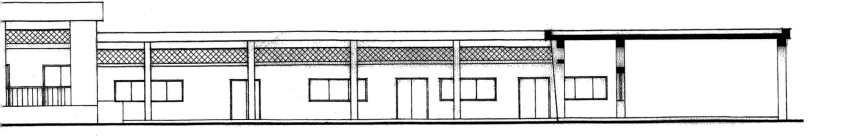

→ HH Sheikh Khalifa
bin Ali Al Thani Palace,
first-floor plan.

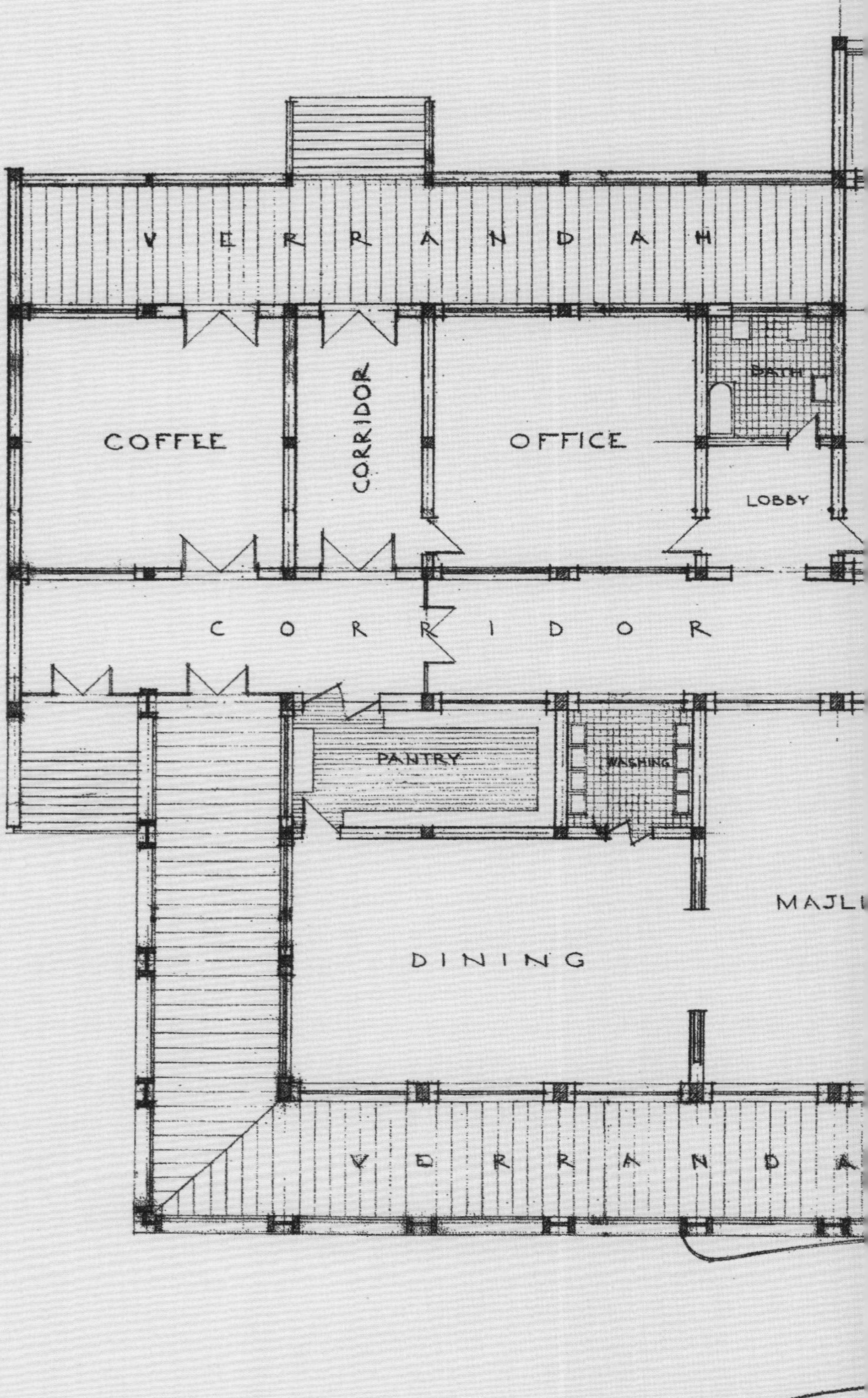

VERRANDAH

COFFEE

CORRIDOR

OFFICE

BATH

LOBBY

CORRIDOR

PANTRY

WASHING

MAJLI

DINING

VERRANDA

→ Front elevation.

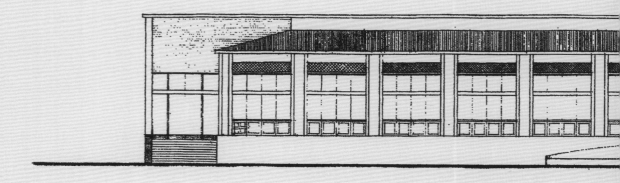

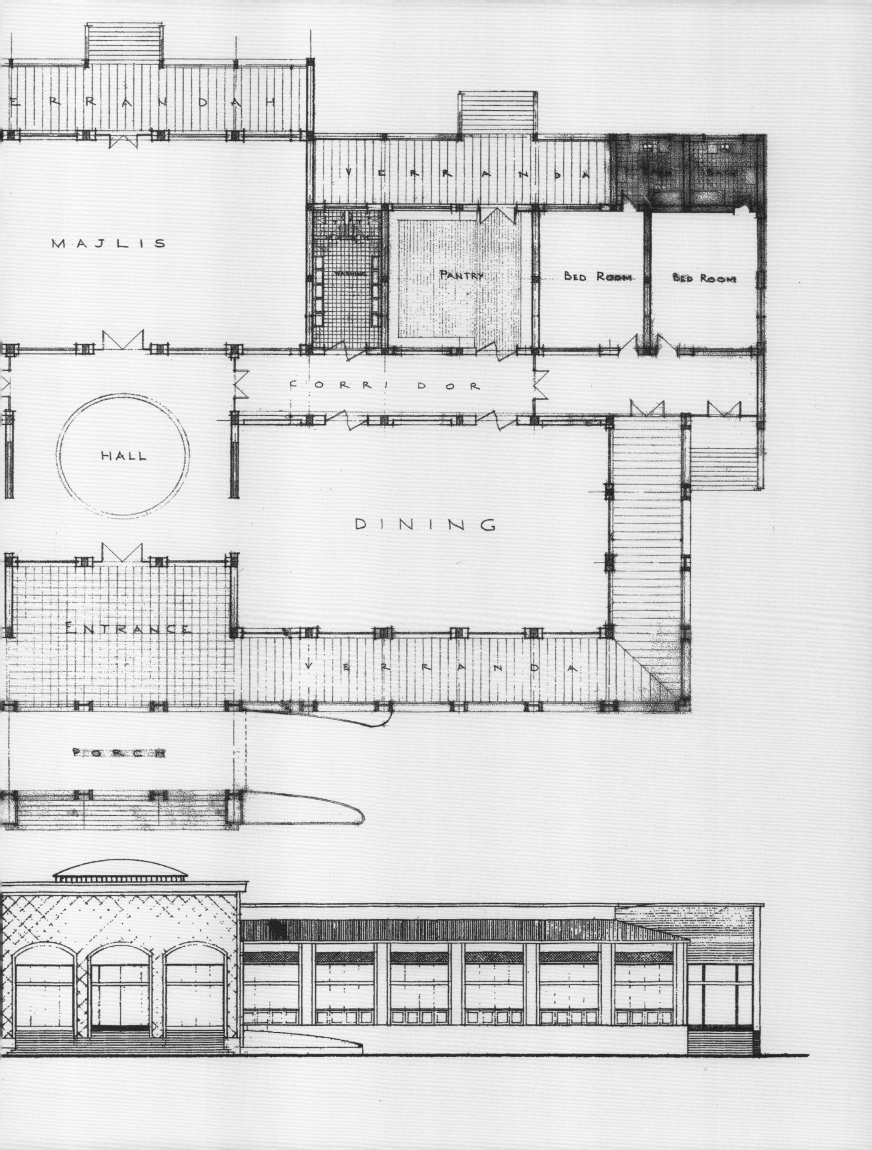

VERRANDAH

VERRANDA

MAJLIS

WASHING

PANTRY

BED ROOM

BED ROOM

CORRIDOR

HALL

DINING

ENTRANCE

VERRANDA

PORCH

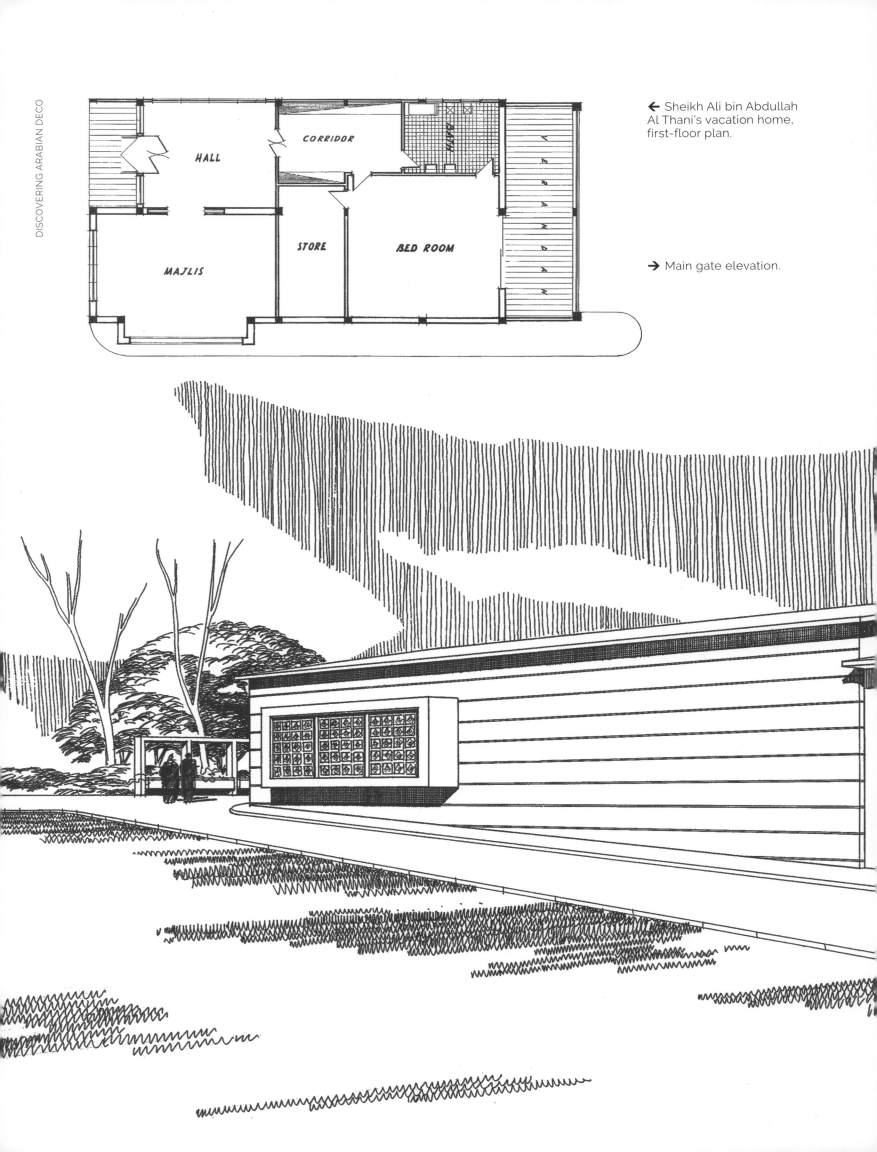

HALL

CORRIDOR

BATH

MAJLIS

STORE

BED ROOM

← Sheikh Ali bin Abdullah Al Thani's vacation home, first-floor plan.

→ Main gate elevation.

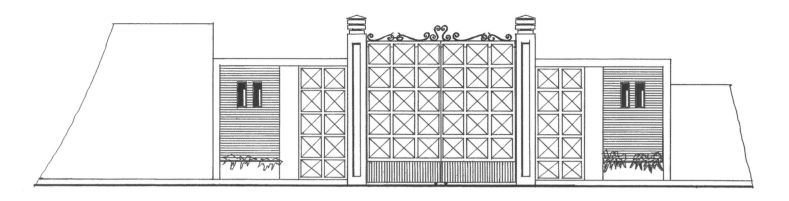

↖ Perspective of Sheikh
Ali bin Abdullah Al Thani's
vacation home.

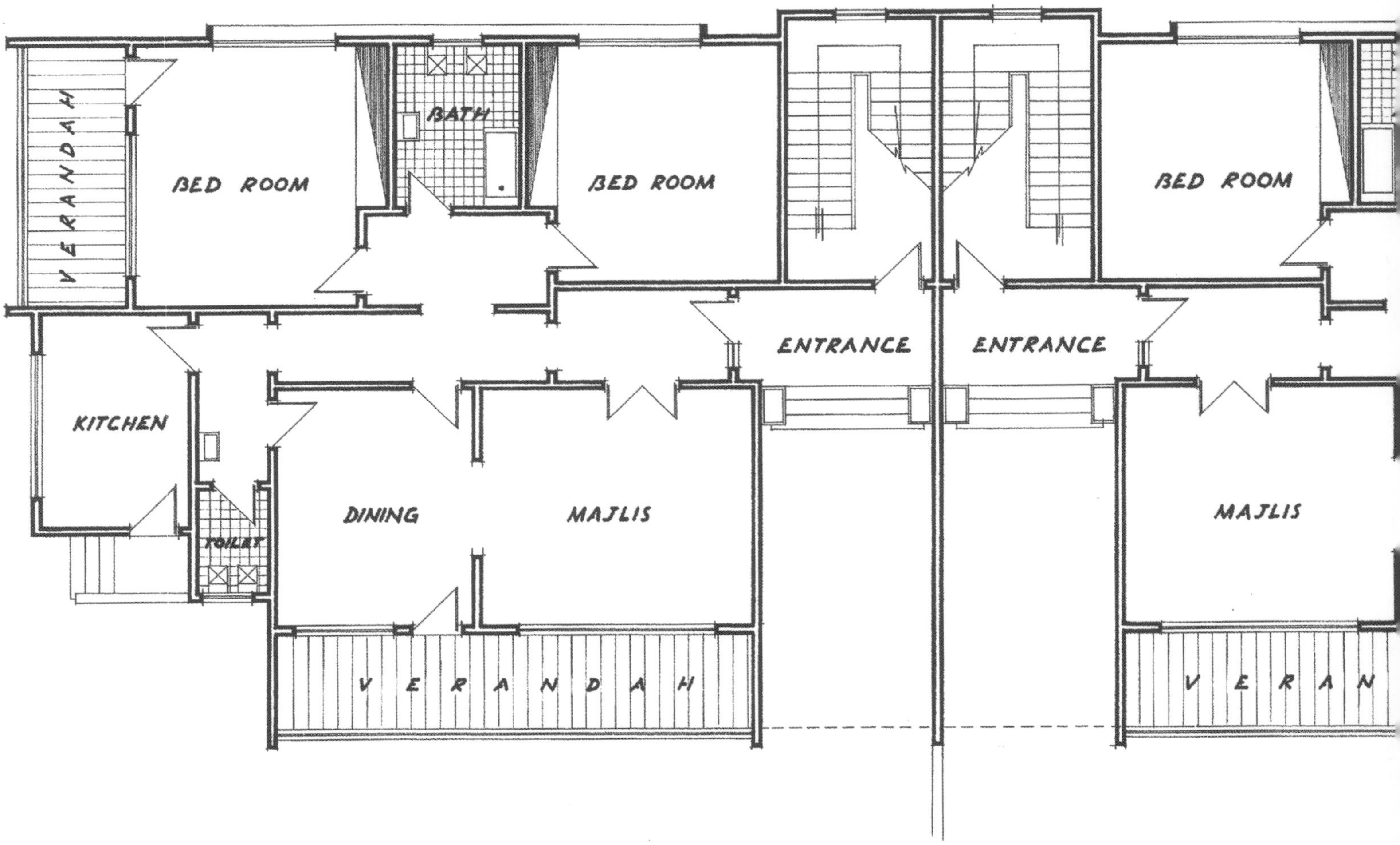

VERANDAH

BED ROOM

BATH

BED ROOM

BED ROOM

ENTRANCE   ENTRANCE

KITCHEN

TOILET

DINING   MAJLIS

MAJLIS

VERANDAH

VERAN

VERAN

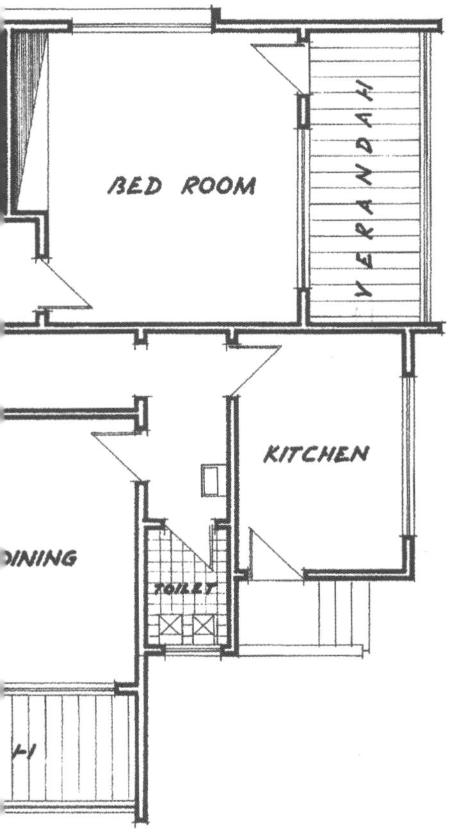

BED ROOM

VERANDAH

KITCHEN

DINING

TOILET

←↓ Villa for Sheikh Ali bin Abdul Aziz Al Thani, floor plan and perspective elevation.

The design of the gate shows the popular steel doors of that time. Another example of an early modern villa was for Sheikh Ali bin Abdul Aziz Al Thani. The twin villas reflected a modern style with vertical and horizontal features and wall cladding.

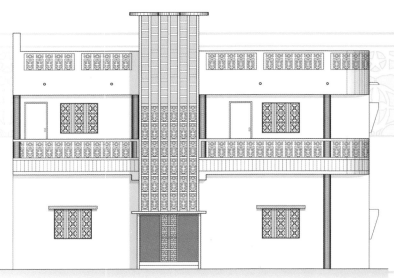

↙ Front elevation of an early-Deco building.

↓ Early-Deco building featuring vertical screen wall and decorated balcony and parapet.

Early Signs of Deco

Various residential and commercial projects in Doha developed in the 1960s with an early sign of the Deco movement in their elevations. They can still be seen today in some apartment buildings in central Doha with a vertical, detailed screen wall above the entrance door and decorated concrete or gypsum balusters on the balcony and parapet.

Another building example of early Deco is Al Maana offices with a *majlis* attached at the back, where the details and carved patterns in the blue, wooden, circular *mashrabiya* and balcony are visually attractive.

Bayt Al Zaman, which was built in the 1950s by Mr. Faraj Al Zaman in Fareej Al Ghanim, also shares similar early-Deco features of decorated balcony and parapet. The Cleopatra Building in Musherib introduced a new feature of the early-Deco period represented by its triangular form and the floating parapet and long extending balcony.

The Cleopatra Building, as it appears in an aerial view from 1966, has a unique triangular form that interprets the early-Deco influence in its form. The attractive features of the floating parapet and the long extension of the balcony also show early-Deco signs.

Another house in old Al Rayyan for Sheikh Jassim bin Ali also represented some signs of early Deco on the main gate, and on the balcony and parapet-railing decorations. Fareej villas also show some signs of early Deco, especially the decorations on the parapet.

→ Al Maana and Partners office building and *majlis* at the back (top) and window detail (bottom).

↑→ Early-Deco feature
of two decorated balconies
of Al Maana and Partners
office building and *majlis*.

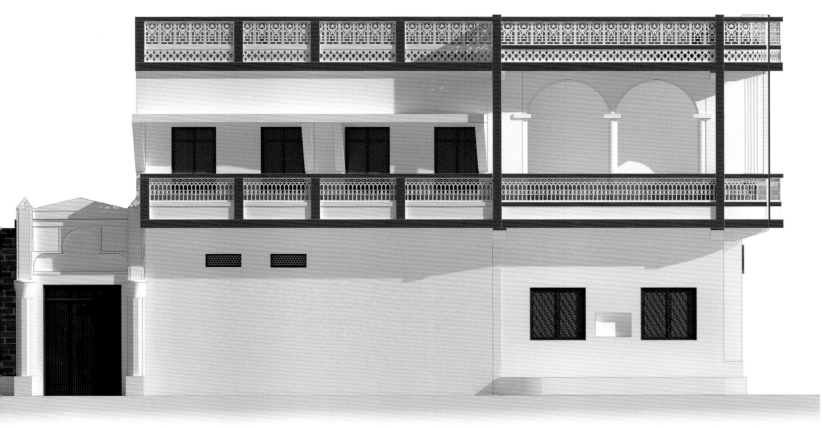

← Bayt Al Zaman with its decorated balcony and parapet. The central entrance is defined by the curved, decorated balcony and parapet.

↓ Front elevation.

↑ Side elevation.

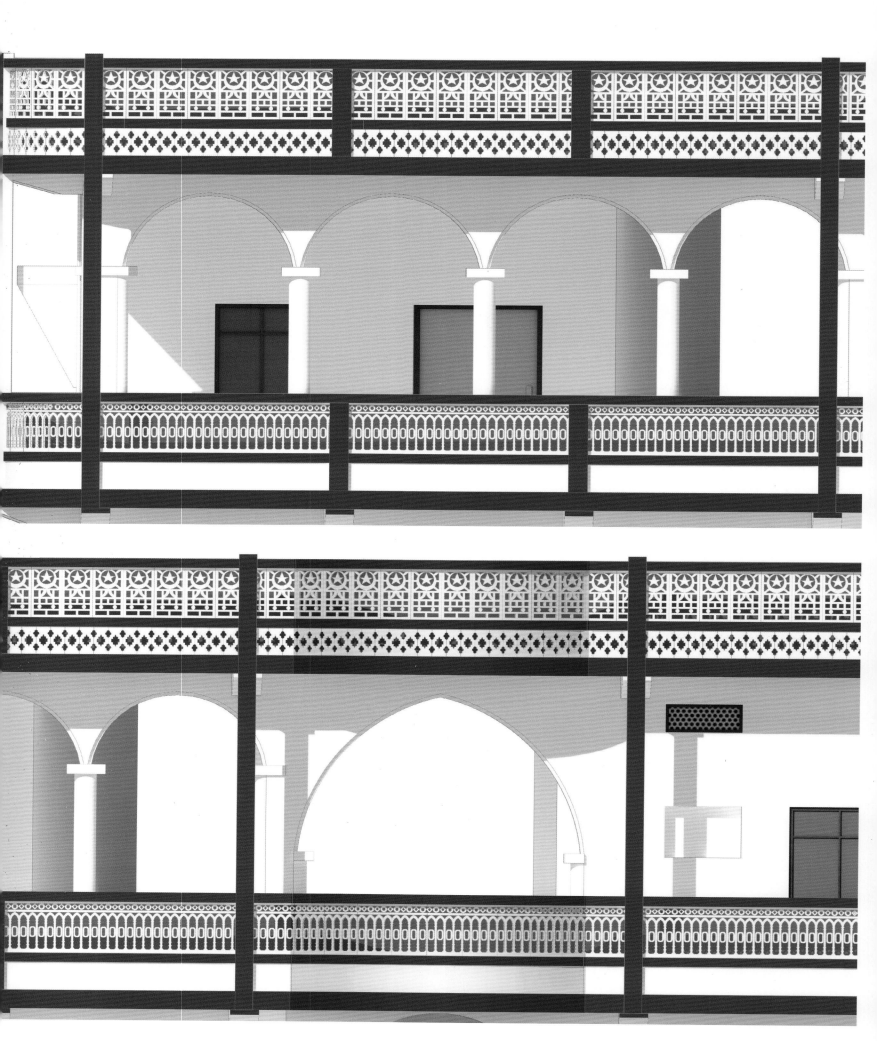

← Bayt Al Zaman balcony and parapet decoration.

→ Aerial view of Cleopatra Building in 1966, showing its unique triangular form.

→ Cleopatra Building, front view showing the main entrance.

↗→ Side views with the early-Deco floating parapet and the long extension of the balcony.

← Early-Deco features in the old house in Al Rayyan for Sheikh Jassim bin Ali.

→ Early-Deco features of the gate for the old house in Al Rayyan for Sheikh Jassim bin Ali (left) and gate front elevation detail (right).

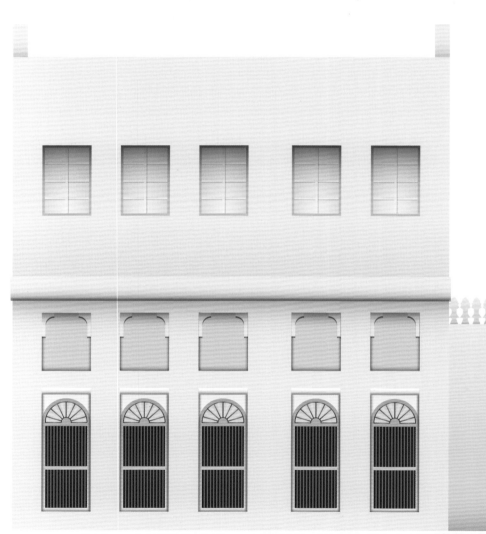

↓ Sheikh Jassim bin Ali's old house front elevation.

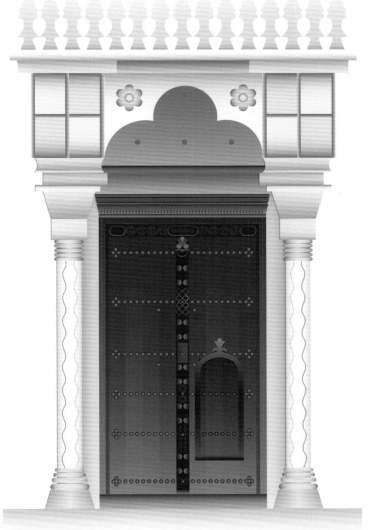

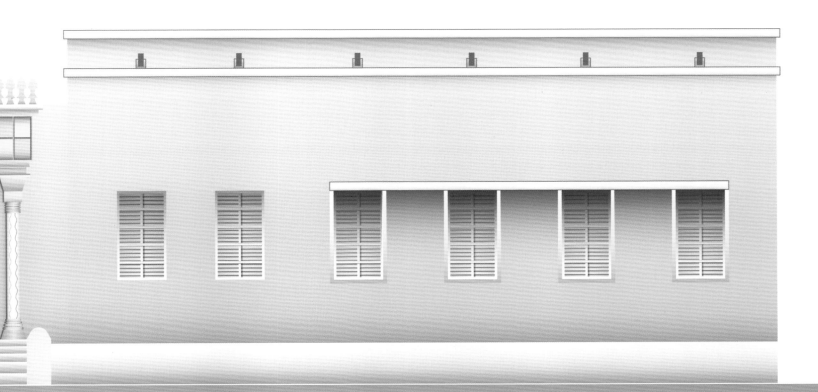

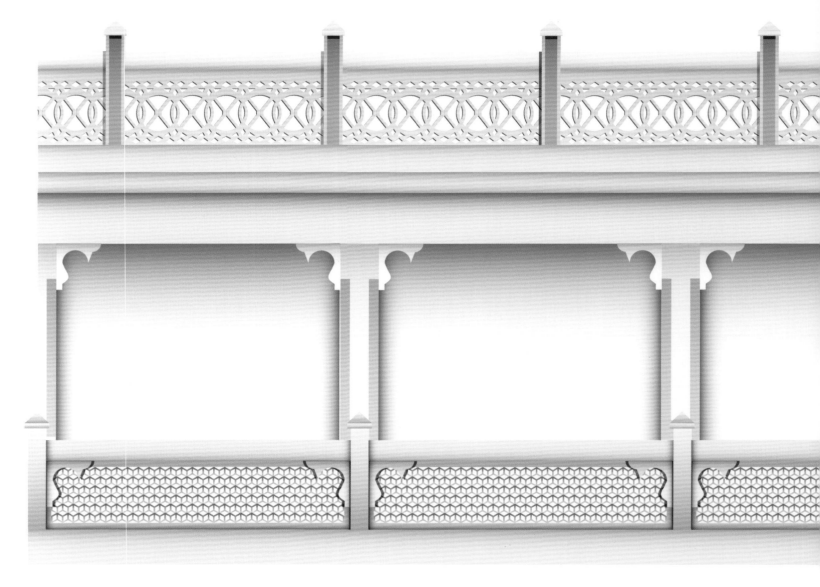

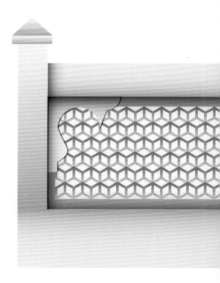

↑ The early-Deco feature of decorated balcony and parapet on the old house for Sheikh Jassim bin Ali in Al Rayyan (above), and the elevation showing them in detail (top).

↑ Detail of the elevation of the decorated balcony.

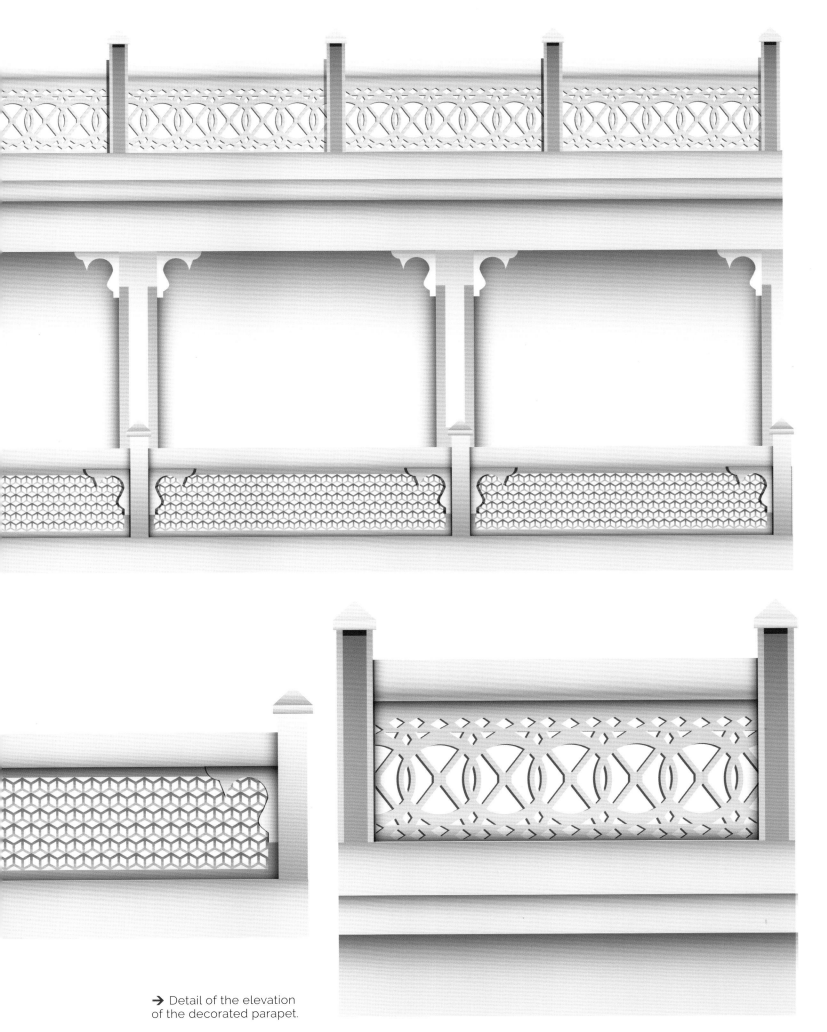

→ Detail of the elevation
of the decorated parapet.

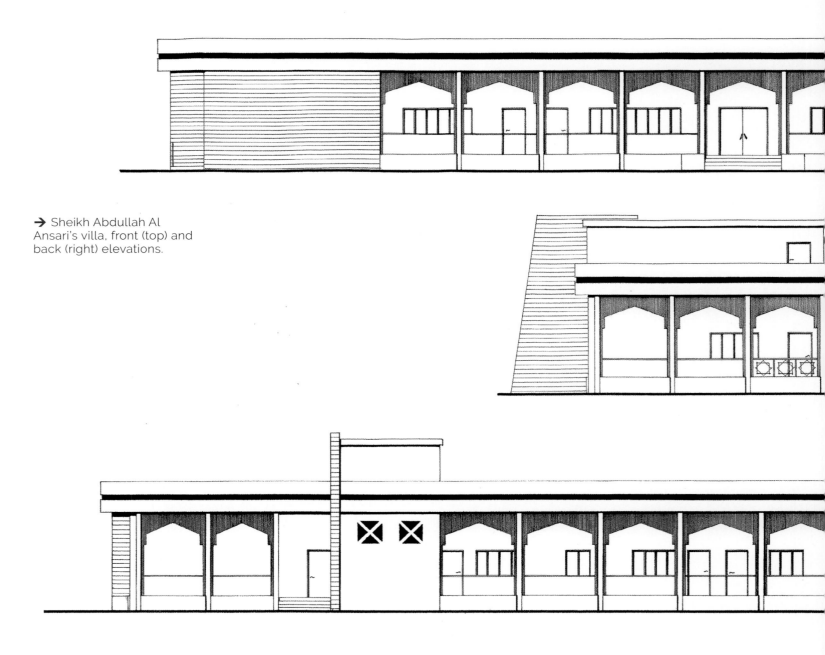

→ Sheikh Abdullah Al Ansari's villa, front (top) and back (right) elevations.

→ Right (above) and left side (right) elevations.

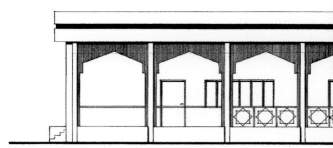

Villas

AEB developed many designs for different types of villas in the 1960s, from small individual villas to twin villas and townhouse villas. Sheikh Abdullah Al Ansari's villa is one of the unique designs that was developed and inspired by the Qatari vernacular. It was a square courtyard concept with a veranda around

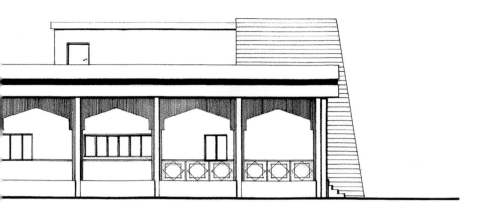

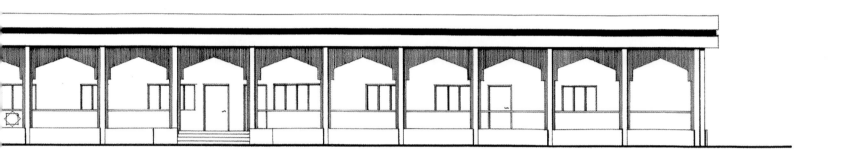

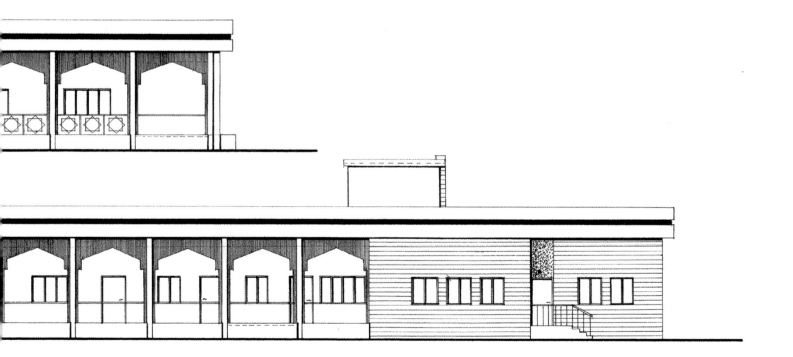

it leading to all spaces as well as an external veranda that had the common feature of pointed arches. This external-veranda design feature was also present in Sheikh Ali bin Jabor's villa but without the courtyard, which was replaced with a long central corridor.

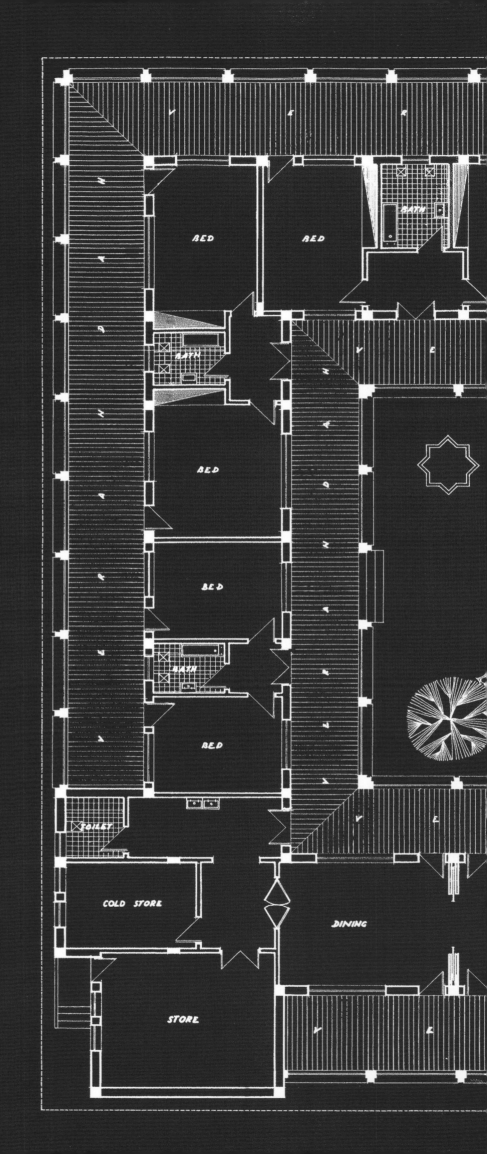

→ First-floor plan
of Sheikh Abdullah
Al Ansari's villa.

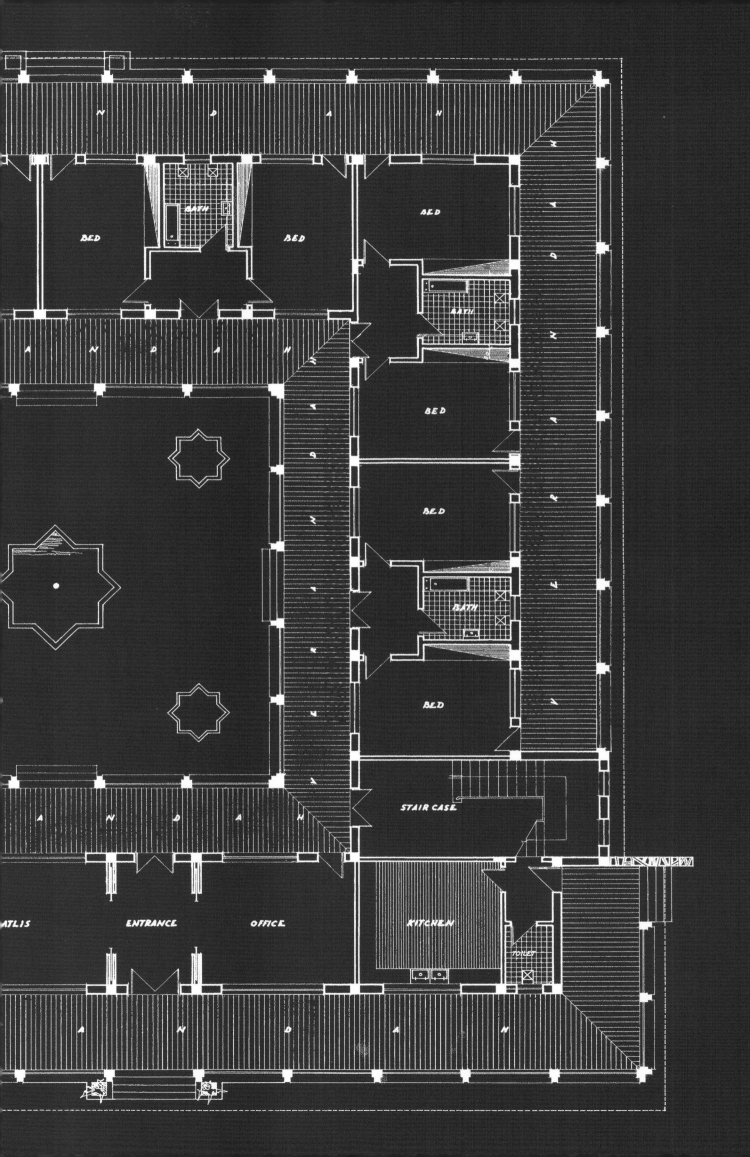

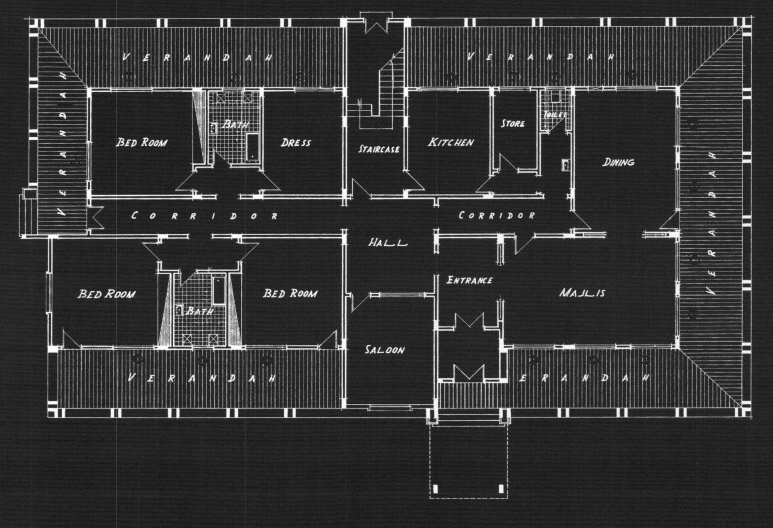

↑ Floor plan of Sheikh
Ali bin Jabor's villa.

↓ Front elevation of
Sheikh Ali bin Jabor's villa.

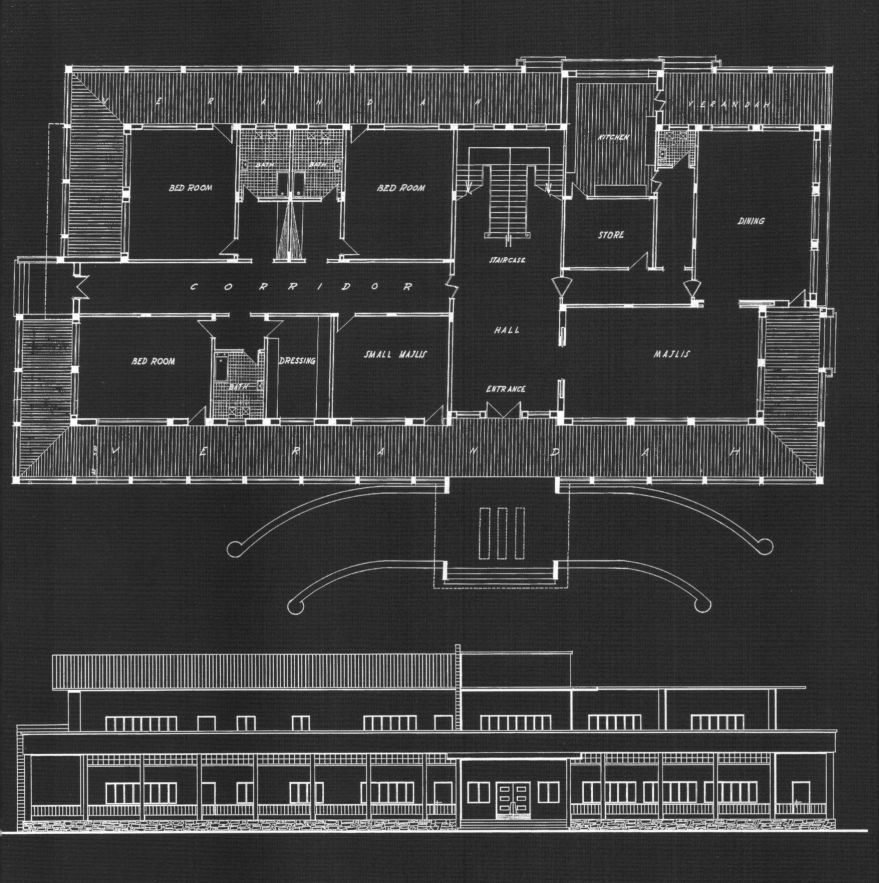

← Boundary wall
elevation of Sheikh
Ali bin Jabor's villa.

↑ Sheikh Saif bin Ahmed's
villa, first-floor plan (top)
and front elevation (above).

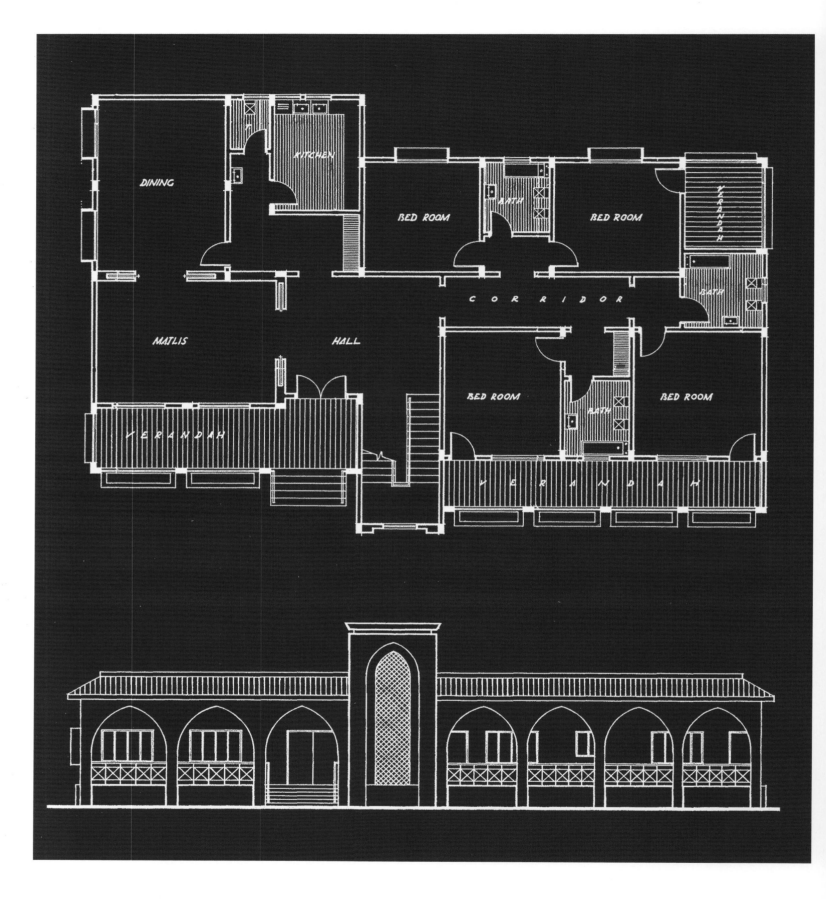

The same design can also be seen in Sheikh Saif bin Ahmed's villa with similar early modern elevation features.

Most of the single-story villas were contemporary designs and have common features like the veranda concept for the Qatari vernacular with small

↑ Ali Al Attiyah's villa, floor plan (top) and front elevation (above).

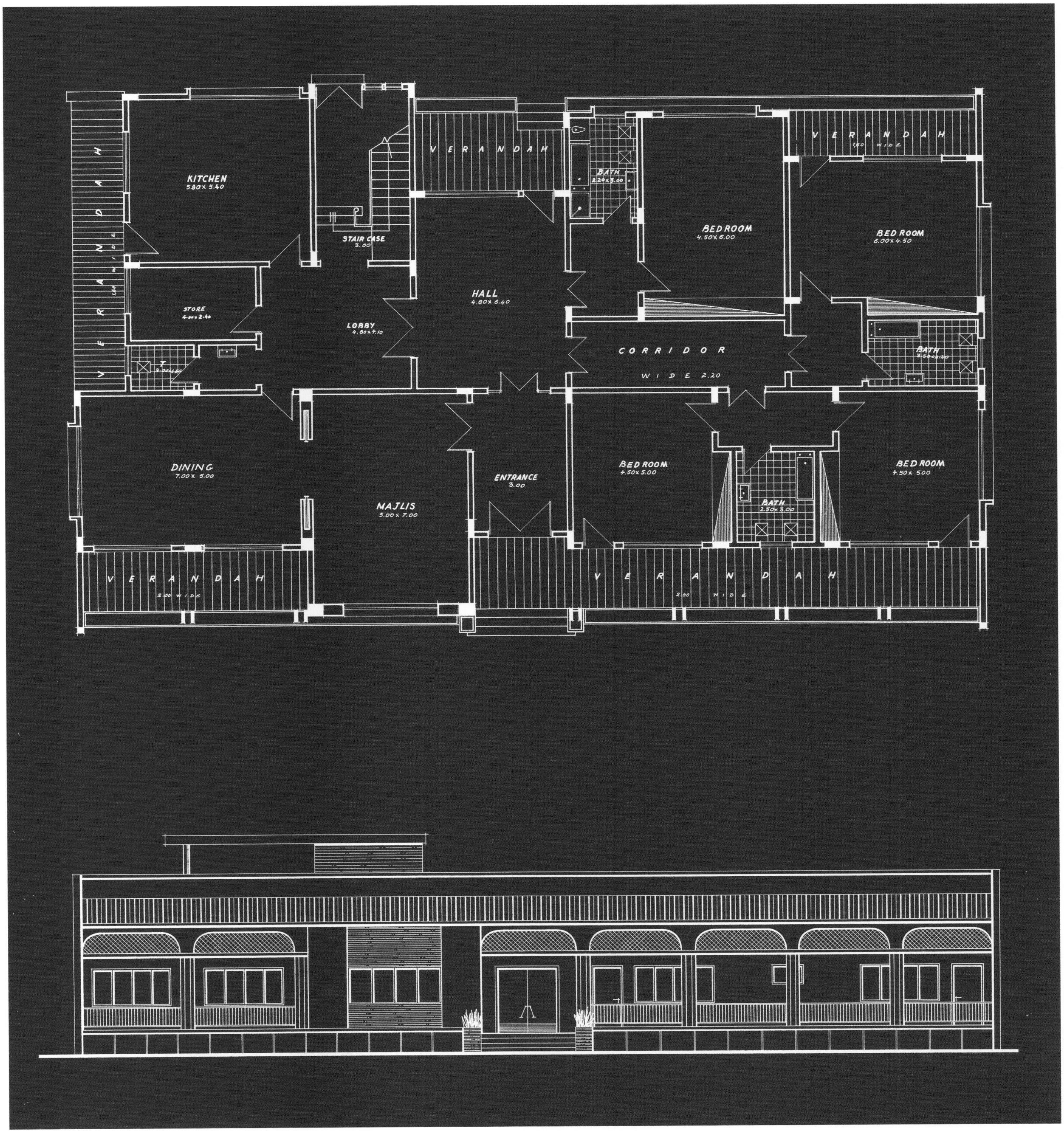
VERANDAH
KITCHEN
5.80X 5.40
STORE
STAIR CASE
3.00
VERANDAH
BATH
HALL
4.80X 6.40
LOBBY
VERANDAH
BEDROOM
4.50X6.00
BED ROOM
6.00X4.50
CORRIDOR
WIDE 2.20
BATH
DINING
7.00X 5.00
MAJLIS
5.00X 7.00
ENTRANCE
3.00
BED ROOM
4.50X5.00
BATH
2.50X3.00
BED ROOM
4.50X 500
VERANDAH
2.00 WIDE
VERANDAH
2.00 WIDE

↑ Mohammed bin Eid's villa, floor plan (top) and front elevation (above).

square openings, screen walls, vertical stone cladding walls, and some with pseudo arches (three-center arch). AEB has also designed villas with the early modern feature of verandas only on the front and back. An example of this design feature can be seen in Ali Al Attiyah's villa and Mohammed bin Eid's.

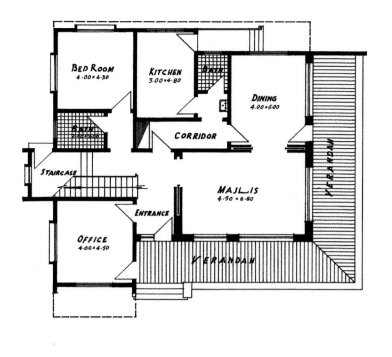

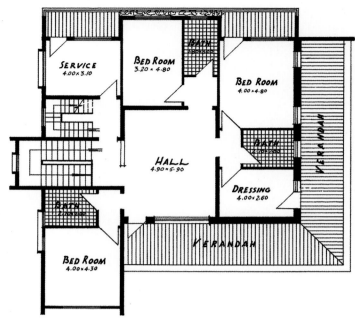

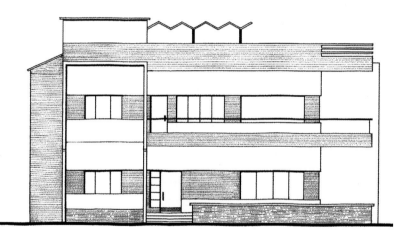

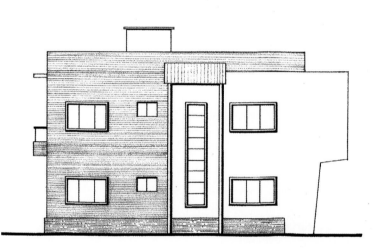

↑ Ahmed Al Malki's villa, first-floor plan (top) and front elevation (above).

↑ Ahmed Al Malki's villa, second-floor plan (top) and side elevation (above).

↗ Rashid bin Sultan Al Kwari's villa, first-floor plan (top) and second-floor plan (middle).

Another example of design was the box-villa concept, where the villa appears in a box form with a veranda at one corner on the ground-level floor, reflecting architectural trends at that time. While multiple-floor villas usually have a balcony on the second floor, large glass openings, and stone cladding, some would also have pointed arches like the ones seen in Al Marmar Palace. This example can be found in villas that belong to Ahmed Al Malki, Rashid bin Sultan Al Kwari, and Hussain Haidar Darwish.

→ Rashid bin Sultan Al Kwari's villa, front elevation (middle) and back elevation (bottom)

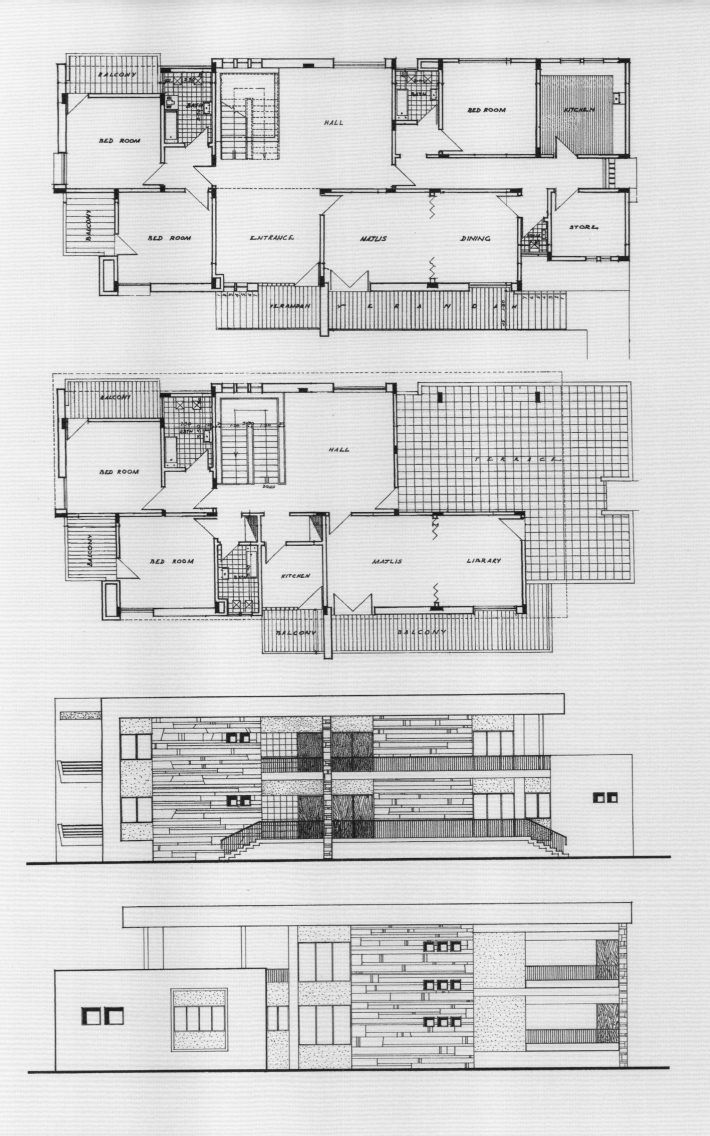

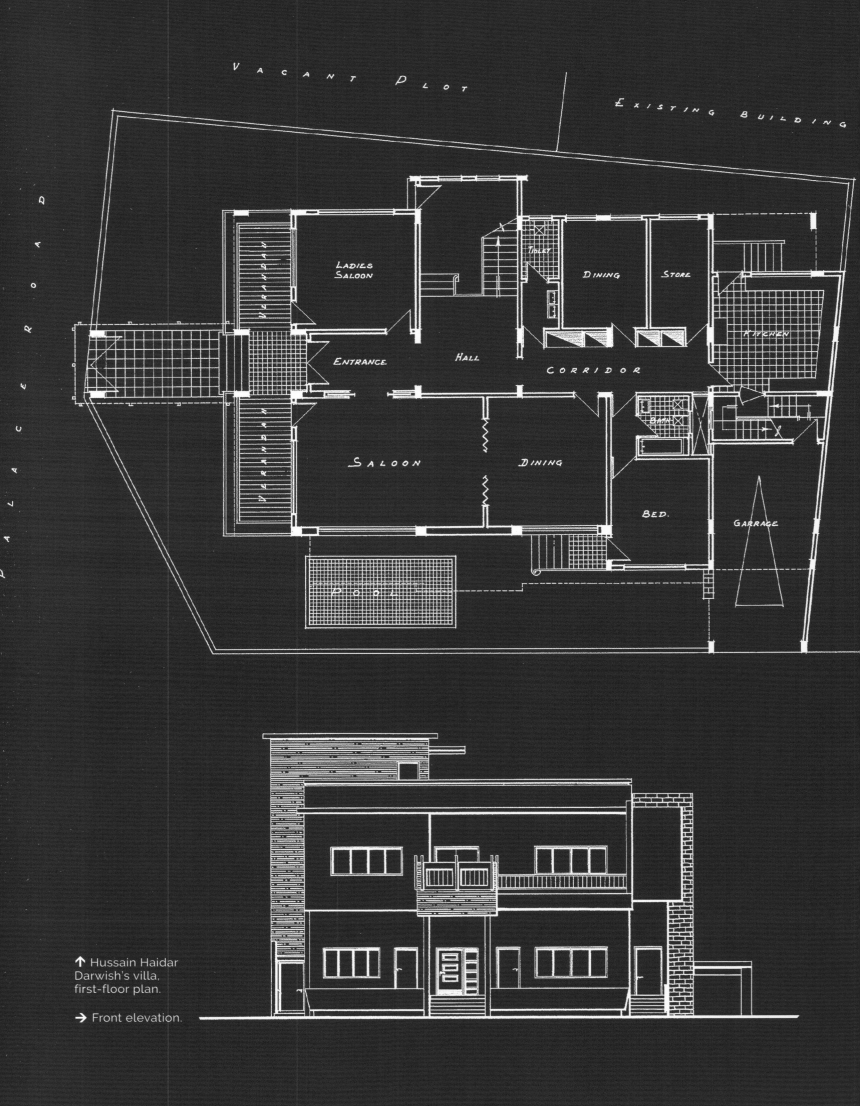

VACANT PLOT

EXISTING BUILDING

PALACE ROAD

LADIES SALOON

TOILET

DINING

STORE

KITCHEN

VERANDAH

ENTRANCE

HALL

CORRIDOR

VERANDAH

SALOON

DINING

BATH

BED.

GARRAGE

POOL

↑ Hussain Haidar Darwish's villa, first-floor plan.

→ Front elevation.

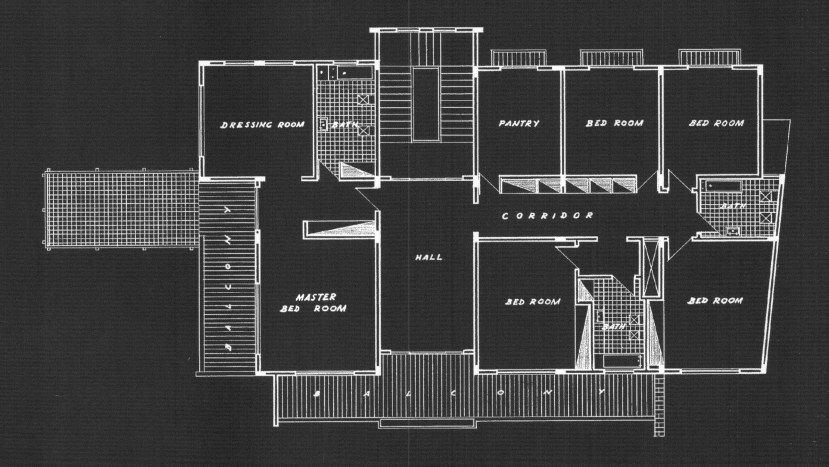

DRESSING ROOM   BATH   PANTRY   BED ROOM   BED ROOM

CORRIDOR

HALL   BED ROOM   BATH

MASTER BED ROOM   BATH   BED ROOM

BALCONY

↑ Second-floor plan.

↓ Side elevation.

Buildings

It's worth noting here that these multipurpose structures were most likely at-tached courtyard houses with commercial elements, due to the density of the population in areas like Al Asmakh. The shops up front were owned by mer-chants who usually leased them out. Some of the unique features of these buildings were the columns and how the gypsum was used to create decorative

↑ Multipurpose building with the early-Deco feature of a decorated parapet (top) and front elevation (above).

→ An example of a smaller multipurpose building with decorated balcony and parapet.

→ Front elevation of the smaller multipurpose building with decorated balcony and parapet.

161

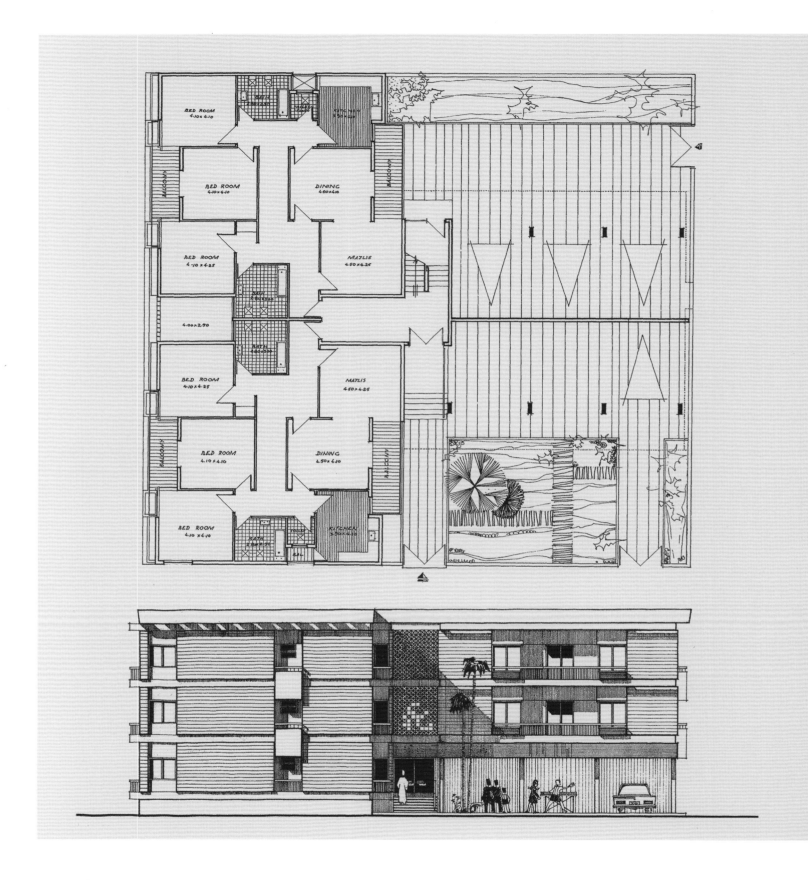

patterns on the balcony railings, the parapets, and above the main entrance door. Other multipurpose buildings had no distinctive decorative features except for the parapet patterns. The oil boom attracted more people to come to Doha for work, which resulted in an increase in the population. This contributed to the development of apartment buildings, which also became a trend in the city.

↑ Hussain Haidar Darwish Building, first-floor plan (top) and front elevation (above).

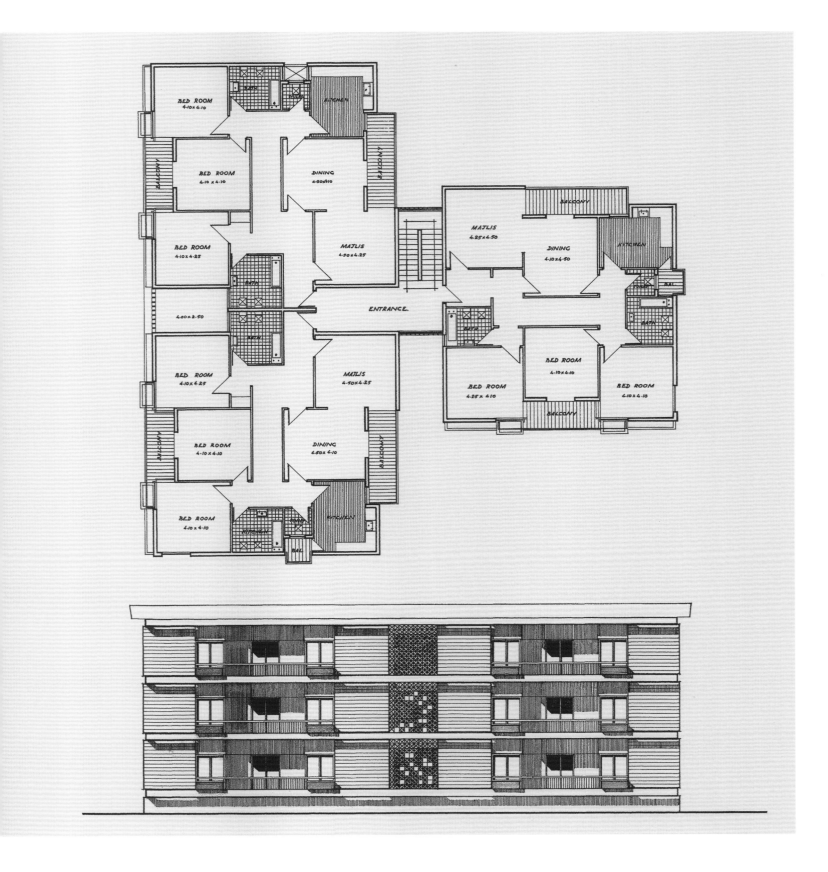

↑ Hussain Haidar Darwish Building, upper floors plan (top) and side elevation (above).

AEB designed an apartment building in 1968 with parking space on the ground-level and multiple levels of apartments. This type of building was designed for Hussain Haidar Darwish, where the design featured small balconies with large glass openings and horizontal cladding patterns with a vertical screen wall above the main entrance. In the same year, AEB also designed

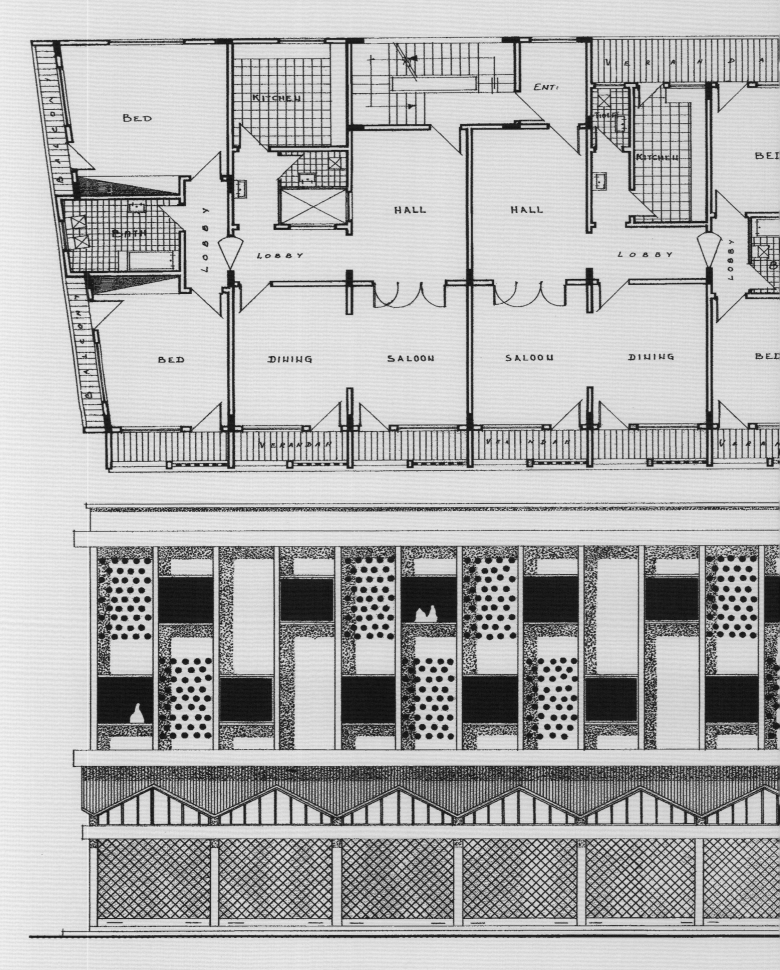

↑ Ali bin Abdullah Al Attiyah building, upper floors plan (top) and front elevation (above).

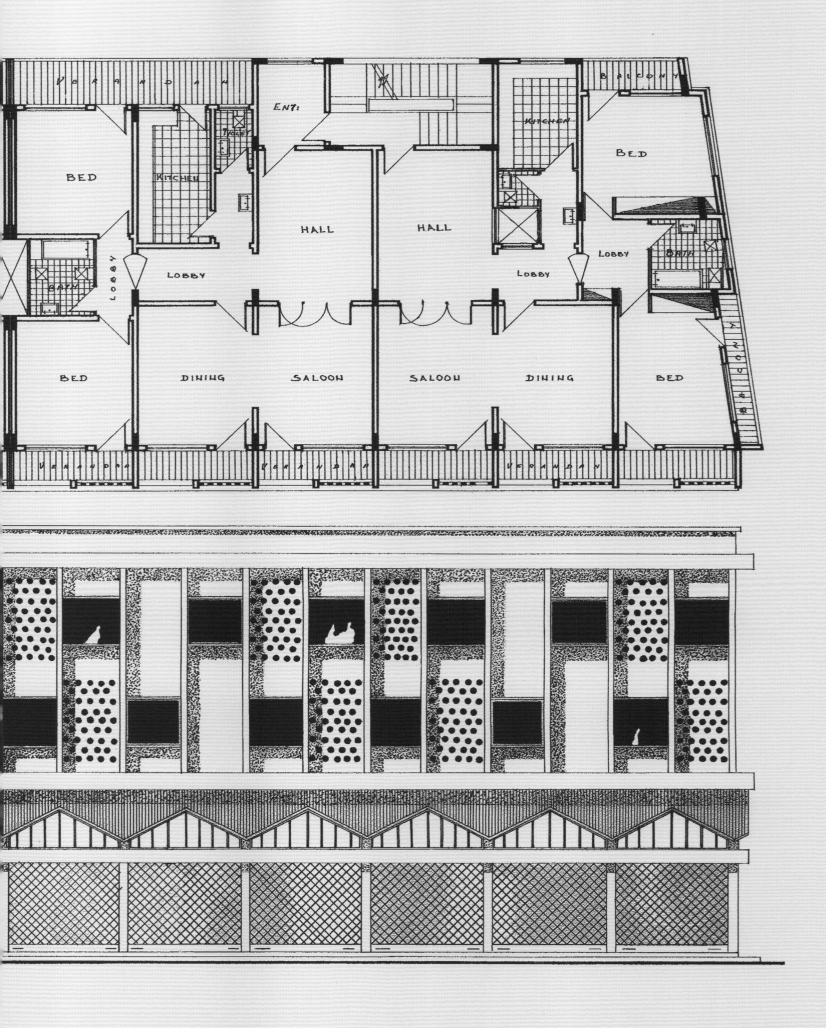

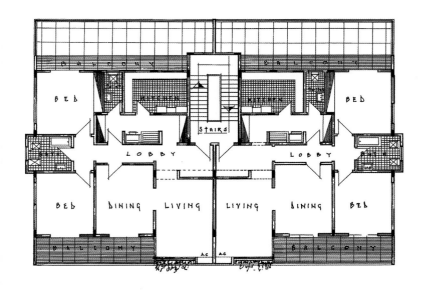

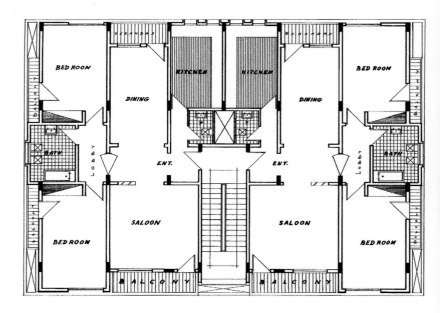

↑ Typical floor plan of Abdel Rahman bin Hamad Al Thani's apartment building (top) and front elevation (above).

↑ Typical floor plan of Mohammed bin Khalid Rabban's apartment building (top) and front elevation (above).

another bigger apartment building for Ali bin Abdullah Al Attiyah with a commercial front on the ground level. The building had unique features organized in a vertical pattern including screen walls and recesses creating shade and small balconies.

AEB designed multipurpose buildings in 1967 and 1968 with a more modern appearance, with stone cladding, in a symmetrical concept where the main entrance is at the center, defined by a vertical screen wall extending above it.

→ Typical floor plan of Mubarak Al Dulaimi's apartment building (top) and front elevation (bottom).

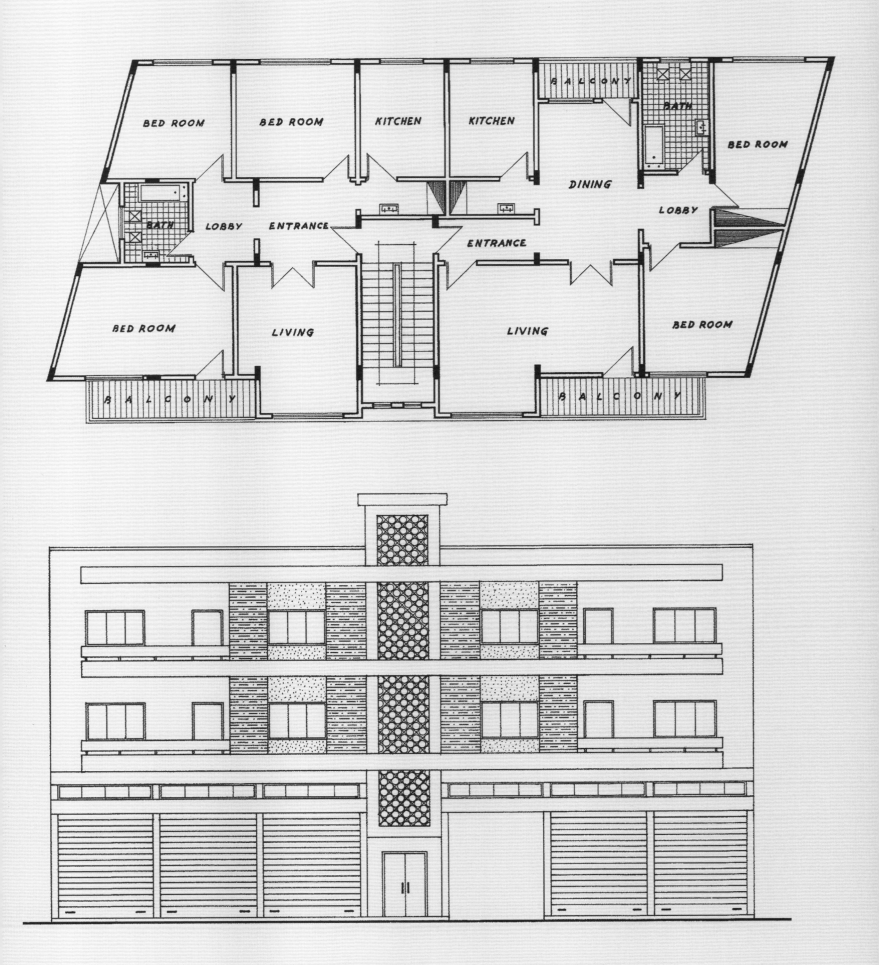

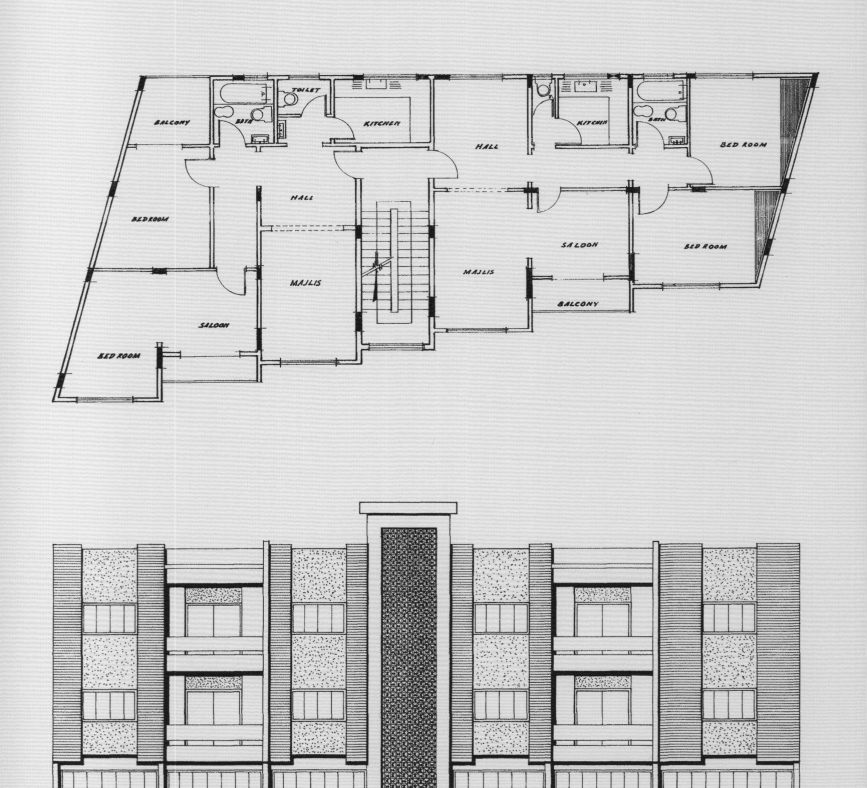

↑ Upper-floor plan for
Mohamed Abdel Rahman
Diab's apartment building (top)
and front elevation (above).

↑ Second and third-floor
plan for Sheikh Khalid bin
Hamad building (top) and
front elevation (above).

← Typical floor plan of
another apartment building
for Mubarak Al Dulaimi
(top) and front elevation
(bottom).

There are two apartments per floor and their elevation features large balconies with big glass openings. This type of design feature appeared in the buildings of Sheikh Abdel Rahman bin Hamad Al Thani, Mohammed bin Khalid Rabban, and Mubarak Al Dulaimi. Other smaller-size apartment buildings were designed with the entrance on one side with the same elevation features mentioned above. This style was applied to the buildings of Sheikh Khalid bin Hamad and Mohamed Abdel Rahman Diab.

Qatari Deco

The Introduction of Deco

Art Deco is a style of visual arts also called *style moderne*, a movement in the decorative arts and architecture that originated in the 1920s and developed into a major style in western Europe and the United States during the 1930s. The milestone of this style was derived from the International Exhibition of Modern Decorative and Industrial Arts held in Paris in 1925. It combines modern design with traditional elements such as exquisite craftsmanship and luxurious materials.

Art Deco was also influenced by the abstract and geometric forms of Cubism and the bright colors and the exoticized crafts and styles of countries such as China, Japan, and Egypt. The decorative aspect and the compositional arrangements also derive from Beaux-Arts architecture, through symmetry, straight lines, hierarchy in the floor plan distribution, and facades divided into base, shaft, and capital—although at this time with more rational volumes and the occasional use of ornaments. During the 1930s, Art Deco became more moderate and sober, incorporating materials such as concrete and stainless steel.

The early signs of the Deco movement began appearing on buildings in Doha in the mid-1950s. Deco started to be used on gates, parapets, balconies, main central entrances, *liwan*, columns, windows, and doors. Many of these designs came to Doha through Lebanese and Egyptian architects. The architects that carried out these designs are unknown, and we hope that they will be known in time. Most of the Deco features in Doha are presented using concrete, steel, and glass.

Art Deco started to appear on gates, parapets, balconies,

← Aerial view of the fish market next to the vegetable market in 1966, at the bottom and at the top of the photo respectively.

The Deco features on the entrance and windows at the fish market.

→ The colorful attraction made by the fish market building.

Between 1963 and 1965 a new fish-market building was constructed close to the seashore and next to the vegetable market to the south. Although the building was longitudinal in a rectangular shape, its architectural significance is reflected in the main entrance and windows. There were two main access points on both the eastern and western sides, emphasized by a concrete offset framing the door with a large, stepped projection at the top, centered with a decorative plaque showing a fish. The windows on the two sides of the entrance with their vertical, tilted, concrete patterns were the first to introduce the Qatari Deco movement in Doha. The building also had a longitudinal central roof projection connected to the two entrances to provide daylight and ventilation.

main central entrances, *liwan*, columns, windows, and doors

Gates

The gate has always been the first architectural encounter that a person experiences externally before it leads to the inside. In the Arabian Peninsula, the gate had a deeper meaning beyond the general notion of an opening that allows transition from one space to another. It symbolized the social, economic, and sometimes political status of the household, which depended on the scale, decorative details, and materials used on the gate. Many of the residential buildings in Doha had very glamorous, ornamented gates.

Many palaces were constructed in the second half of the 1950s in the western area next to the Amiri Diwan. One of the large outstanding palaces located on Al Rayyan road and directly next to the Amiri Diwan was for Sheikh Fahad bin Ali, built between 1953 and 1956, and known as Fahad Palace.

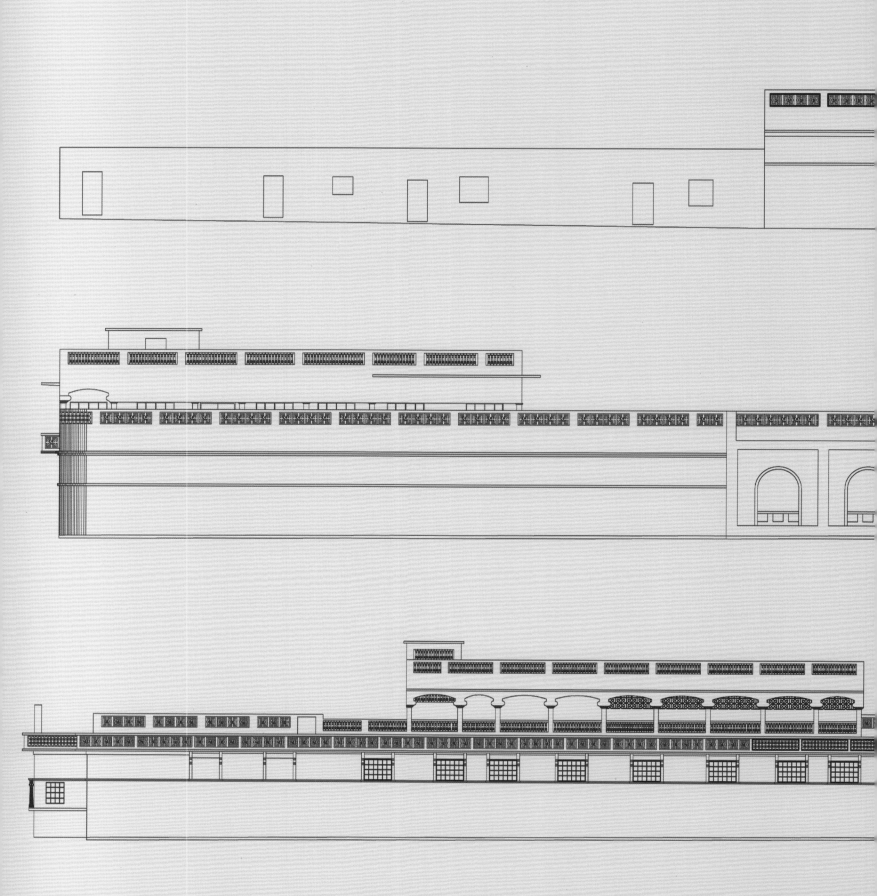

↑ Sheikh Fahad bin Ali
Palace, front elevation (top).

↑ Back elevation (middle)
and side elevation (above).

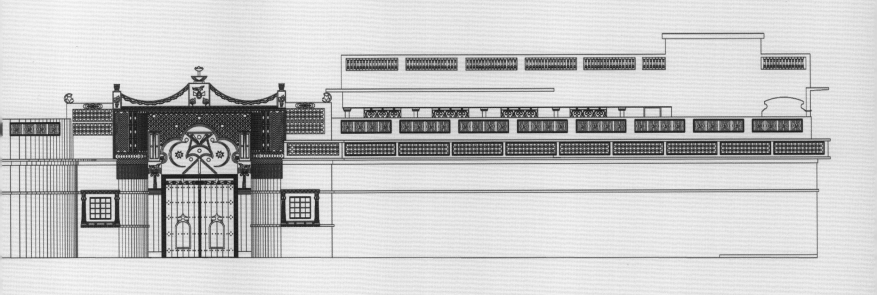

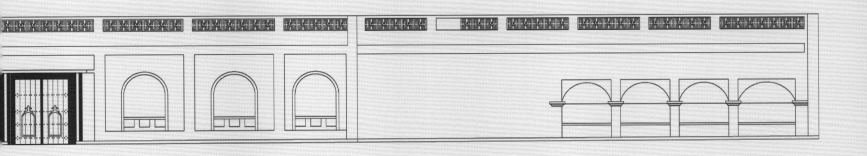

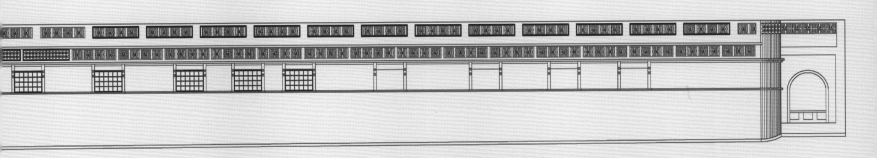

→ Gate of Sheikh Fahad
bin Ali Palace.

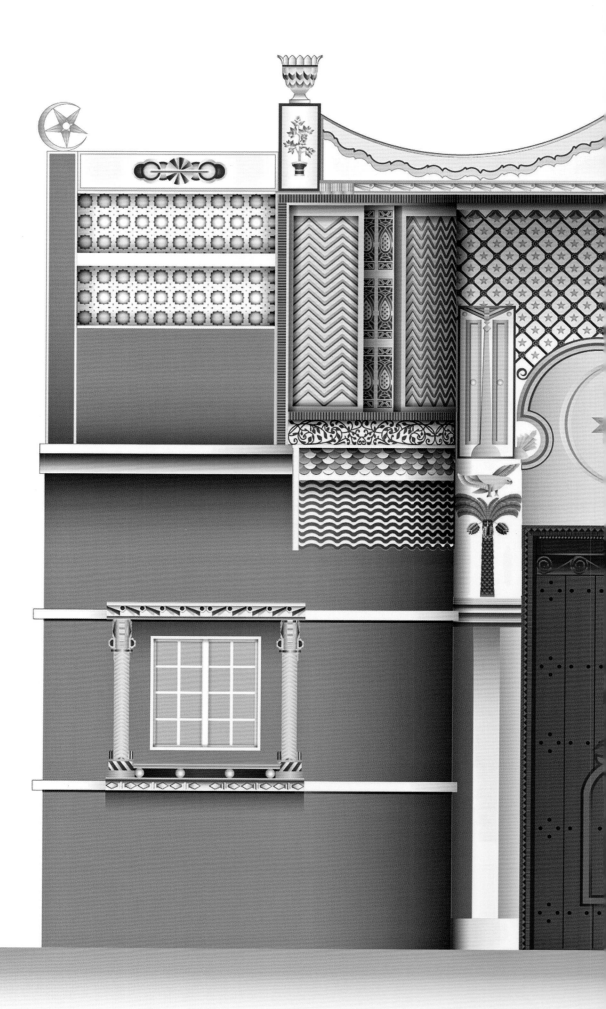

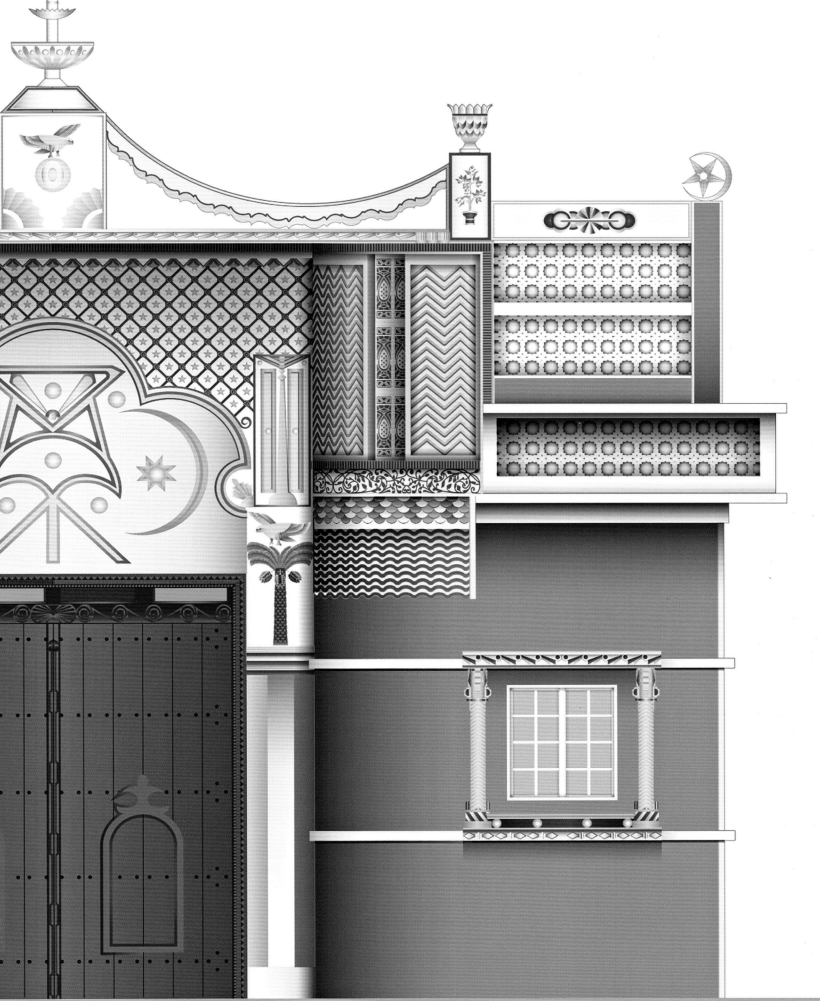

← Gate of Sheikh Fahad bin Ali Palace.

↓ → Sheikh Fahad bin Ali Palace, the detailed decoration above the wooden door of the gate (bottom), and the detailed ceiling decoration above the wooden door (right).

Following pages
↓ Arabian influence on the decoration of a date palm and a falcon on the left side of the gate of Sheikh Fahad bin Ali Palace.

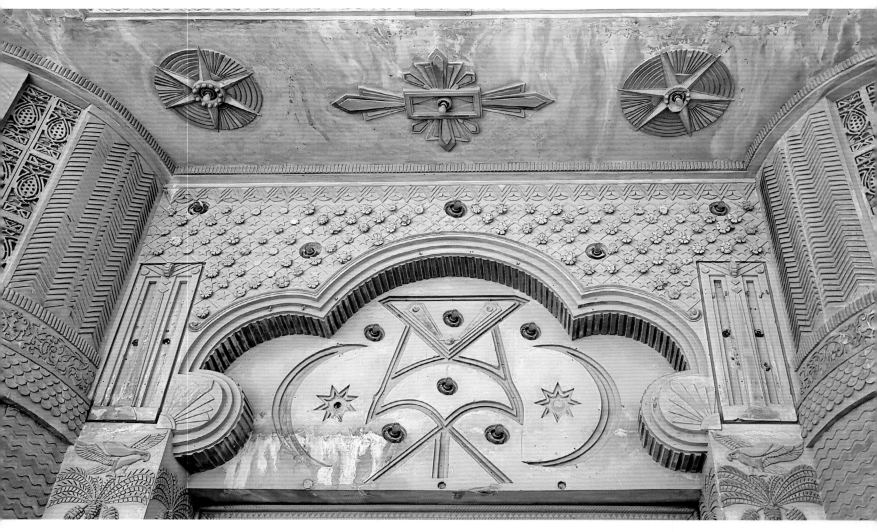

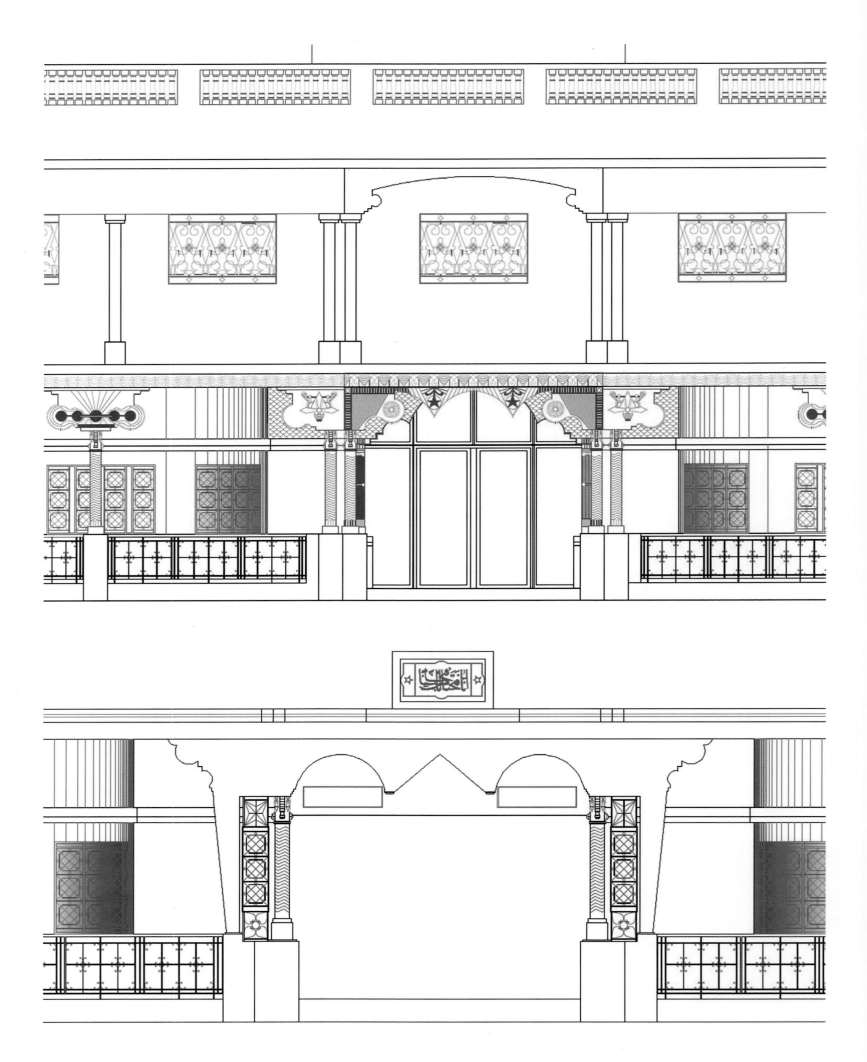

↑ View of the *liwan* with decorated columns and cantilevers at Sheikh Fahad bin Ali Palace.

← Sheikh Fahad bin Ali Palace, decorated *liwan* detailed elevation (top) and the main decorated *liwan* entrance elevation (bottom).

↓ Rendered view of the *liwan* with decorated columns, entrance, and cantilevers at Sheikh Fahad bin Ali Palace.

The palace was built on an irregular large plot consisting of three main parts: the main entry gate, the palace building with an open courtyard, and an old graveyard surrounded by a series of shops. The palace had no decorative details at the time it was built, they were only added later in the 1960s. The main gate is located on the west boundary wall, while walking toward it decorative screen patterns can be noticed on top of the wall. Its scale doubles in size with two different motifs when reaching the gate. The gate is secured by guard rooms on both sides with a glass window framed by an ornamented canopy and two columns. The curved wall of the guard room leads to the main two-fold wooden door simply decorated with horizontal copper nails and a small access door at the center of each fold (known locally as *farkhah*). The wooden door is placed in the center of a colorful relief-carved frame consisting of a variety of plants, classic, and geometric patterns. One interesting ornament that is culturally related to Qatar is the palm tree with a falcon on top of it above the columns on both sides of the door. The falcon relief is also presented at the top center of the gate. Passing through the gate, the open courtyard can be seen, enwrapped by the decorative veranda of the palace building.

↑ The gate of a palace in Al Rayyan.

← View of the *liwan* with decorated columns and cantilevers at Sheikh Fahad bin Ali Palace.

The veranda shows three different levels of decorative enrichment in three parts of the palace, indicating the use and importance of each one. When walking along the veranda, the first two-story building has the most detailed decoration, followed by a less decorated part, and finally with no decoration at all. The relief carvings presented on various walls of the palace with different density and details indicate the importance of the Deco movement in representing social status in Qatar. The cantilever on the first floor is a decorated *liwan*, a common feature of Deco.

Another palace in Al Rayyan was also influenced by the Deco movement but on a different level when compared to the gate of Fahad. The gate had a veranda-like concept of a series of ogee (onion-shaped) arches like the one in the Amiri Diwan new annex. The arches are decorated with dynamic steelwork while the columns have a Corinthian crown. The entrance arch is larger in width with two-fold decorated steelwork. The arches are topped with a geometric pattern followed on top by an ornamented zigzag cornice.

The main-entrance arch is also defined by the decorated segment on top of it. The boundary wall on the right side of the gate is topped with a decorative metal grill. The use of these arches again indicates the influence the Amiri Diwan design had on introducing the Qatari Deco to other palaces. Passing through the main gate, the palace building can be seen with an adaptation of the veranda concept but without any decorations. Instead, decoration is more present on the grill patterns as used on the gate, windows, and railings. The zigzag cornice on the gate was also

↑ Elevation of the gate of a palace in Al Rayyan (top) and detail of the steelwork motifs of the arches on the gate sides.

➔ Elevation of the steelwork motifs for the arches on the sides of the gate.

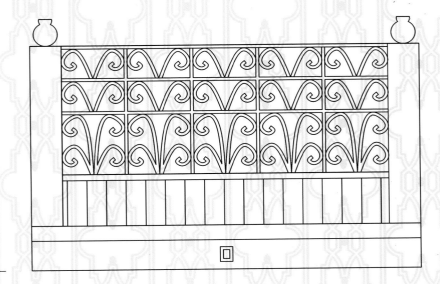

↑ Elevation of the steelwork motif on the main gate.

↗ The steelwork motif and zigzag decoration on the right-side wall to the gate.

used for the parapet on the roof. The palm tree symbolizing Qatari culture was also represented but in the form of sculptural lighting features on the roof. The palace has a room on the upper level to catch the breeze. The room is framed by two concrete cantilevers: the first has the same metal grill pattern as the palace in its square opening; the second has four pointed glass openings with a Deco pattern on the glass at the top. The small dome of the minaret is decorated with light bulbs extending down from its apex.

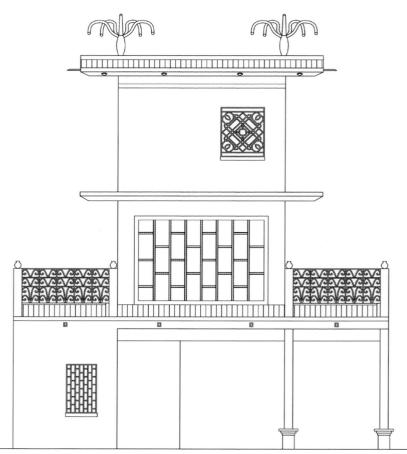

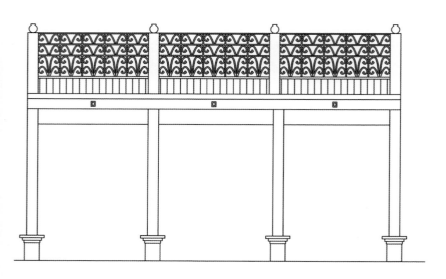

↖ The balcony and window steelwork motifs in a palace in Al Rayyan.

← The palace building with the same gate-decoration motif.

↑ Elevations showing that the same gate decoration motifs are also used in the palace building (top), and that the balcony steelwork motif is the same as on the gate (above).

↑ The lights, shaped
to resemble a palm tree,
indicate the influence of
the Deco movement (top).

The steelwork-pattern
drawing for the window
grilles (above).

→ The minaret dome
is decorated with light
bulbs extending down
from its apex.

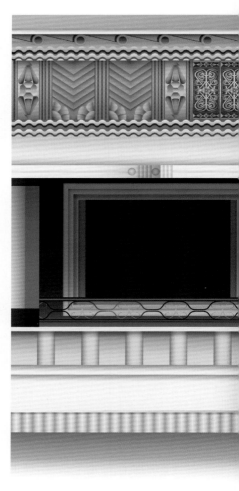

Sheikh Mohammed bin Hamad's *majlis* is one of the most decorated palaces of its time. It was constructed between 1952 and 1959 in the western area of the Amiri Diwan (currently in Al Bida' park). The building has an interesting, large rectangular plan with chamfered corners in addition to being surrounded by a double-column veranda. The main entrance is at the center of the south facade defined by a double-column portico supporting a pediment ornamented with arabesques and rosettes. The frieze above the veranda is wrapped around the *majlis* with a series of low-relief sculptured bands and medallions. The ornamented series on the frieze starts from both sides of the entrance with a branch of roses followed by a palmette band, then by a rosette, then two chevrons with flowers

↖ The *majlis* of Sheikh Mohammed bin Hamad in Al Bida' (top) and the entrance (bottom).

↓ Front elevation.

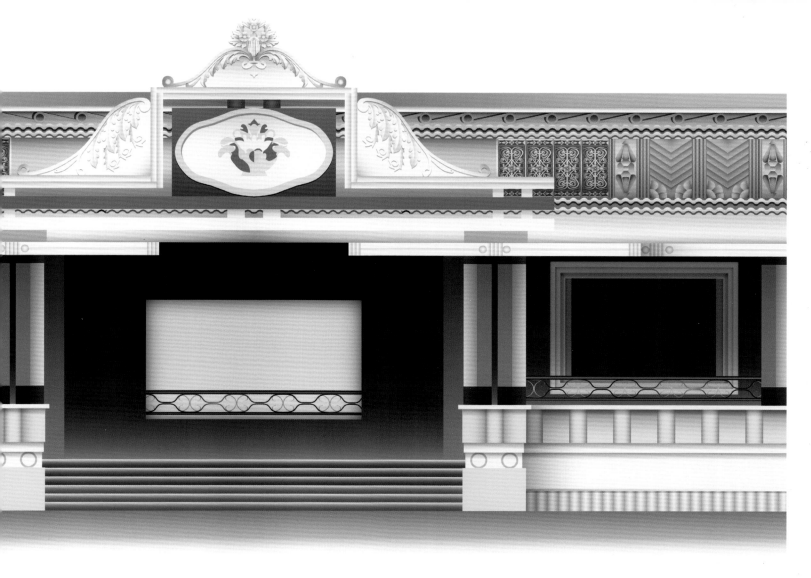

↑ Elevation
of the entrance.

in the corner, then another rosette, then a palmette band again, and then a band motif. This ornamented band pattern repeats symmetrically on the frieze— except for the chamfered corners, which are ornamented with a circle-bound star expanding around abstract eagle wings and crowned with a flower vase. Below the wings are flower branches reaching the corner rosette. A small tower, part of the *majlis* complex, is also fully ornamented with a series of simple decorated bands toward the central medallion, which is decorated from the top with an ivy leaf, then a rosette bound by a flower festoon, and finally by a simple vertical motif. The variety of ornaments used with a series of patterns and gradual scale and density also indicate another representation of the Deco movement in Qatar.

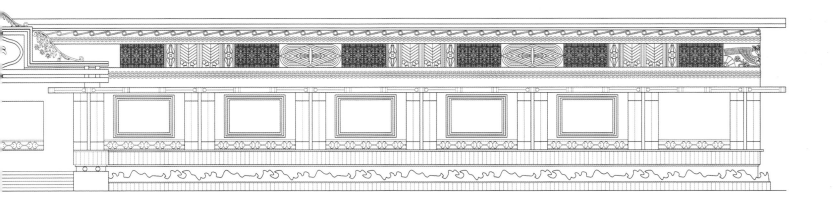

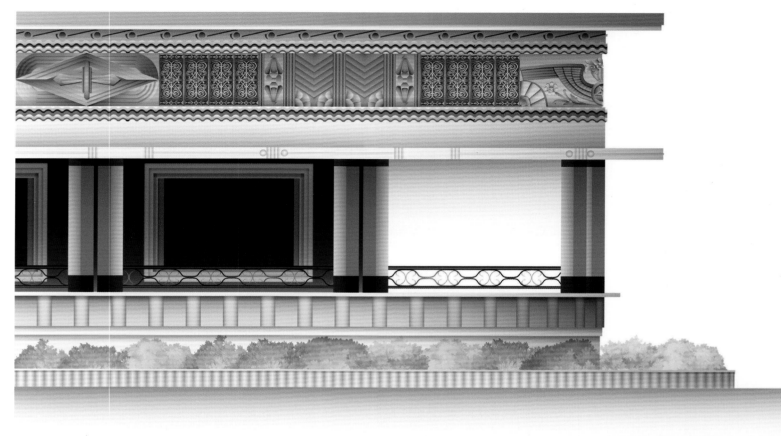

↑ Sheikh Mohammed bin Hamad's *majlis*, elevation of the right side (top) and view of the right corner (above).

↗ View of the left corner.

→ Decorative medallion on the ceiling of the *majlis* (left) and pattern drawing (right).

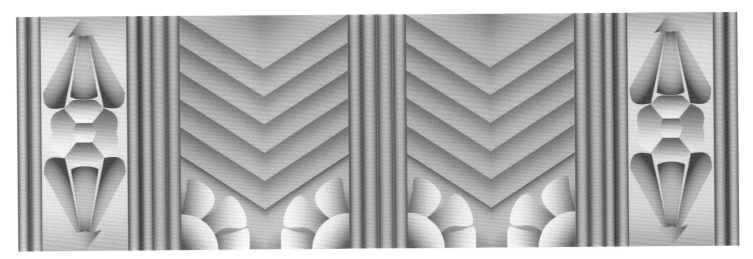

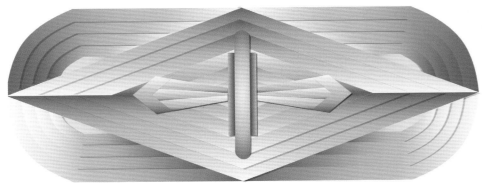

↑→ Some examples of
the ornamental medallion
series on the frieze.

193

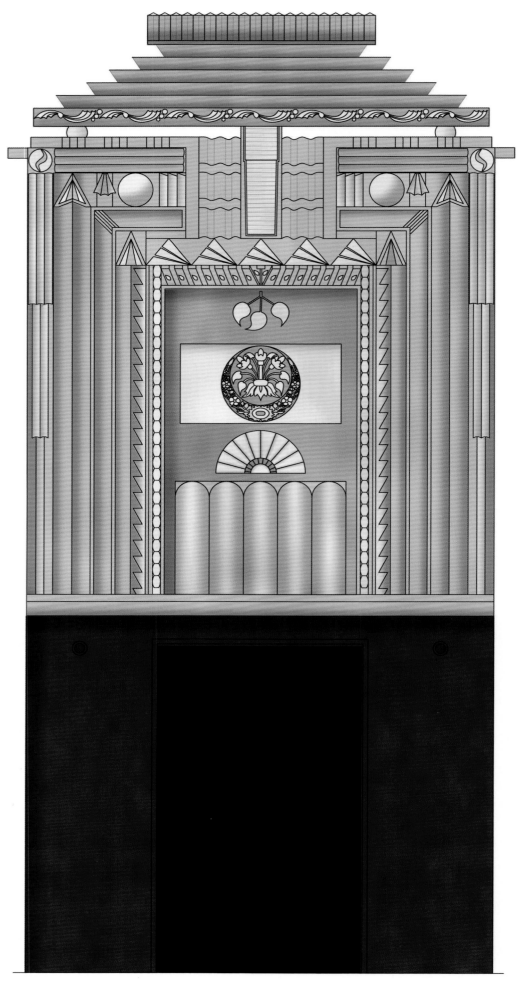

← Elevation of the fully ornamented tower of Sheikh Mohammed bin Hamad's *majlis*.

→ A small tower, part of the *majlis* complex, is also fully ornamented.

← The gate of Al Attiyah
Palace as it appears today,
also known as Musheireb
Palace.

Al Attiyah Palace, also known as Musheireb Palace, is also known for its attractive, decorative gate. The portico gate is supported by two cylindrical columns decorated at the top with a band motif and crowned with a helix. The trefoil-like arch is decorated on the two bottom sides of the helix with various flower vases. The rest of the arch is ornamented with symmetric foliage and topped with a cornice and crowned with a decorative parapet.

→ Gate-front elevation
of Al Attiyah Palace the way
it originally looked.

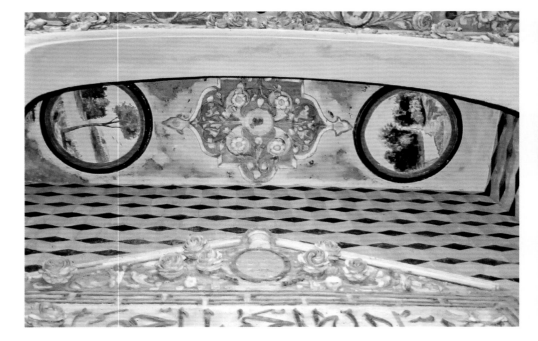

↖ The decorative details and paintings of the Qatari natural landscape on the gate ceiling at Al Attiyah Palace.

↑ Cylindrical columns decorated at the top with a band motif and crowned with a helix.

↖ The decorative details on the gate.

← The decorative details and calligraphy on the inner part of the gate.

→ Detail of the gate decoration at Sheikh Ghanim bin Ali Palace.

↑ Gate of Sheikh Ghanim bin Ali Palace.

The two-fold metal gate is ornamented with grid patterns of a simple row of rosettes, while the top row is a grill of leaf-like ornaments. The wall above the gate is decorated with a mosaic of rhombus patterns and centered with a fret-band frame with the calligraphy caption بسم الله الرحمن الرحيم ("In the name of Allah the Merciful") and topped with a pediment decorated with foliage and centered with an elliptical shining rock. The ceiling of the portico is decorated with moldings with foliage and sided by two circular bands with paintings showing the Qatari natural landscape. The side walls of the portico are decorated with a foliage framed and centered with a star wrapped by a garland of flowers. Another gate similar in form but with less decorative details is for Sheikh Qassim bin Ali in Old Al Rayyan. Although it has less decoration, it is attractive with its large wooden two-fold door decorated with copper nails.

The most famous gate in Doha for its interesting combination of decorations is the one at Sheikh Ghanim bin Ali Palace. The gate has two guard rooms at the sides with semicircular front walls, each with two rectangular windows with an ornamented grill. The gate appears as a portal that is gradually decorated from the bottom to the top. The cylindrical columns on the sides are decorated

with a rosette motif, while the tympanum is decorated in the center with a star framed by two types of rosettes and on its two sides it has a large rosette with three branching leaves. The spandrel is decorated with a combination of foliage, stars, rosettes, and band motif. The portal is crowned at the top with a symmetrical sculpture of two large fishes looking toward the central star.

↑ Gate front elevation of Sheikh Ghanim bin Ali Palace.

200

The metal gate, however, has an interesting ornament, where it can be divided into three parts. The lower part is decorated with rhombus shapes, the middle part is decorated with a band motif, and the top part with a modern ornamental pattern. The neon lights accent the relief carvings on the wall creating an enchanting contrast of color at night.

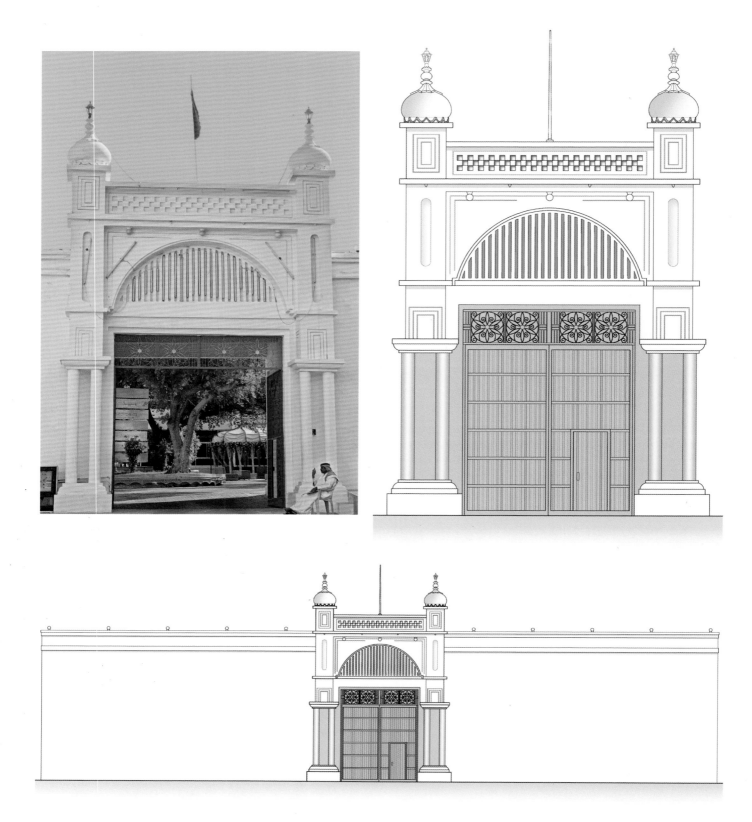

The gate of Sheikh Suhaim bin Hamad Palace has a simple form inspired by the Deco movement, where it also appears as a portal with simpler decorative elements. The gate is sided by two cylindrical, double columns topped with a frieze decorated with a centric, rectangular pattern. The tympanum above the metal gate is decorated with simple vertical lines. The parapet is ornamented with checkered patterns and edged by the same columns as the crown below with a small onion dome on top.

↖ Gate of Sheikh Suhaim bin Hamad Palace.

↑ Gate elevation (top) and front boundary wall elevation (above).

→ Front view (top) and left-corner view (bottom) of Salim Al Jaber's house in Al Jasrah.

Salim Al Jaber's house in Al Jasrah is another example of the influence of the Deco movement represented in its facade. The two-story rectangular form building with chamfered corners on the upper floor is symmetrical with the main entrance at the center giving a portal-like appearance. The first floor is ornamented with a grid and a chevron pattern at the corners, while the second-floor cantilever is ornamented by brick rendering below the window strip and glass bricks on top.

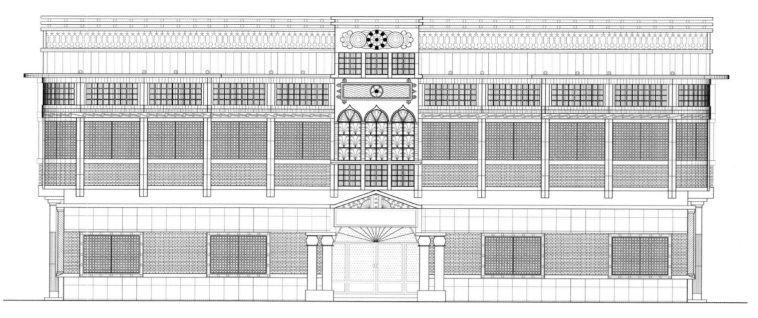

↑ Salim Al Jaber's house, the front elevation.

↑ The central, projected vertical decoration defining the entrance.

↗ Front elevation of the central, projected vertical decoration.

→ The parapet decoration of the building.

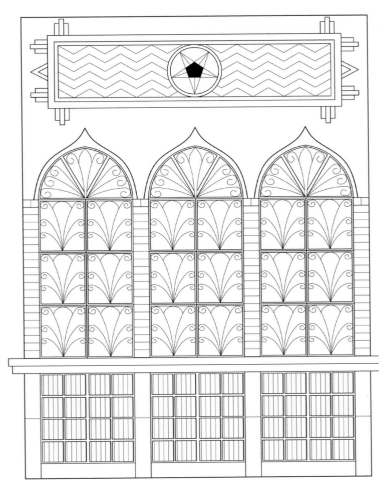

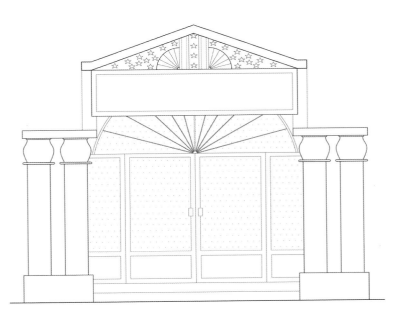

↖ Upper part of the vertical decoration above the entrance (top) and top decoration of the vertical projection of the entrance (middle).

↑ Drawing of the decoration above the entrance (top) and elevation of the entrance (above).

← The date palm decoration on the side of the projection of the entrance at Salim Al Jaber's house.

The building is crowned at the top with two parapets, one as a baluster and the other like a bead-molding pattern. The main entrance is emphasized by portal-decoration details that could be divided into two parts. The first part on the ground-floor level with the main entrance door has a double column on both sides with a plain rectangular frame crowned by a pediment and decorated with stars. The second part is a *mashrabiya*-like projection with three windows and a decorated metal grill and glass blocks on the lower part. On top of the three windows is a chevron decoration with a star in the center. This is followed by three other square openings of glass blocks and topped by a molded combination of stars and rosettes. The palm tree is another important decoration connected to Qatari culture and it appeared again on the side.

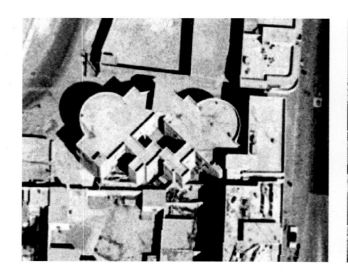

← Aerial view of the Deco villa in Al Asmakh in 1966 (left) and view of the right corner (right).

→ View from the left corner of the villa.

↑ Side view of the Deco villa in Al Asmakh.

↗ Details of the decoration on the balcony (left and right).

← View of the entrance of the villa.

A new form of the Deco movement appeared in an apartment building in the southeastern corner of the Al Asmakh district. The luxury apartment building not only had noteworthy decoration but also an artistic asymmetrical, unique, curved form, which was unorthodox at that time. The main visual attraction of the building is the semicircular, decorated veranda and balcony on top with double columns, which is a typical Deco motif. The boundary wall has the same semicircular form as the veranda and is ornamented at the top with a screen railing with vertical openings and a geometric band motif. The balcony is adorned and divided into two parts: the first is with a star band as a background and formed at the top and bottom with a chevron-band motif;

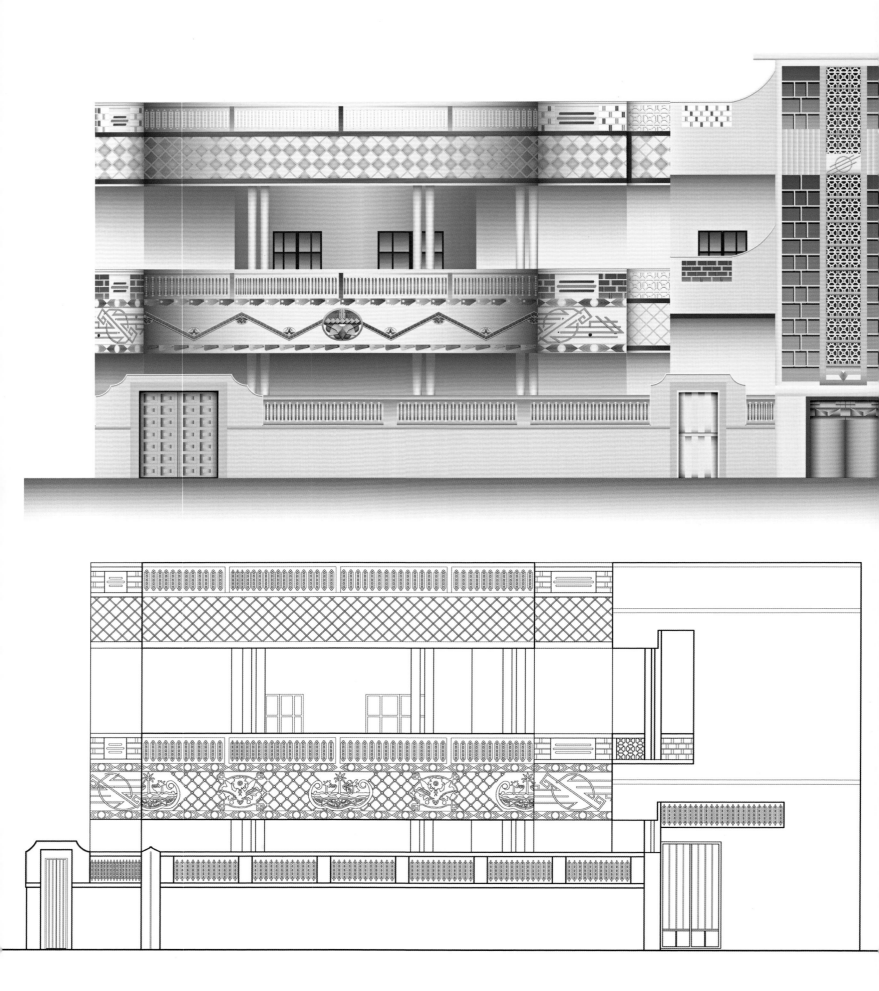

↑ Deco villa in Al Asmakh,
front elevation (top).

↑ Side elevation
of the villa (above).

→ Example of a decorative
medallion on the balcony.

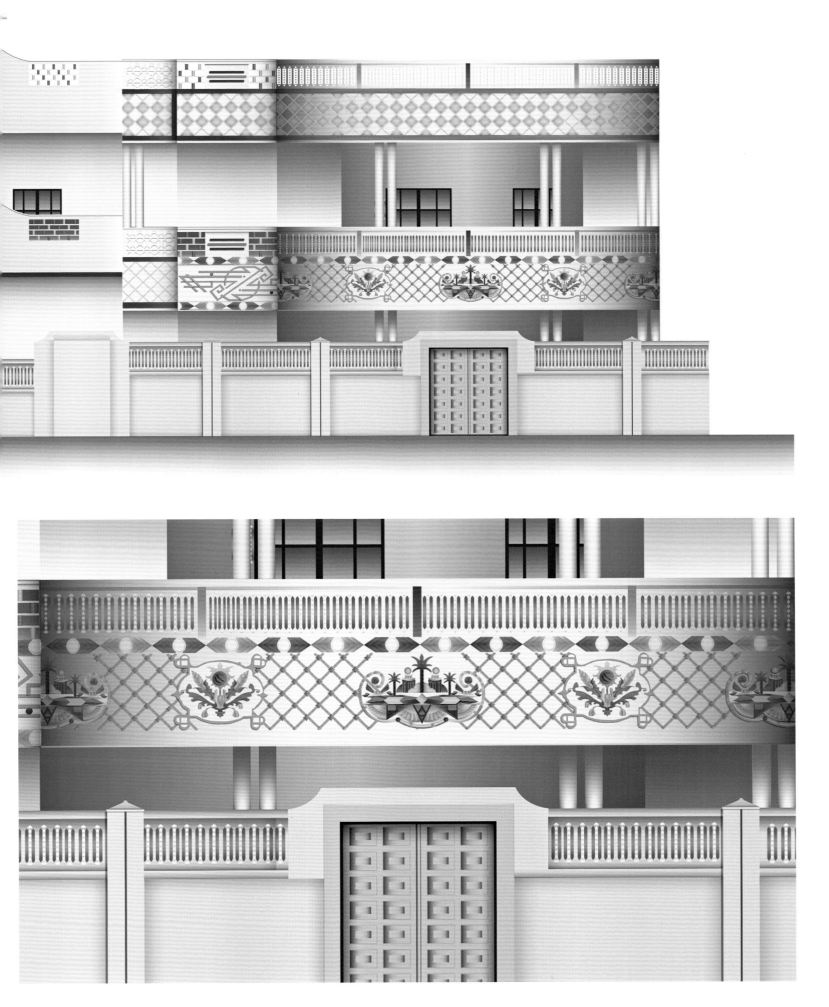

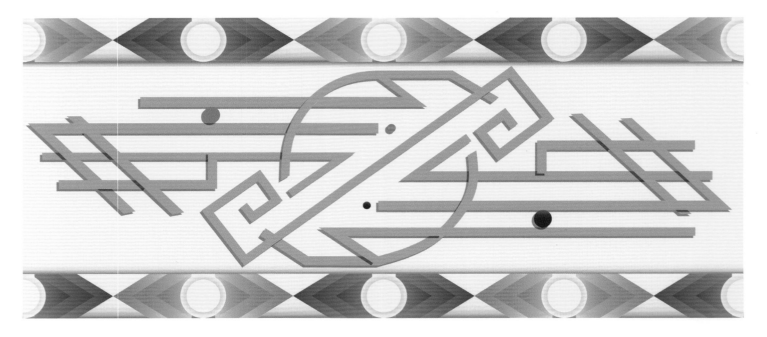

↑→ Deco villa
in Al Asmakh, patterns
of decorative medallions
on the balcony.

← Examples of a decoration
plate from the balcony.

← Deco villa in Al Bida', now demolished.

the background is ornamented with three molds—a rosette with a leaf, an oasis with a palm tree, and a half-geometric rosette. The second part is the balcony railing, which is like the one used for the top of the boundary wall. Beyond the semicircular decorated veranda and balcony, the two sides continue with the same decoration, except that the mold is free geometric art and the railing on top changes to a simple horizontal layer connected by colorful abacus-like elements. The frieze is adorned with rhombus patterns as a background and formed at the top and bottom with a chevron-band motif. The parapet above it is a railing with the same balcony and boundary wall design.

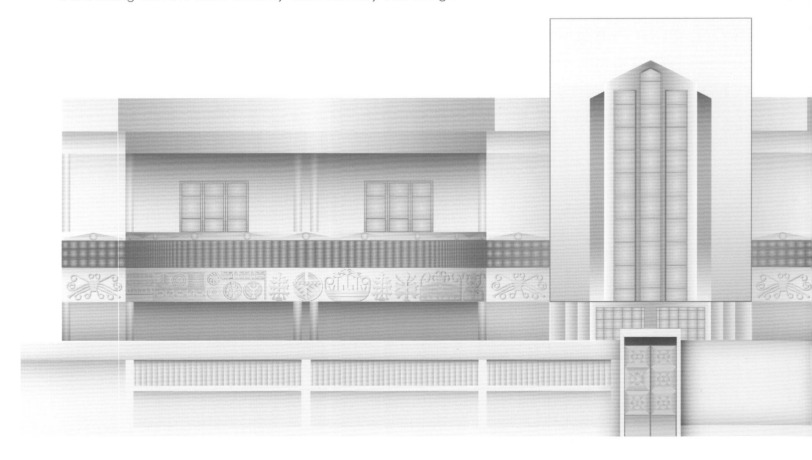

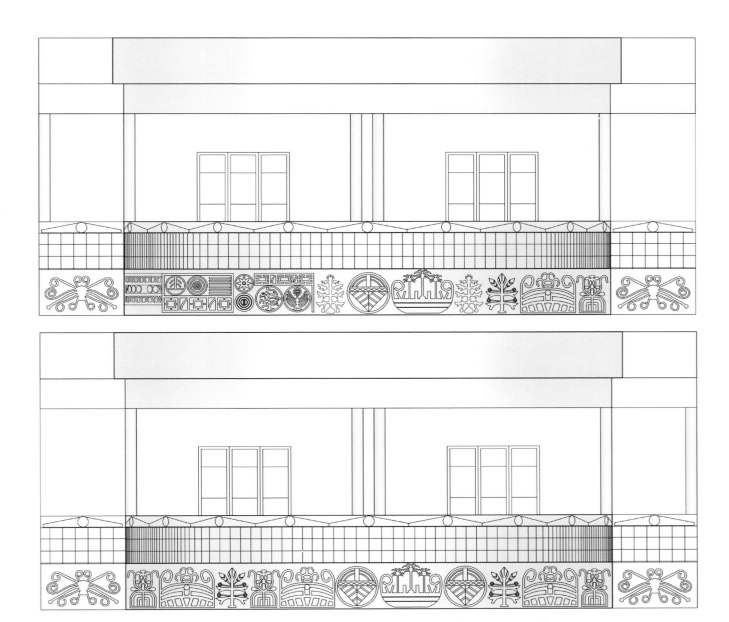

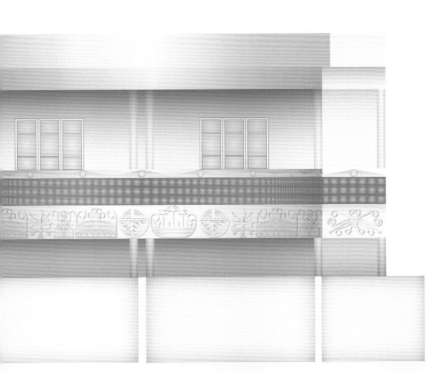

← Front elevation
of the demolished Deco
villa in Al Bida'.

↑ Elevation of the right-side
balcony (top) and of the
left-side balcony (above).

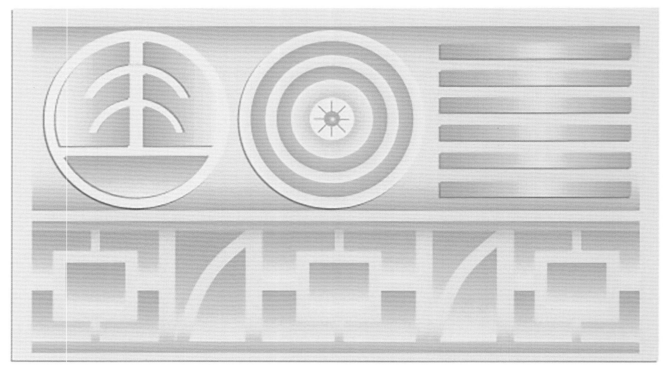

←↑ Patterns of the decorative medallions on the balcony of the demolished Deco villa in Al Bida'.

Another modernist Deco villa with a central staircase similar to the one in Al Asmakh was in Al Bida' with a double-column veranda and decorated balcony; however, there were three differences: (a) the decorative band was only molding without any background or band motif on the top and bottom, (b) the balcony railing had three rows of glass blocks above the decorative bands, and (c) the parapet was plain with no ornamentation.

217

↗ Decoration of right-side (top) and left-side (bottom) balcony of the demolished Deco villa in Al Bida'.

Another villa in Al Bida' also has its decoration focused on a polygon-like projection facade, with a band and plant motif on top of the window opening and molds of rosettes with leaves, or a star or eagle, below the window. The window grilles are also ornamented with plant and free-form ornaments. A vertical, rosette mold is also visible at the center of the semicircular facade between the two polygon-like window projections. The villa is crowned with a decorated parapet using a balustrade.

The Deco movement also had a simpler appearance in some of the residential buildings in the high-density districts. This simplicity appeared not only on the metal gates and early modern railings of the balcony and parapet but also the external plaster with horizontal lines or smudges, or the use of glass blocks, screen walls, and band motifs.

↖ View of another Deco villa in Al Bida'.

← View of the right corner of the villa.

→ View from the left corner of the villa.

↓ Steelwork and decoration on the windows on right and left side of the villa.

↑ Front elevation
of the Deco villa in Al Bida'.

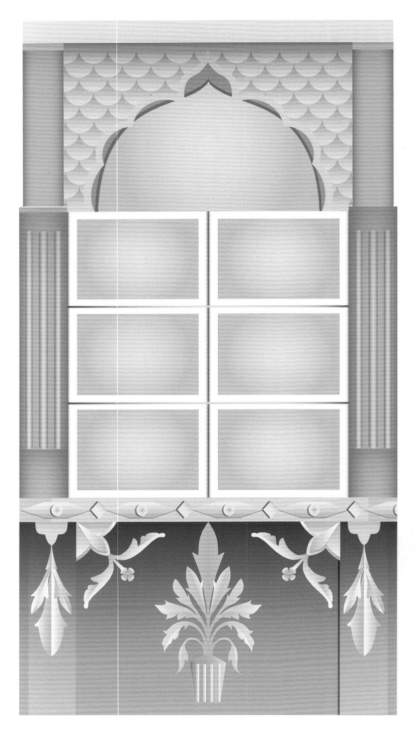

↑ Deco villa in Al Bida',
decoration of the window
on the left side.

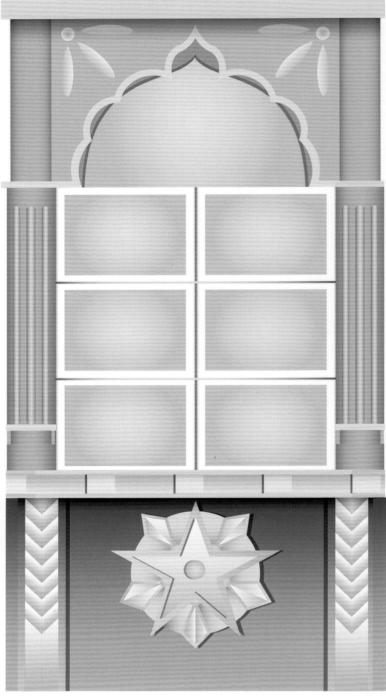

↑ Decoration of the
window on the right side
of the villa.

The Deco style appeared in villas not only on metal gates, early

↑ Decoration and steelwork of the window on the right side.

↑ Steelwork decoration on the door of the villa.

modern balcony railings, and parapets but also on windows

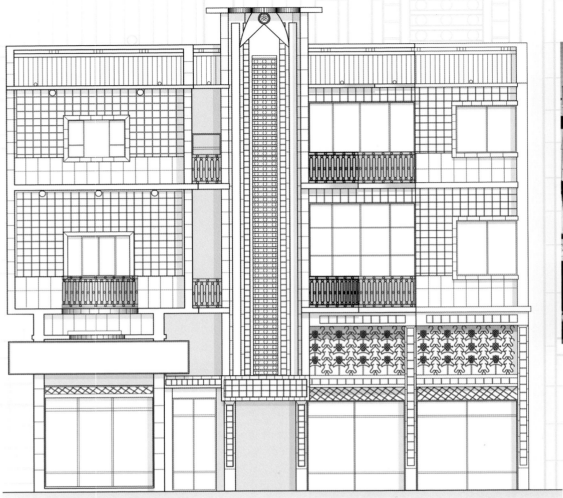

↑ Apartment building
influenced by the Deco
movement.

← Front elevation of the
apartment building.

↑ Steelwork decoration
on the building elevation.

→ Residential building influenced by the Deco movement.

→ Front elevation of the residential building.

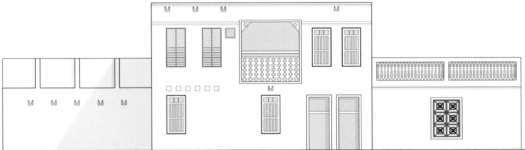

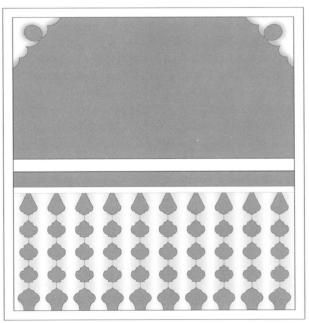

←↑ Decorated balcony and drawing of the decoration motif on the residential building.

↑ Deco movement influences are evident in the wall texture and screen at a residential building.

↑ Residential building influenced by the Deco movement in the balcony and parapet decorations.

↑ Evident Deco movement influences in balcony decoration and wall texture at a residential building.

← Mosque in Al Mansura influenced by the Deco movement as evident in the decorated entrance with a small minaret and crescent screen wall (left) and the crescent screen wall above the entrance (right).

← The decorated entrance with a small onion dome at the top.

The mosques were also influenced by the Deco movement, such as the one in Al Mansura with its gate not only decorated with Islamic screen molds but also crowned with a small minaret. Another example is a canopy mosque gate with a small onion dome on top. Moreover, the same mosque also has the external projection of the decorated *mihrab* attractively visible on the street. The tall minaret with its rhombus openings and small, parapet details also gives a visible attraction to the mosque from afar. This indicates how the Deco style contributes to introducing the mosque visually for the people in high-density districts.

→ Another mosque influenced by the Deco movement, which is evident in the decorated entrance with a small onion dome at the top.

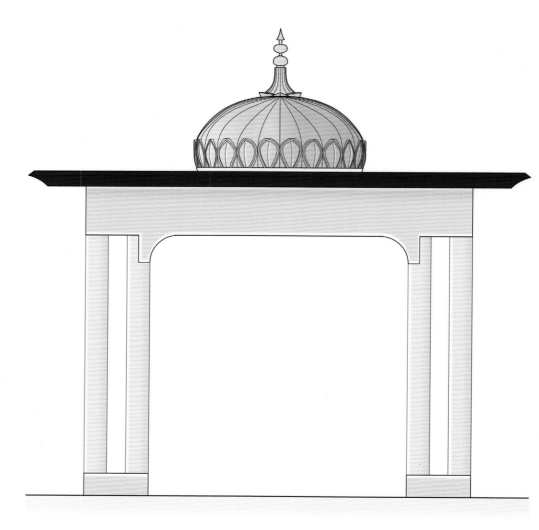

← Elevation of the decorated entrance with a small onion dome at the top.

→ The *mihrab* influenced by the Deco movement (top) and the *mihrab* perspective (bottom).

Minaret elevation influenced by the Deco movement.

↓ Detail of the decorated small onion dome at the top of the entrance.

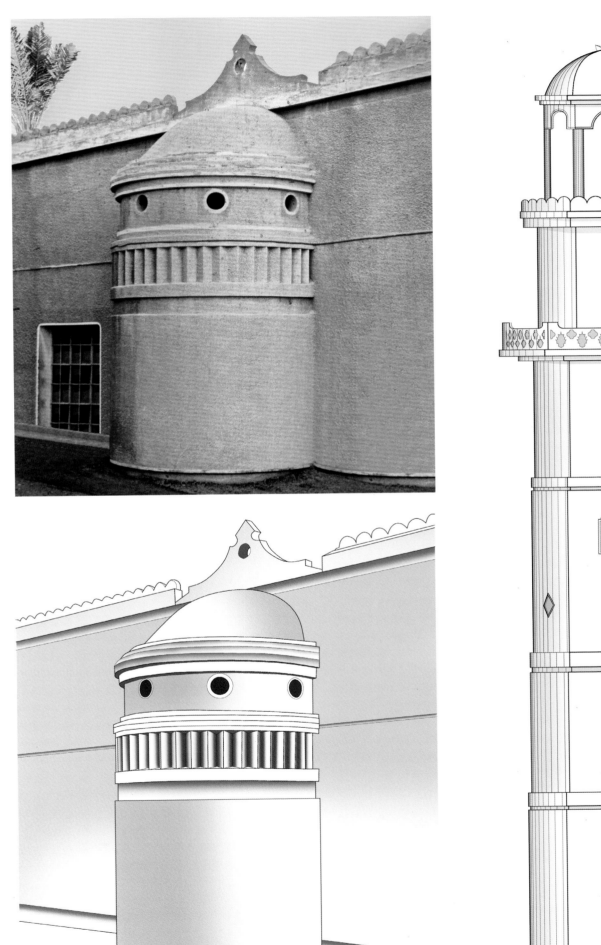

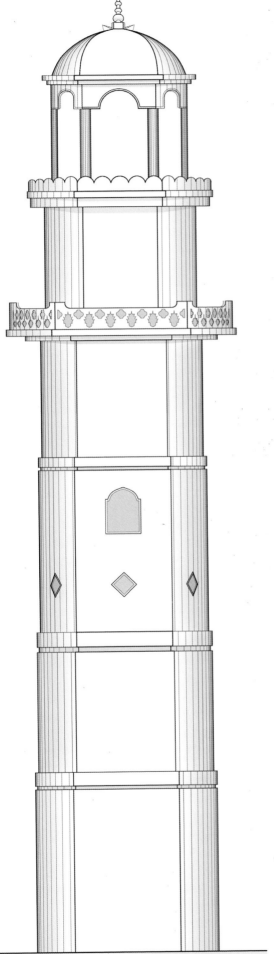

The increase of metal shops in the industrial areas in Doha in the 1960s contributed to the increased use of metal doors on residential buildings. The steel door became a trend that replaced wooden doors. These metal doors, one or two folds, large or small, wide or narrow, were also influenced by the Deco movement. The metal decorations on the doors are always found to be either in a network pattern or single or multiple units, and as a unique mirror art. The decorations are artistic impressions of a rose, leaf, star, bird, or butterfly, or are geometric, or circles, and free-form. These decorated doors could be found in single or multiple colors, but the most common are blue, black, white, and green. Some gates are associated with a canopy, which may indicate the social status of the family.

→ Decorated steelwork door influenced by the Deco movement.

↙↓ Gates with a modern and simple decoration influenced by the Deco movement.

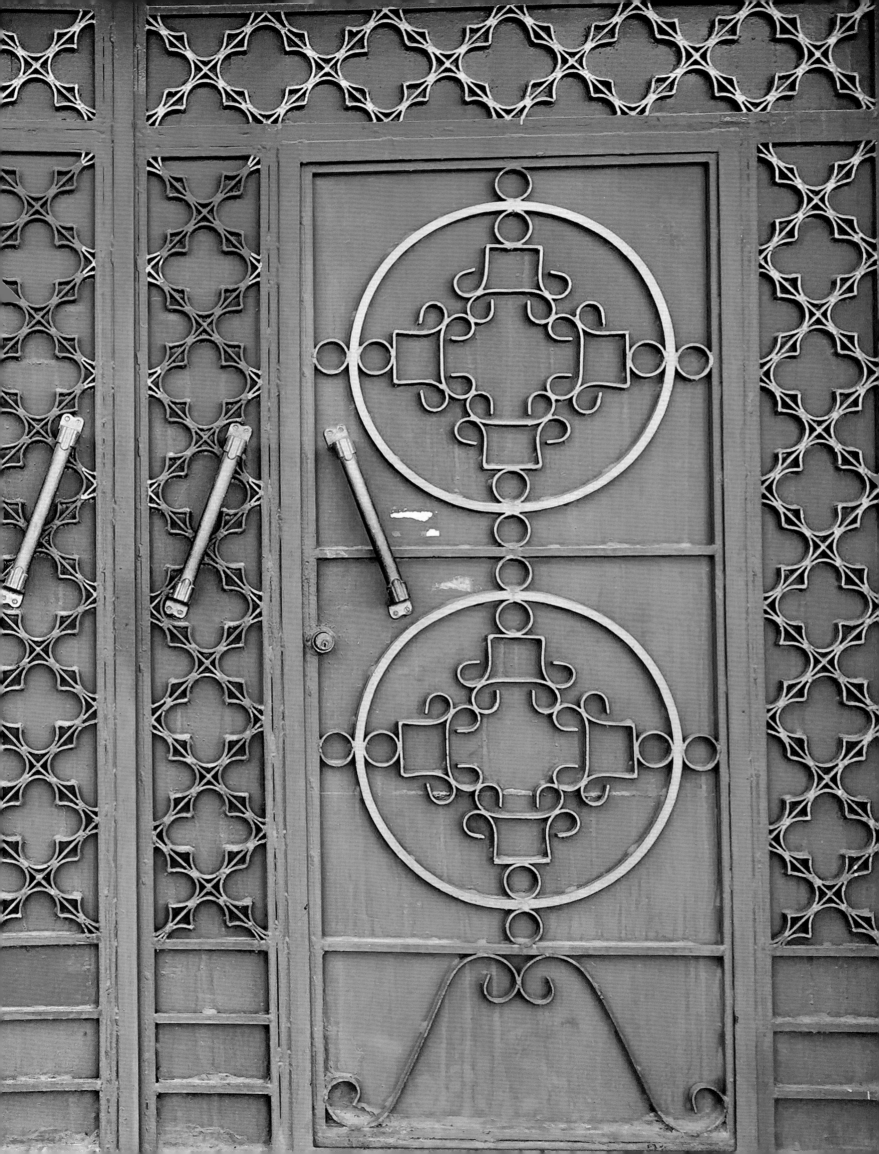

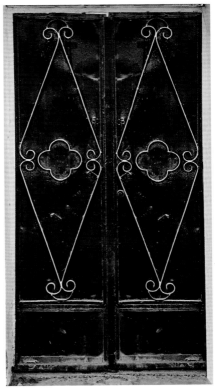

←↑ Some doors decorated with steelwork motifs that are influenced by the Deco movement.

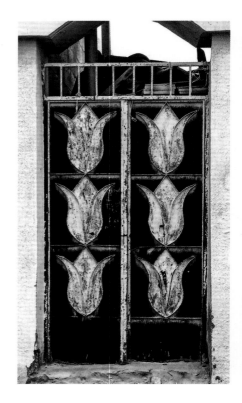

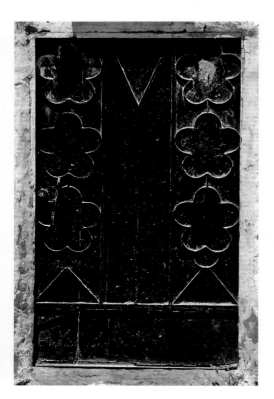

↑→ Examples of doors
decorated with steelwork
motifs influenced by
the Deco movement.

←→ More examples of decorative steelwork door motifs influenced by the Deco movement.

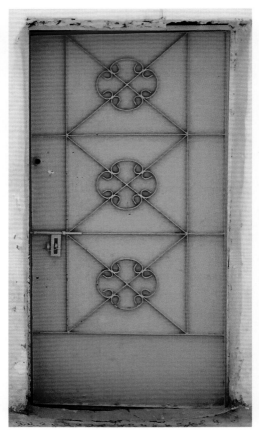

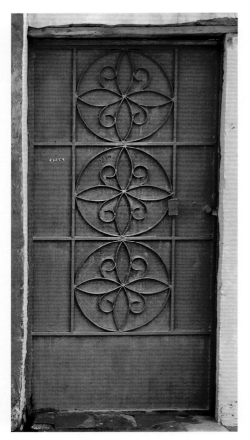

↑→ Additional examples of doors decorated with steelwork motifs inspired by the Deco movement.

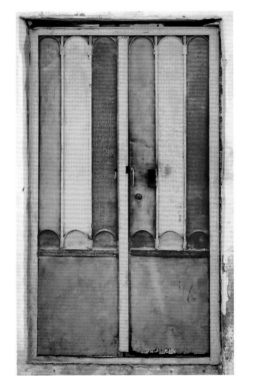

← ↑ Other examples of the Deco movement influence on decorative steelwork motifs.

COMMON PATTERNS-FLORAL

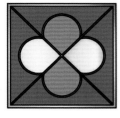
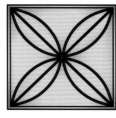

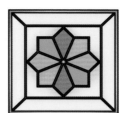

COMMON PATTERNS-GEOMETRIC

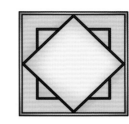
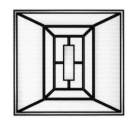

↑ Examples of typical Deco-movement floral and geometric steelwork patterns.

Conclusion

The 1960s brought new prospects to Qatar that contributed to a dramatic increase in oil revenues leading to urban development. Urban development led to better conditions and an improved quality of life in Qatar. This process started with establishing centralized administration systems to take control of its affairs. It introduced a new type of large-scale multistory government buildings within a large plot. In addition to establishing new entities for fishing, transport, and the media, there was a major expansion in all services and infrastructure, including new urban road features like landscaped roundabouts. However, the most significant theme in the 1960s was the beginning of the Qatari Deco movement in existing and new buildings. The Deco style became a trend that symbolized functional, social, and economic status for the building and its owner. It also introduced new decorative materials and ornaments during the pre-oil period. It is an architectural signature for buildings of the 1960s that was and, in some cases, still is present in governmental, commercial, residential, public, and religious buildings in Qatar.

CHAPTER 4

The significance of this decade, when compared to the two previous ones, was not only the new efficient government, the financial boom, the quality of buildings produced, and the magnitude of construction, but also globalization.

MODERN ARCHITECTURE

Introduction

The two decades following the oil discovery (1950–1970) witnessed a form of change for each decade: urban transition in the 1950s and urban necessity in the 1960s. However, the issue of the Qatari constitution in 1970—aimed at forming the ministerial cabinet—and the declaration of independence as a state in 1971, without a doubt introduced the decade of prosperity in its modern and urban history.

The dawn of modern prosperity started with the establishment of an efficient central administration of the first cabinet that included ten ministries in 1970. These ministries are Ministry of Finance and Oil, Ministry of Education, Ministry of the Interior, Ministry of Justice, Ministry of Public Health, Ministry of General Works, Ministry of Work and Social Affairs, Ministry of Industry and Agriculture, Ministry of Transport, and Ministry of Electricity and Water. This was followed by the establishment of two ministries in 1971: Ministry of Foreign Affairs and the Ministry of Economy and Trade. Three other ministries were established in 1972: the Ministry of Media, the Ministry of Municipal Affairs, and Ministry of Defense. Each ministry was designated with tasks, responsibilities, and the authority to develop the country in a planned approach and putting it into effect.

This decade also witnessed a significant boom in oil revenues due to the unprecedented increase in oil prices. In 1972, the oil revenues increased tremendously, reaching 600 million US dollars, and it doubled in 1973. After one year, in 1974, the revenues almost tripled, reaching 1.6 billion US dollars, because of the increase in the oil price to 12.5 dollars a barrel. Moreover, the 25 percent equity ownership of the oil companies by the Qatari government, and the increase in oil production and prices, in addition to government control on oil marketing, all contributed to the increase in revenues. The expansion of the oil industry also included the establishment of a new refinery in Um Said near the oil tanks, in 1972, which also contributed to increasing production and revenues.

Another contribution from the oil fields came by using the gas associated with it to operate the oil stations, electric power plants, desalinated water plant, and fertilizer factory, in addition to the discovery of the world's biggest gas field, north of Doha, in 1971. All these factors contributed to a financial boom accompanied by economic prosperity, which took Qatar to a new level of modernity.

The significance of this decade, when compared to the two previous ones, was not only the new efficient government, the financial boom, the quality of buildings produced, and magnitude of construction, but also globalization. The new Qatari Government started attracting international experts by commissioning western planning consultants for master planning and local consultants to ensure cultural continuity. In 1972, the Government commissioned the first western consultant, the British-based Llewelyn Davis, to develop a detailed study on Doha. The comprehensive study was based on the first census, in 1971, to identify the challenges facing its urban development and how to accommodate population growth, in addition to commissioning the Arab Engineering Bureau (AEB) to design many of the governmental buildings, urban landmarks, and many other projects in the financial and private sectors. This phase of development was driven by a proper planning vision that was bridged between international and local expertise. The development in this decade also witnessed new sectors such as entertainment, private press, shopping malls, and a university.

Urban Planning

In 1972, the Ministry of General Works (Ashghal) contracted the British-based Llewelyn Davis consultants for two years, to propose a new master plan for Doha, and later renewed their contract twice, until 1978. The six years of work carried out by Llewelyn Davis included a comprehensive study of the urban challenges, population growth, building regulations, services, redevelopment of populated areas, and a proposal for a new master plan for the city. Llewelyn Davis based his study on the first census of 1971 and a basic map of Doha from 1968.

The efforts during these six years were crystallized in three master plans. The first was a development plan (1972–1992), the second was a reconstruction plan (1974–1999), and the third was a complex plan. The proposed development plan in 1972 included a general urban and architectural plan, a report on population structure and growth, detailed planning for residential zones, detailed planning for central Doha, road network plans, land-use plans, and planning and construction bylaws. The reconstruction plan came out in 1974 as a two-year revision of the first proposal, which included more detailed planning on the road network and land use.

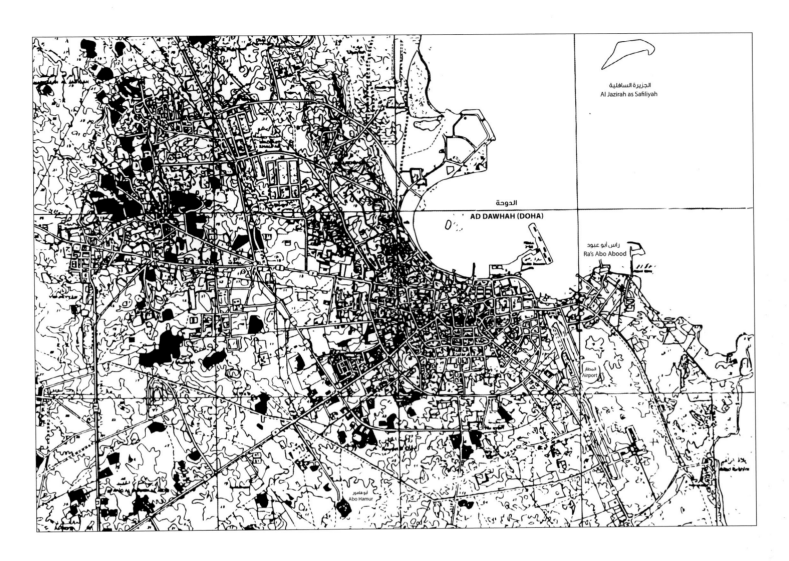

الجزيرة السافلية
Al Jazirah as Safliyah

الدوحة
AD DAWHAH (DOHA)

راس أبو عبود
Ra's Abo Abood

مطار
Airport

أبو هامور
Abo Hamur

↑ Map of Doha in 1968
used by Llewelyn Davis
for his study.

The third proposed master plan was presented in 1976 with major changes considered regarding the first two proposals. These changes to the plan
accommodated the many modifications that accompanied development in
the city. These changes included (a) the great and unexpected development
in the international oil market, (b) reclamation on the seafront bringing attraction to the heart of Doha, (c) the increased number of cars in the city, and (d)
the establishing of many national projects in different stages of planning and
execution that greatly influenced development. All these changes made the
sophisticated master plan flexible, to accommodate the fast and continuous
changes in the city's urban form. For example, the master plan included keep-
ing the idea of the ring roads and introducing new linear connection roads beyond the city center. In addition, a huge reclamation area of 630 hectares was
introduced on the northern side of the Corniche (Al Dafna). Moreover, the distribution of land use insured the achievement of building attractive commercial centers within the city, the visual and architectural connection between the
central commercial area and the newly developed land in the north, comfortable residential areas, and the proximity of the industrial areas to the city center.

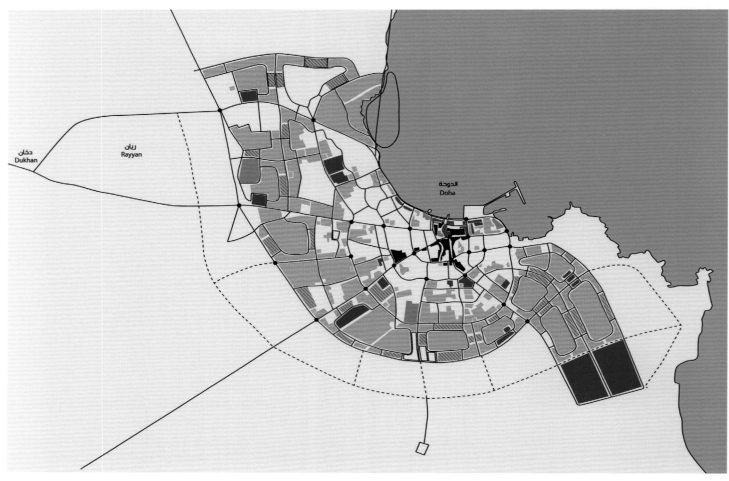

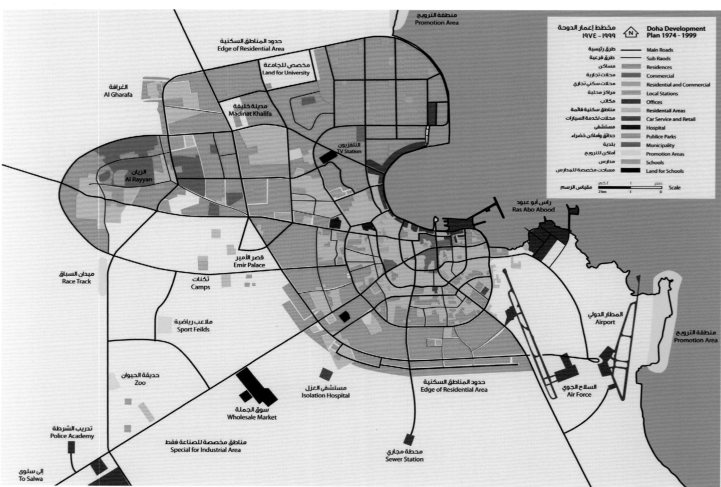

منطقة الترويج
Promotion Area

حدود المناطق السكنية
Edge of Residential Area

مخصص للجامعة
Land for University

الغرافة
Al Gharafa

مدينة خليفة
Madinat Khalifa

التلفزيون
TV Station

الريان
Al Rayyan

رأس أبو عبود
Ras Abo Abood

ميدان السباق
Race Track

قصر الأمير
Emir Palace

ثكنات
Camps

ملاعب رياضية
Sport Feilds

المطار الدولي
Airport

منطقة الترويج
Promotion Area

حديقة الحيوان
Zoo

مستشفى العزل
Isolation Hospital

حدود المناطق السكنية
Edge of Residential Area

السلاح الجوي
Air Force

تدريب الشرطة
Police Academy

سوق الجملة
Wholesale Market

محطة مجاري
Sewer Station

إلى سلوى
To Salwa

مناطق مخصصة للصناعة فقط
Special for Industrial Area

مخطط إعمار الدوحة ١٩٧٤ - ١٩٩٩		Doha Development Plan 1974 - 1999
طرق رئيسية		Main Roads
طرق فرعية		Sub Roads
مساكن		Residences
محلات تجارية		Commercial
محلات سكني تجاري		Residential and Commercial
مراكز محلية		Local Stations
مكاتب		Offices
مناطق سكنية قائمة		Residentail Areas
محلات لخدمة السيارات		Car Service and Retail
مستشفى		Hospital
حدائق وأماكن خضراء		Publice Parks
بلدية		Municipality
أماكن للترويج		Promotion Areas
مدارس		Schools
مساحت مخصصة للمدارس		Land for Schools

مقياس الرسم ٢.٥كم Scale

دخان
Dukhan

ريان
Rayyan

الدوحة
Doha

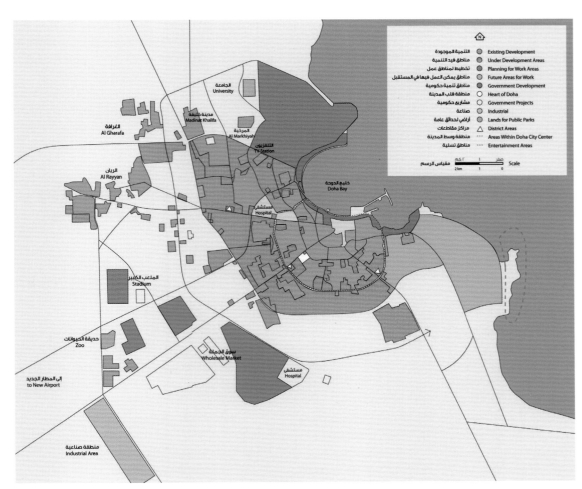

← Llewelyn Davis's first proposal—master plan development for Doha (1972–1992).

↙ Llewelyn Davis's second proposal— reconstruction plan for Doha (1974–1999).

→ Llewelyn Davis's third proposal—complex plan for Doha (1976–1999).

↓ Llewelyn Davis's third proposal—complex plan for central Doha.

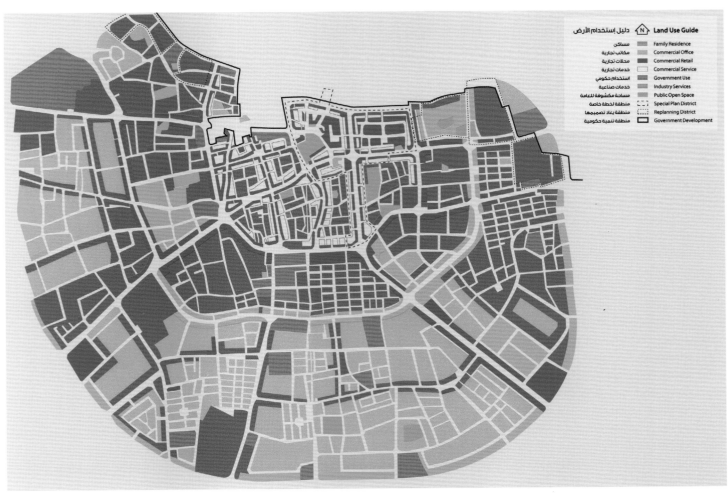

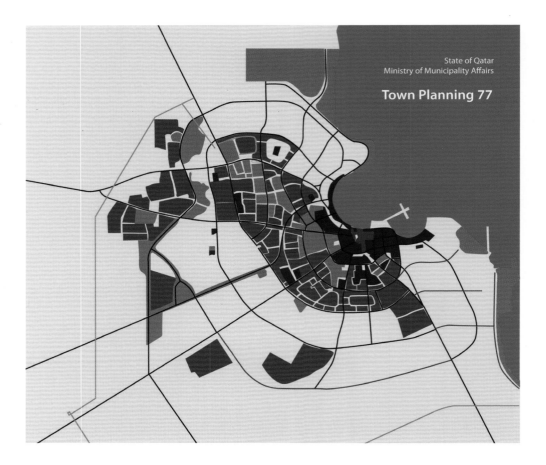

← Town planning No. 77, issued by the Municipality, is a compilation of all Llewelyn Davis's proposals.

In early 1977, an American planning consultancy known as William L. Pereira Associates was appointed to continue after Llewelyn Davis, developing the extension of the landfill area in the northern part of the city known as the New District of Doha or the West Bay. This new district aimed not only at enhancing Doha's image of prosperity and development but also at providing a well-planned infrastructure and services area for large national projects. Pereira started by studying the area and the population projection with a conclusion that the new area would hold a capacity of ninety-six thousand to one hundred twelve thousand people. This was followed by creating a road network that was perfectly connected to the city center. This was achieved by

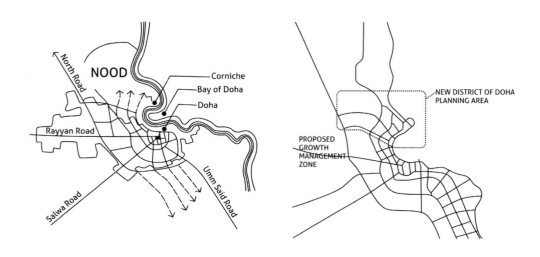

← William L. Pereira's planning area for the new location of the Doha district (right) and road connection network between the ring road of central Doha and the new district (left).

→ New district of Doha land-use plan by William L. Pereira.

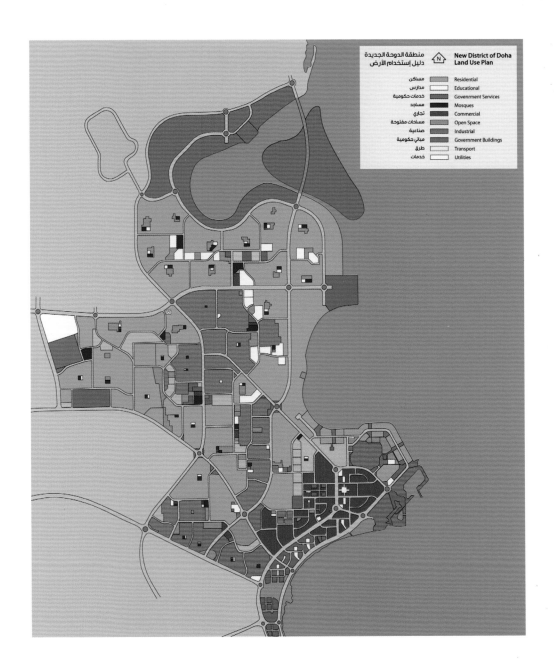

connecting the long ring road axes to the liner roads extending north, which are parallel to the coastline. The land use was designed in a gradual direction from the highest to the lowest density. The services and activities would extend linearly through the various residential blocks and complexes starting from the main service center located at the southeast of the area. The main service center area was also directly connected to the governmental building zones by the Corniche. The proposal for the north Corniche included an area for embassies and ministries, a business district with a park, and a large hotel for conferences. The master plan also included a plan for Qatar University and staff housing and a new residential district toward the west.

Shankland Cox, the Hong Kong-based consultant, was appointed in 1979 to assess the previous master plan proposals with emphasis on the population projection. The scope of Cox's work was to establish the proper plot size for housing, to limit the construction around the city that resulted in economic issues, to provide a flexible plan to accommodate change, a housing district design for a diverse community, the distribution of services and public facilities throughout the city, and the definition of retail areas all over the city. Based on the above-mentioned scope, Cox started his planning study to develop his first scheme that he called phased reconstruction master plan, which focused on the southern extension of the city. Later, he added another planning study to cover the whole city from the university in the north to the new southern extension. Regarding the road network, Cox depended on defining the road axes on Davis's two master plans of 1974 and 1975, and Pereira's master plan of 1977. However, Cox added the road network extension between Doha and Al Wakra and the fourth ring road, which resulted in a new network design.

↙ Phased reconstruction master plan of Doha and the new southern district by Shankland Cox.

↓ The talking-clock roundabout in Al Mirqab Al Qadeem.

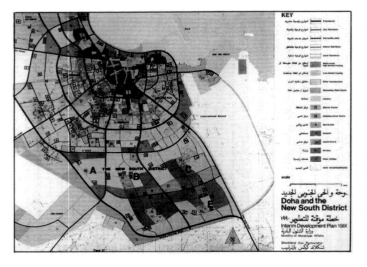

↙ Layout of Sohem bin Hamad Al Thani roundabout tower.

↓ Elevation of Sohem bin Hamad Al Thani roundabout tower.

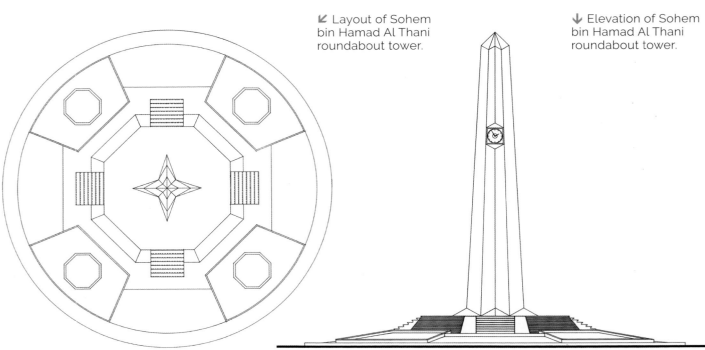

This city also witnessed landscaped roundabouts with public art as monuments, reflecting new modern features added to its road network and urban development. One of the memorable examples of such monuments in people's minds in the early 1970s was the talking-clock roundabout. It was an oval-shaped roundabout located in an area called Al Mirqab Al Qadeem. The oval, landscaped roundabout with the large talking clock became an attraction where people would gather at the roundabout to hear the clock telling the time. AEB also contributed to designing some of these roundabouts in the early 1970s. One roundabout was designed as a star-shaped obelisk with a pyramid on top that had a clock in it. The star-shaped obelisk was placed at the center of a raised, octagonal platform that had steps rising from four directions. Another roundabout was designed as an abstract of a concrete, offset starfish surrounded by flower beds in the form of petals. The flower beds are surrounded by white marble and are finished with colored tiles.

↓ Site plan (below) and general layout (below right) of the abstract of a concrete, offset, starfish roundabout.

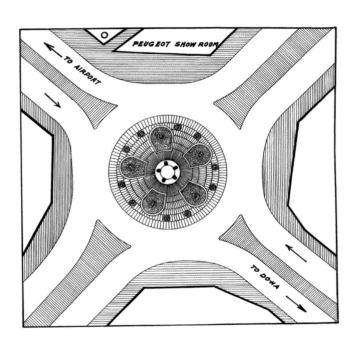

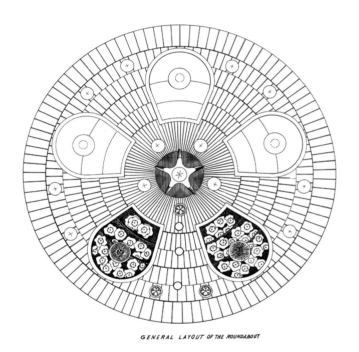

GENERAL LAYOUT OF THE ROUNDABOUT

→ Elevation of the abstract of the starfish roundabout.

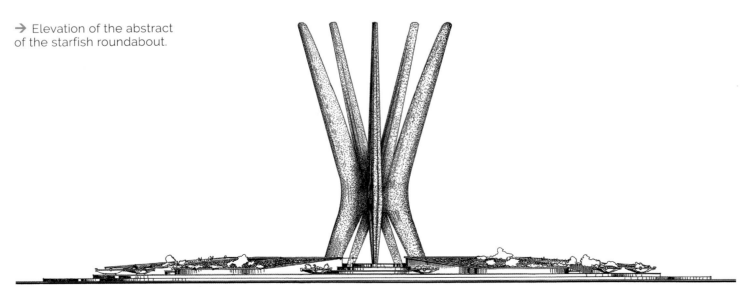

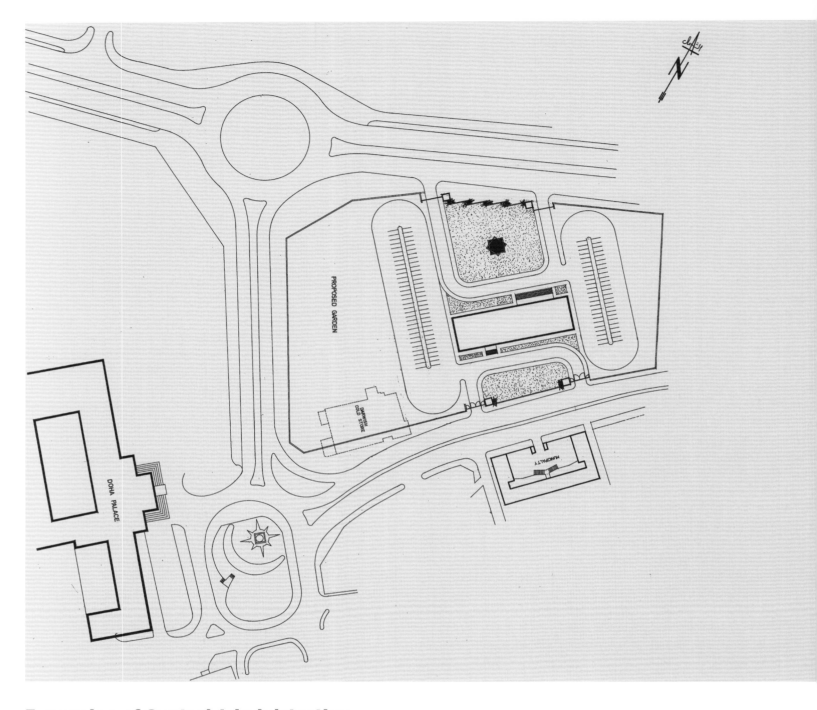

PROPOSED GARDEN

DARWISH COLD STORE

DOHA PALACE

MUNCIPALITY

Expansion of Central Administration

The establishment of the Ministry of Foreign Affairs in 1971 was an important statement by Qatar, opening up to the world for international relations. The site chosen for the new Ministry building was next to the Amiri Diwan and opposite Dar Al Hokuma, which indicates its importance. AEB had the privilege of designing the Ministry of Foreign Affairs building for that site and presented three design proposals in 1974. The first proposal showed a contemporary approach with modern pointed arches that protrude, overlaying the typical administrative-building windows in a double-loaded corridor with offices on both sides. The second proposal had three flat, rounded arches, which became a trend and a tendency that appeared in many apartment buildings.

↑ The site plan of the Ministry of Foreign Affairs.

↗ First-floor plan of the Ministry of Foreign Affairs.

→ The Ministry of Foreign Affairs printed on the back of a one Qatari Riyal banknote.

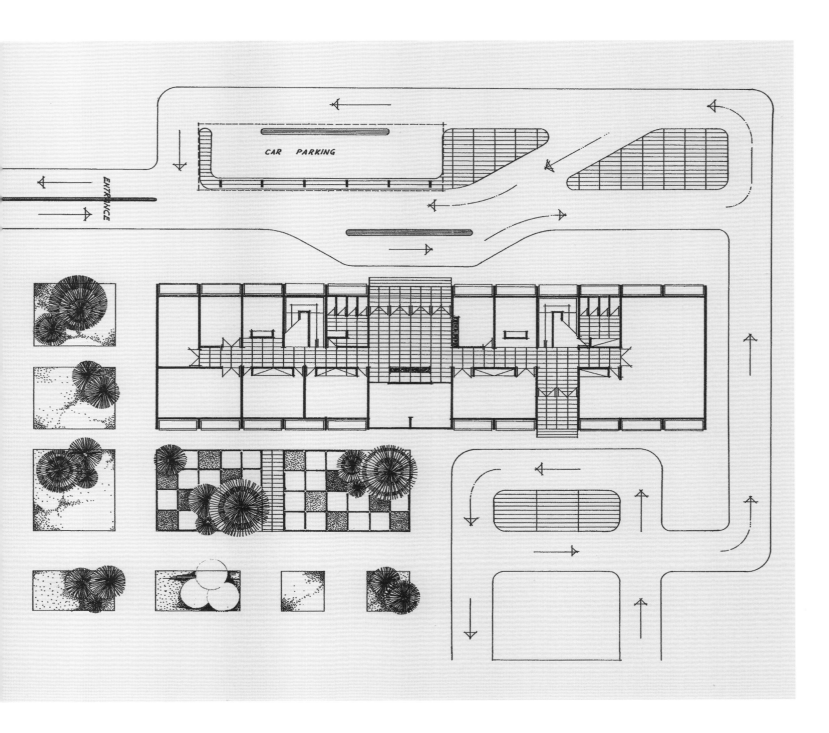

It could also be perceived as an influence from cities like Baghdad and Cairo. The third proposal, which was chosen for construction, seemed to contain elements from both proposals, especially the pointed arches that were influenced by the Diwan. The same arches were also evident in important palaces leading to a belief that they were a strong trend at that time. The arches in their circular or pointed form were devised to give the designs an Arabic touch. Another important element in this building was the *mashrabiya* and their patterns. The Ministry building was also celebrated by printing it on the back of one Riyal banknotes issued by the National Central Authority that was established in 1973.

↗ Perspective of the proposed building for the Ministry of Foreign Affairs.

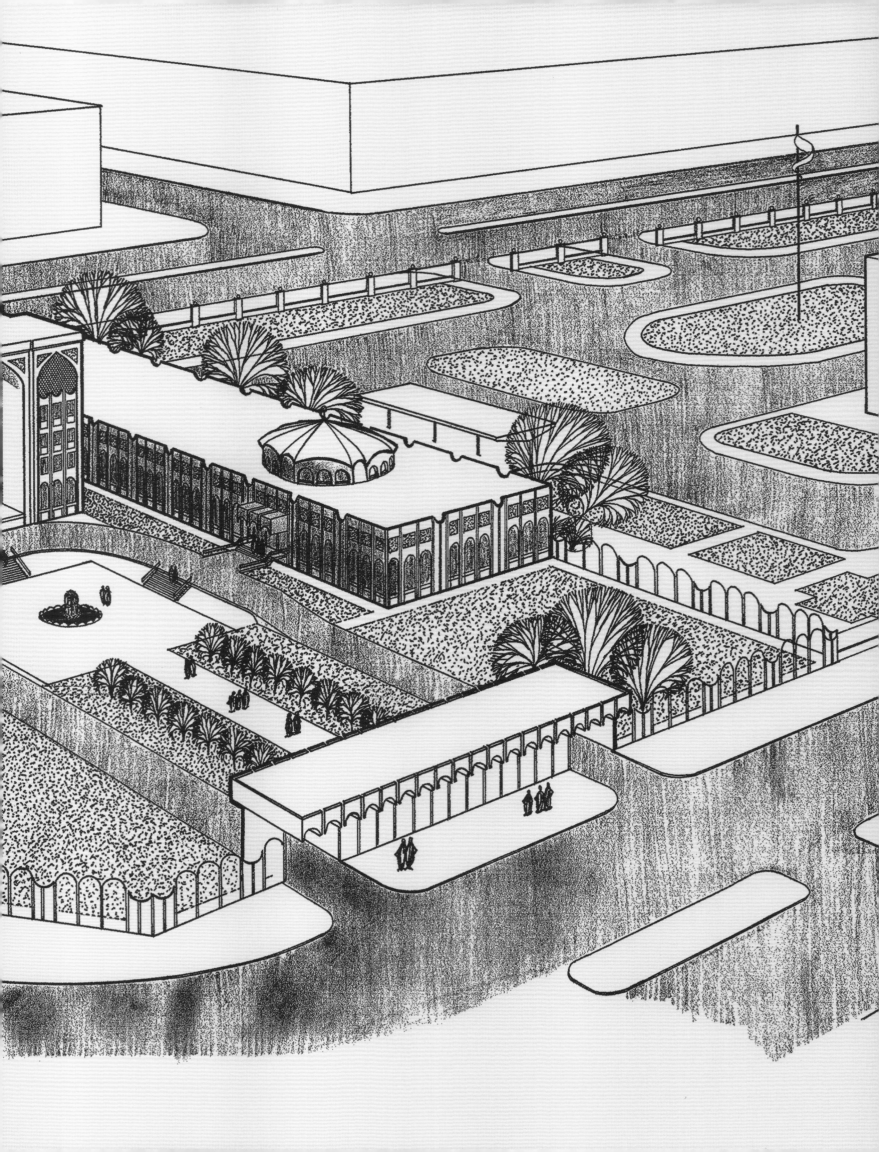

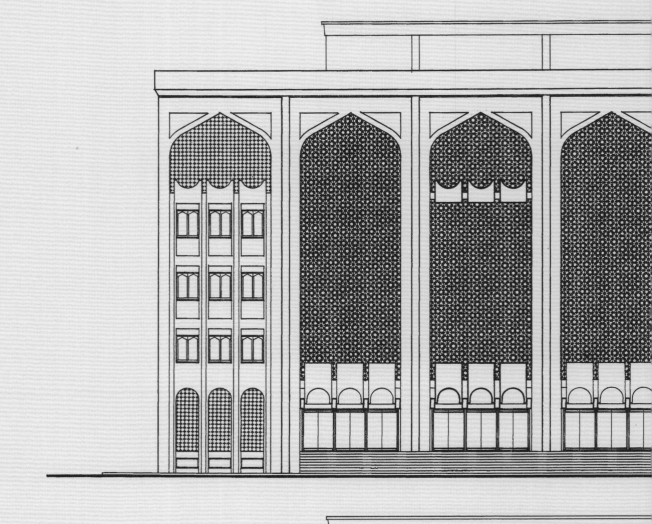

→ Ministry of Foreign Affairs, main elevation.

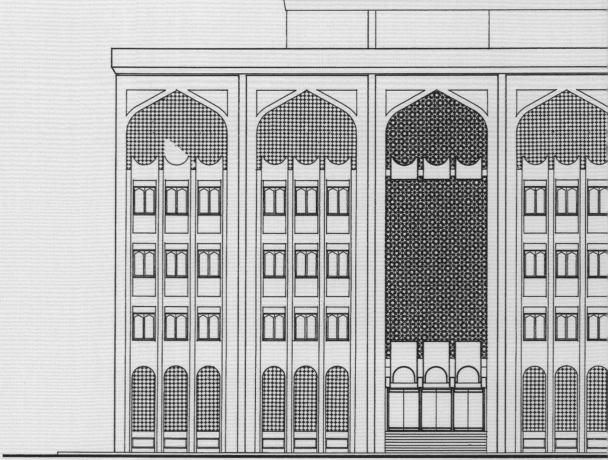

→ Back elevation.

← Proposed interior perspective for the Ministry of Foreign Affairs.

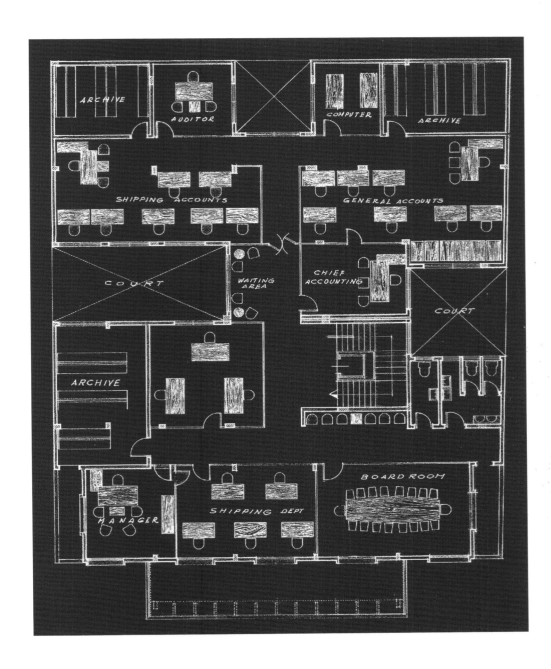

→ Third-floor plan of the Qatar National Navigation & Transport building.

↓ Front elevation of the Qatar National Navigation & Transport building.

AEB prepared a design for the Qatar National Navigation & Transport building as a second modification proposal. The design combined a typical building mass focused on a central entrance, using a form of screening that could be an influence carried forward from the *liwan* tradition, giving shade to the windows. This method became widely used seemingly after John R. Harris used a similar design philosophy to shade the windows for Al Rumailah Hospital. Another important expansion project desired by the Government in the early 1970s was for the State Hospital, which was previously known as Al Rumailah Hospital. AEB prepared three design proposals for the 150-bed expansion to the existing hospital building.

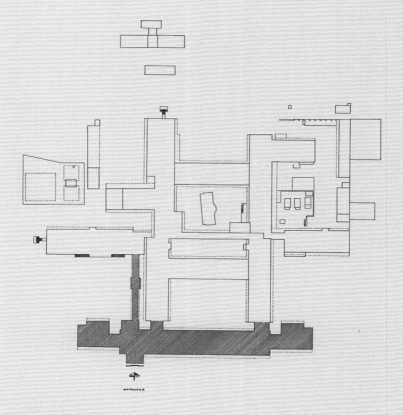

↑ State Hospital,
first proposal by AEB
for the new extension.

↓ East elevation (below),
and west elevation (bottom)
for the new extension.

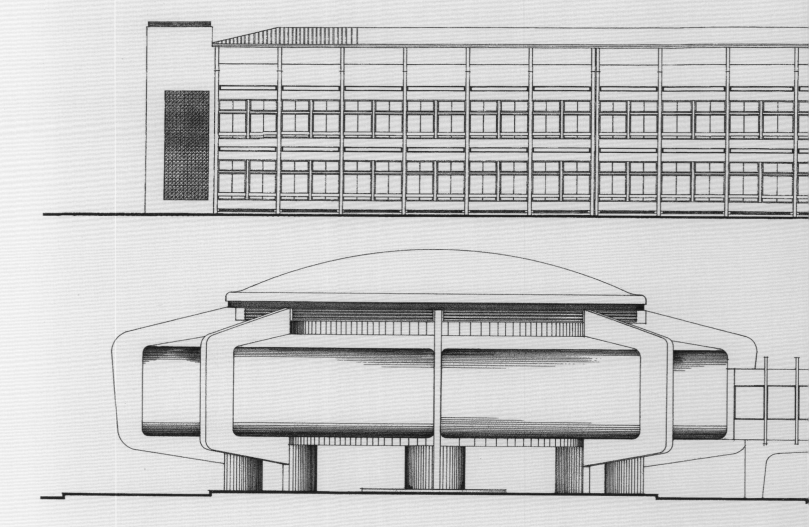

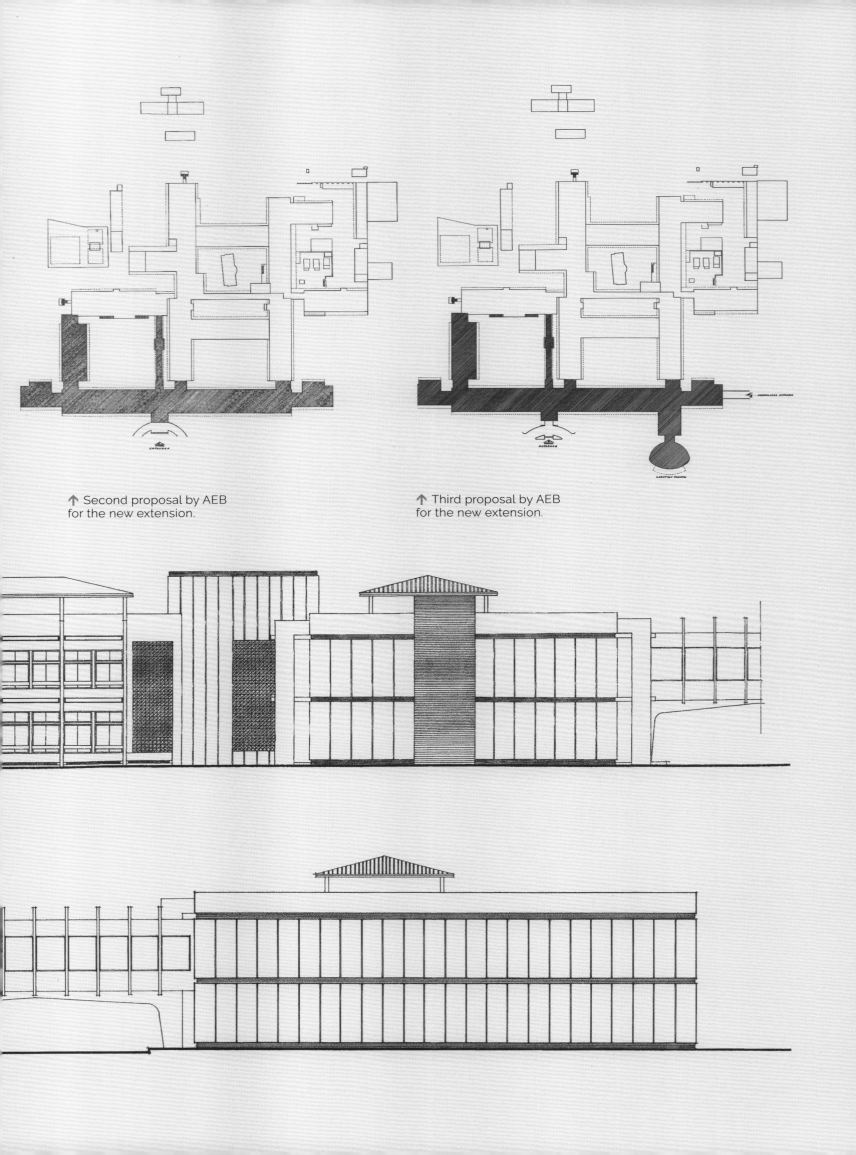

↑ Second proposal by AEB
for the new extension.

↑ Third proposal by AEB
for the new extension.

↑ Perspective of the
new annex extension to
Al Rumailah Hospital.

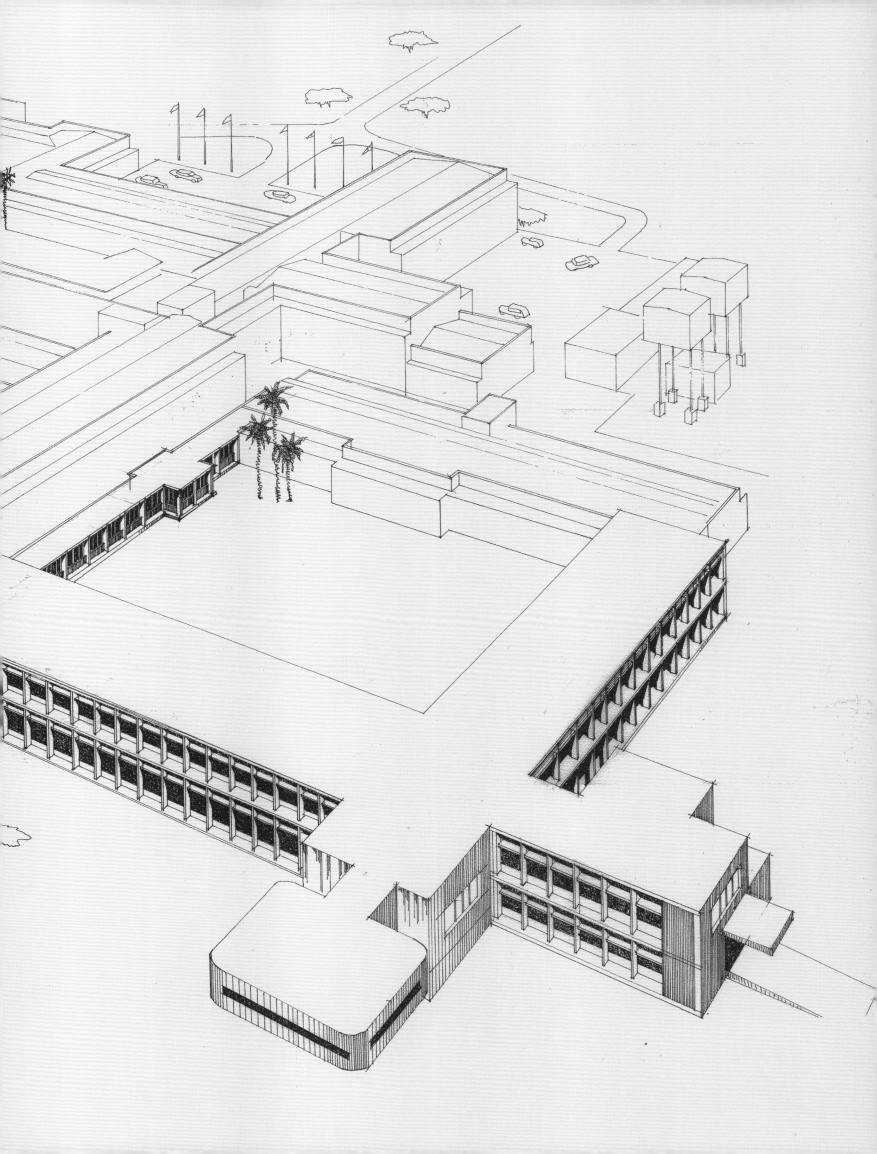

The new extension was proposed to be attached to the existing building on the north side, connecting two parallel annexes perpendicularly and creating a new courtyard. The first proposal was a simple linear annex connecting the building at three access points, while the second proposal was an L-shape, connecting the building from four access points. However, the third proposal was similar to the second but with an extra spaceship-like wing projecting toward the north that would function as an operating theater. The elevation for the extension was proposed to be the same as the existing building except for the operating theater annex.

→ The Gulf Hotel during construction in 1972.

↘ Aerial view of the Gulf Hotel operational after completion.

↓ Recent photo of the Doha Palace Hotel.

Urban & Architectural Features

Hospitality

The hospitality sector also flourished during this decade, when AEB designed the Doha Palace Hotel in 1972. It was designed to reflect a typical modern building with a slight reminisce of the spirit of Qatari Deco,

In this decade, new building typologies appeared in Doha

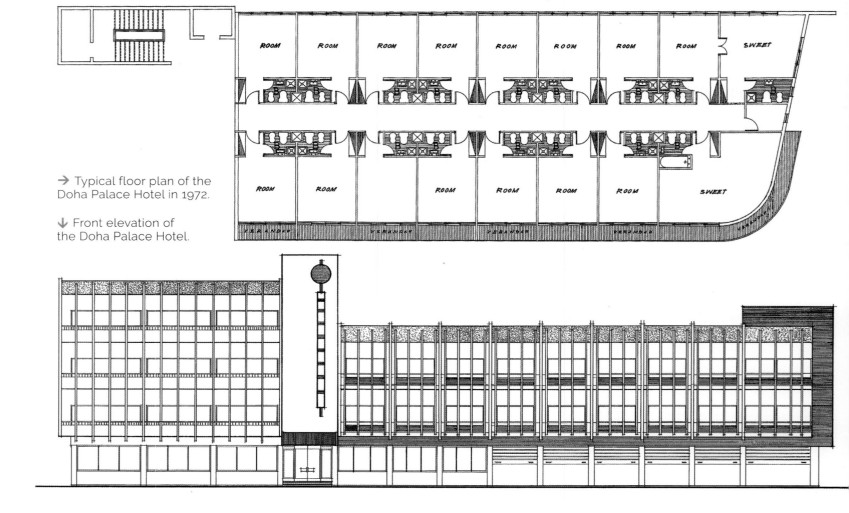

→ Typical floor plan of the Doha Palace Hotel in 1972.

↓ Front elevation of the Doha Palace Hotel.

shown in the protruding columns on the first floor, in addition to the feature cutting vertically through the facade. The hotel building still exists today and was restored with *mashrabiyas* added to the upper floors and red granite to the first floor. Another hospitality building built in 1972 with the best view of the Corniche was the Gulf Hotel. The pillars of the first floor uniquely resemble a Y-shape forming an arcade and have seven floors above. Some of the prominent features of this design are the balconies and the absence of a curtain wall, which became a trend in Qatar soon after. The orientation of the building and the shading provided show a good response to the environment.

marked by mass, scale, function, modernity, and globalization

It is currently part of the Marriot hotels and is closed for restoration to its original state. The Gulf Hotel is a project that reflects the unity of GCC countries—as similar hotels were built across the GCC under the same name in the 1970s (in Bahrain, Oman, UAE, Abu Dhabi, Qatar) with the purpose of exhibiting that unity. Some argue that it was named after Gulf airways due to its flight connections to most of the GCC Countries.

↓ The Gulf Cinema under construction in the early 1970s (left) and after construction completion (right).

The establishment of Qatar Cinema and Film Distribution Company in 1970 and the Ministry of Media in 1972 contributed to bringing media and entertainment to Doha. One of the entertainment projects in the mid-1970s was the construction of the Gulf Cinema on the C-Ring road. It was designed by the Iraqi Aga Khan award winner, the architect Rifat Chadirji, who is also known as the father of modern Iraqi architecture. The symmetrical building was impressive at the time with a grand entrance at the center and two large-screen theaters opposite each other projecting their films from the roof. This was the first public cinema in Doha that brought international film entertainment to the people apart from home television.

Although Qatar started sports—and specifically football—in the 1940s, it was in the 1970s that it quickly established itself as a growing center for football activities by constructing buildings for clubs. For example, the Al Rayyan Club was established in 1967 and later, in the 1970s, the economy allowed the Government to start funding sports in the country, and they considered constructing a building for them. AEB proposed a design for the club in 1971 in a simple L-shaped form, where the entrance is defined by a three-pointed arch canopy. The club consists of a hall leading to the offices, a lounge, and entertainment section with a pool table and table-tennis rooms. The lounge is surrounded by a veranda overlooking the sports fields.

→ The Al Rayyan Club, site plan designed by AEB in 1971 (top right) and floor plan.

→ Perspective of the Al Rayyan Club.

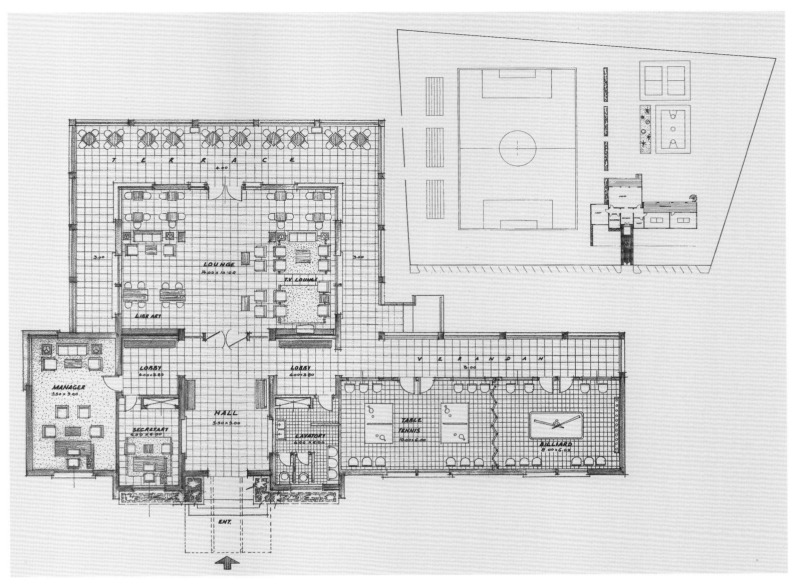

← Aerial view of the Qatar Central Bank after construction in 1977.

Banks

The 1970s also witnessed prosperity in the financial sector by establishing new banks including Bank Al Mashreq, Arab Bank Ltd., Commercial Bank of Qatar, and Qatar Central Bank. In 1971, AEB designed Bank Al Mashreq, where the geometry of the architecture was modern with strong horizontal and vertical lines. These focus on shading in the side elevation of the building, where the glare is reduced by using a horizontal feature on the window. Another design by AEB was made for Arab Bank Ltd. where it gave that sense of modern architecture with large glass windows and horizontal and grid features in its elevation. AEB designed the Commercial Bank of Qatar in 1977. The design shows a typical building mass around a central entrance, perhaps influenced by the *liwan* tradition, shading the windows. Qatar Central Bank was constructed in 1977 in a landfill area by the Corniche Road. The mass of the building was visually attractive with its unique feature of curtain walls that were the first at the time.

↓ Perspective view of Bank Al Mashreq.

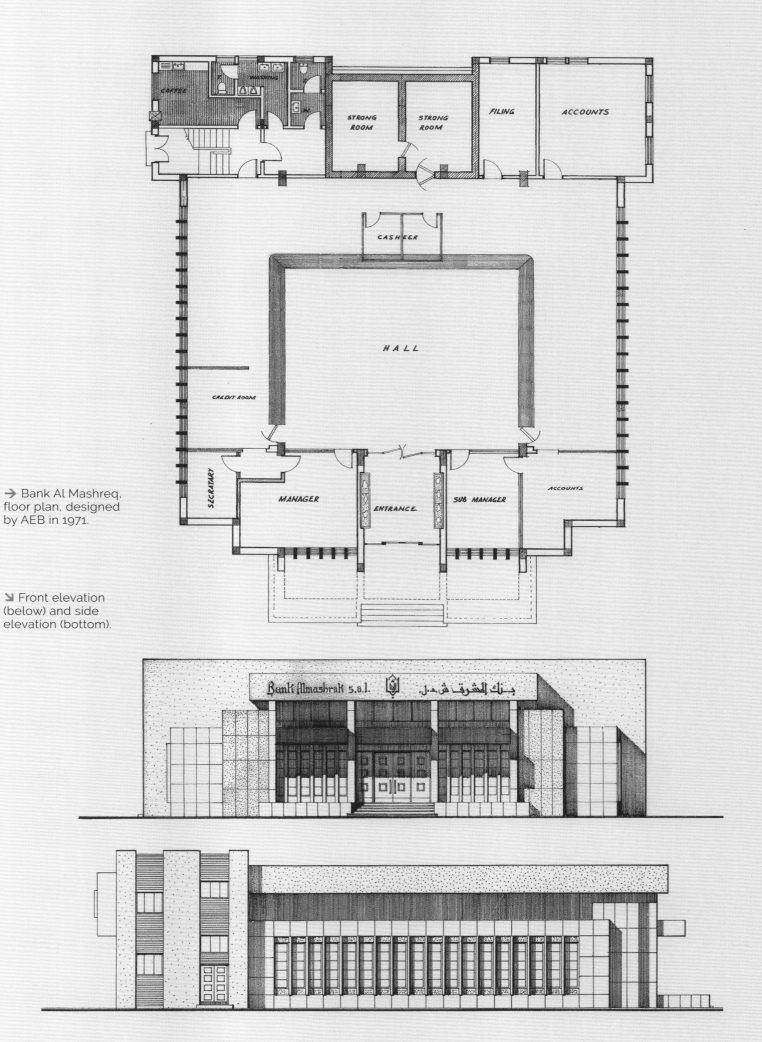

→ Bank Al Mashreq,
floor plan, designed
by AEB in 1971.

↘ Front elevation
(below) and side
elevation (bottom).

COFFEE

WASHING

STRONG
ROOM

STRONG
ROOM

FILING

ACCOUNTS

CASHEER

HALL

CREDIT ROOM

SECRETARY

MANAGER

ENTRANCE

SUB MANAGER

ACCOUNTS

Bank Almashrak s.a.l.   بنك المشرق ش.م.ل.

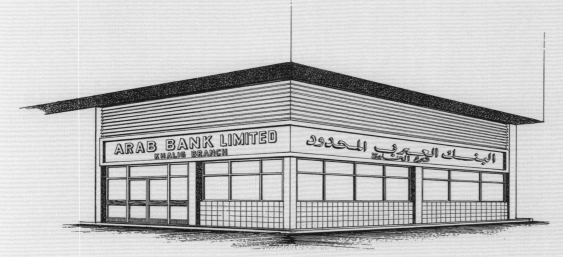

← Arab Bank Ltd, perspective view.

↑ Front elevation.

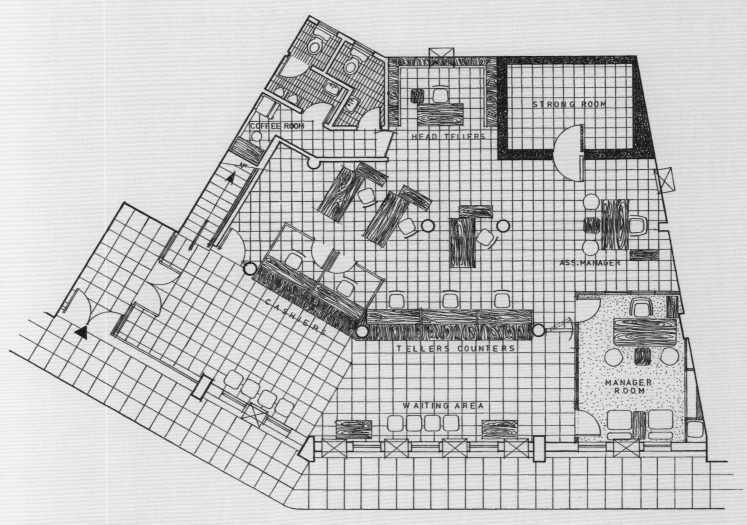

→ Floor plan designed by AEB.

KHALIG ROAD

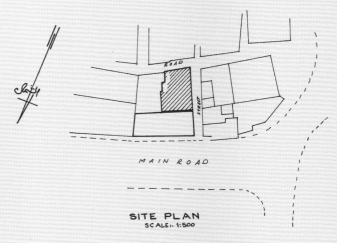

SITE PLAN
SCALE:- 1:500

↑ Site plan of the Commercial
Bank of Qatar in 1977.

↑ Commercial Bank
of Qatar, front elevation.

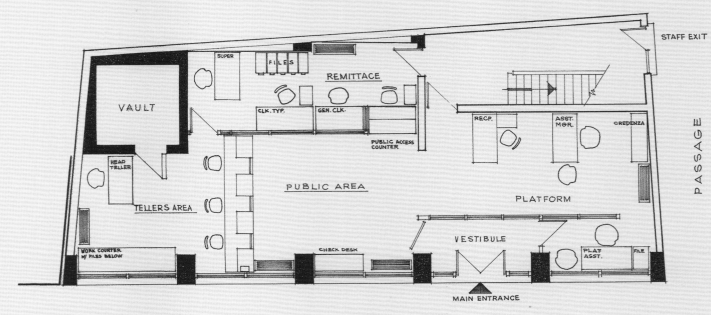

↑ First-floor plan.

MAIN ROAD

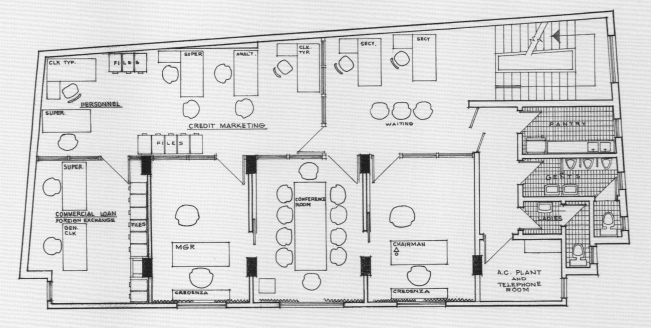

↑ Second-floor plan.

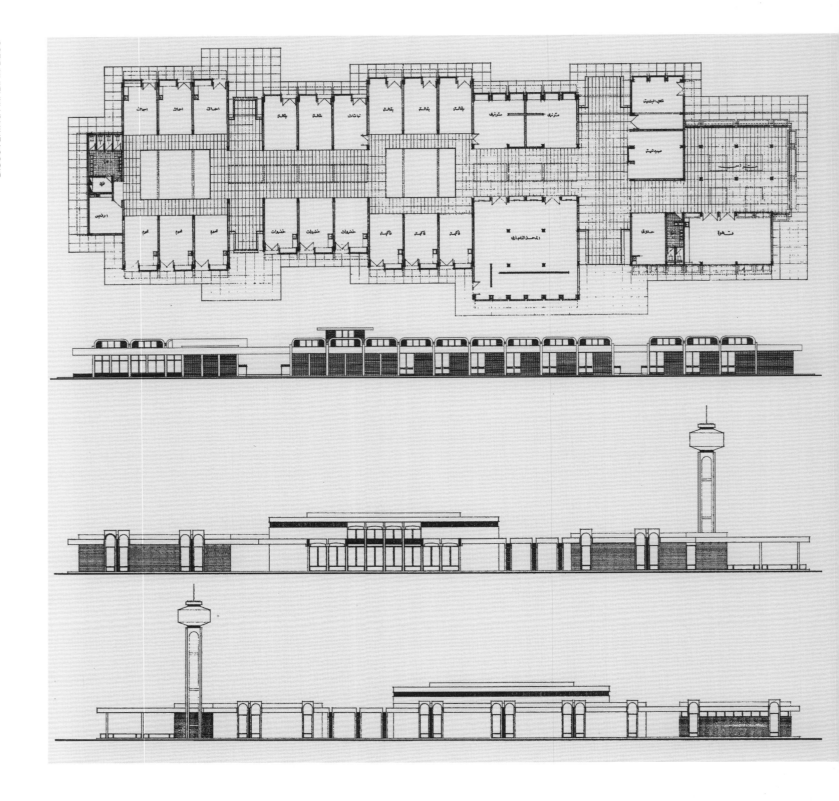

Retail

Building towns became popular in the 1970s in the GCC countries, where there was a strategy to relocate the population from the older parts of the city to new, planned ones. When Khalifa Town Center was first planned out, the Government saw a need to add retail to it: AEB proposed the design for it in 1972. The proposed linear and double-loaded commercial design was the beginning of shopping centers. However, the access points to retail spaces were from the outside, unlike what is common now, which is through an inner corridor.

↑ Khalifa Town Center by AEB in 1972, floor plan (top) and back elevation (middle).

Municipality Shopping Center designed by AEB in 1973, front elevation (middle) and back elevation (bottom).

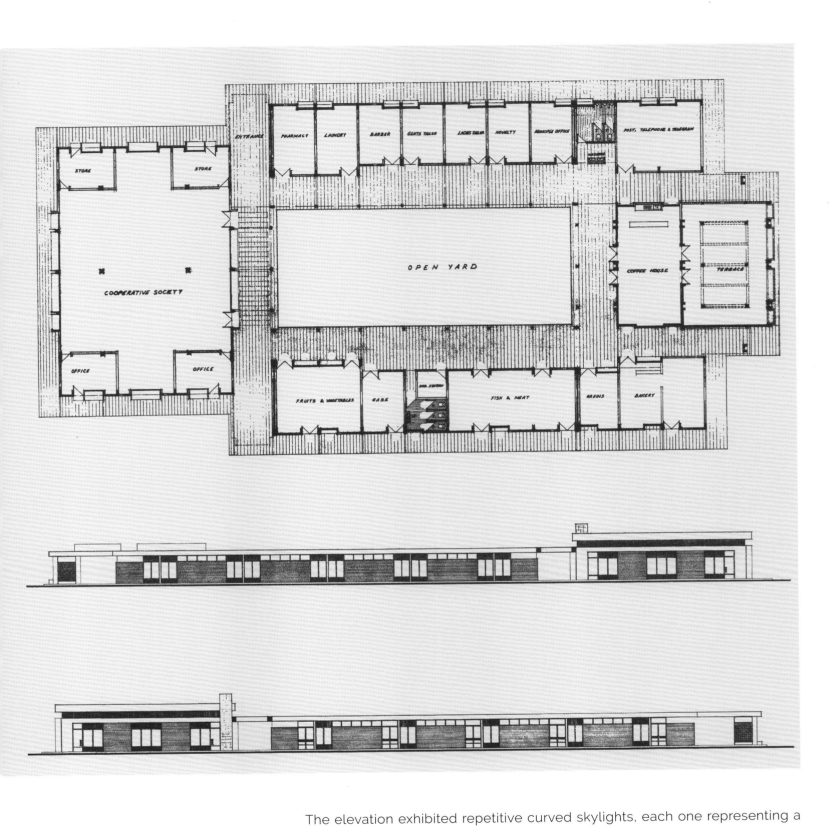

PHARMACY	LAUNDRY	BARBER	GENTS TAILOR	LADIES TAILOR	NOVELTY	MUNICIPAL OFFICE	POST, TELEPHONE & TELEGRAM

STORE   STORE

ENTRANCE

COOPERATIVE SOCIETY

OPEN YARD

COFFEE HOUSE   TERRACE

OFFICE   OFFICE

FRUITS & VEGETABLES   CAFE   SUB. STATION   FISH & MEAT   GRAINS   BAKERY

↑ Cooperative Society retail designed by AEB in 1973, floor plan (top), front elevation (middle), and back elevation (bottom).

The elevation exhibited repetitive curved skylights, each one representing a retail unit. Another shopping center design by AEB in 1973 was for the Municipality Shopping Center, where the concept was a central, rectangular, and covered courtyard with shopping units surrounding it on all sides. The humbleness of the elevation is compensated by the visual attractiveness of the water-tank tower with its modern feature creating a landmark for the Shopping Center. Another Municipality Shopping Center designed by AEB in 1973 had a similar concept to the previous one with the slight difference of having an open courtyard in the center enwrapped by a veranda that leads to the retail units. This design shows the beginning of Cooperative Society retail established by the Government. The building would usually have the Cooperative Society as an anchor and the rest of the retail units would be leased. The elevation has the linear concept of modern simplicity and exhibits horizontal skylights.

Companies

The private sector also prospered with the economic boom and had a share of the modern architecture in the 1970s. For example, the Peugeot Workshop & Showroom for Almana Company was designed in 1974 by AEB with a modern

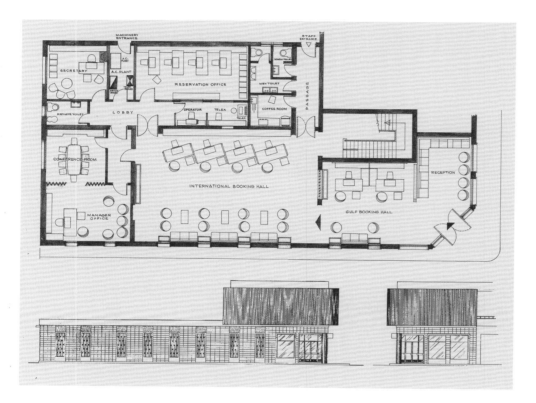

← Al Darwish, floor plan of the booking office designed by AEB in 1974 (top), side elevation (bottom left), and front elevation (bottom right).

↓ Perspective view of the booking office for Al Darwish.

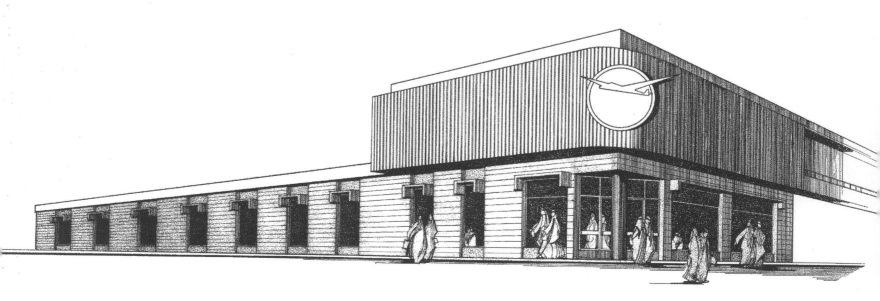

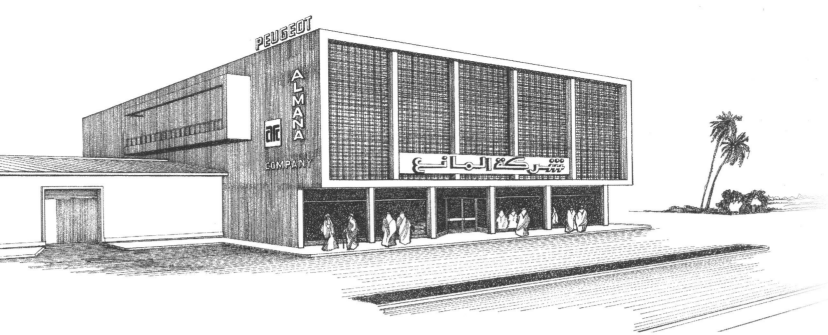

↑ Peugeot Workshop
& Showroom for Almana
Company, perspective
view.

→ Second-floor plan
designed by AEB in 1974
(right), front elevation
(bottom left), and side
elevation (bottom right).

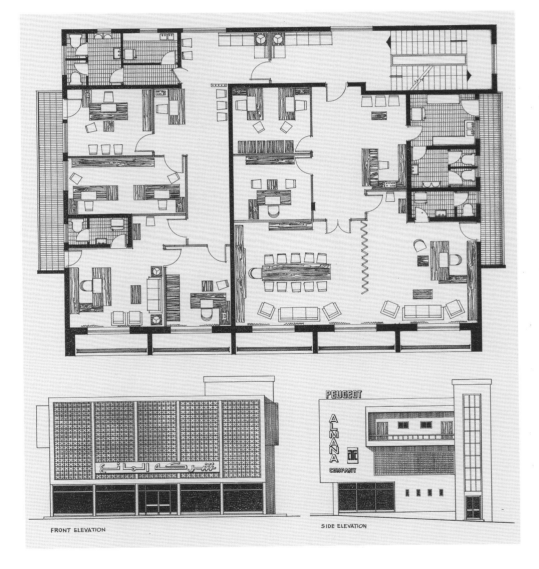

FRONT ELEVATION

SIDE ELEVATION

sense of regular mass with a concrete frame, and was detailed with screen features. Another example is the booking office for Al Darwish, which was also designed by AEB in 1974. The elevation shows the vertical window with a protruding shading feature that became a trend of the time.

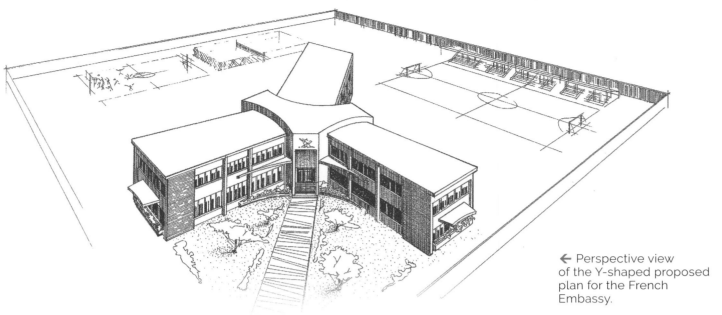

← Perspective view of the Y-shaped proposed plan for the French Embassy.

Embassies

Qatar's newly established international relationships through the new Ministry of Foreign Affairs resulted in the construction of many embassy buildings in the 1970s. Some designs for embassies were proposed by AEB, including the French Embassy facilities, MISR (Egypt) Embassy and Ambassador's Residence, and the Ambassador of the Kingdom of Jordan's Residence.

AEB made three design proposals for the French Embassy facilities in 1974, the first in a Y-shape

↓ Perspective view of the fan-shaped proposed plan for the French Embassy facilities.

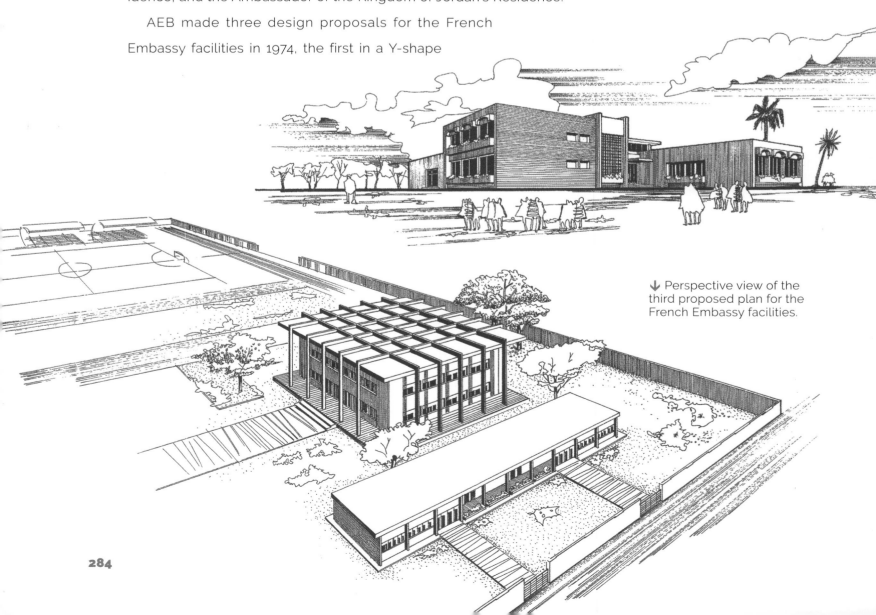

↓ Perspective view of the third proposed plan for the French Embassy facilities.

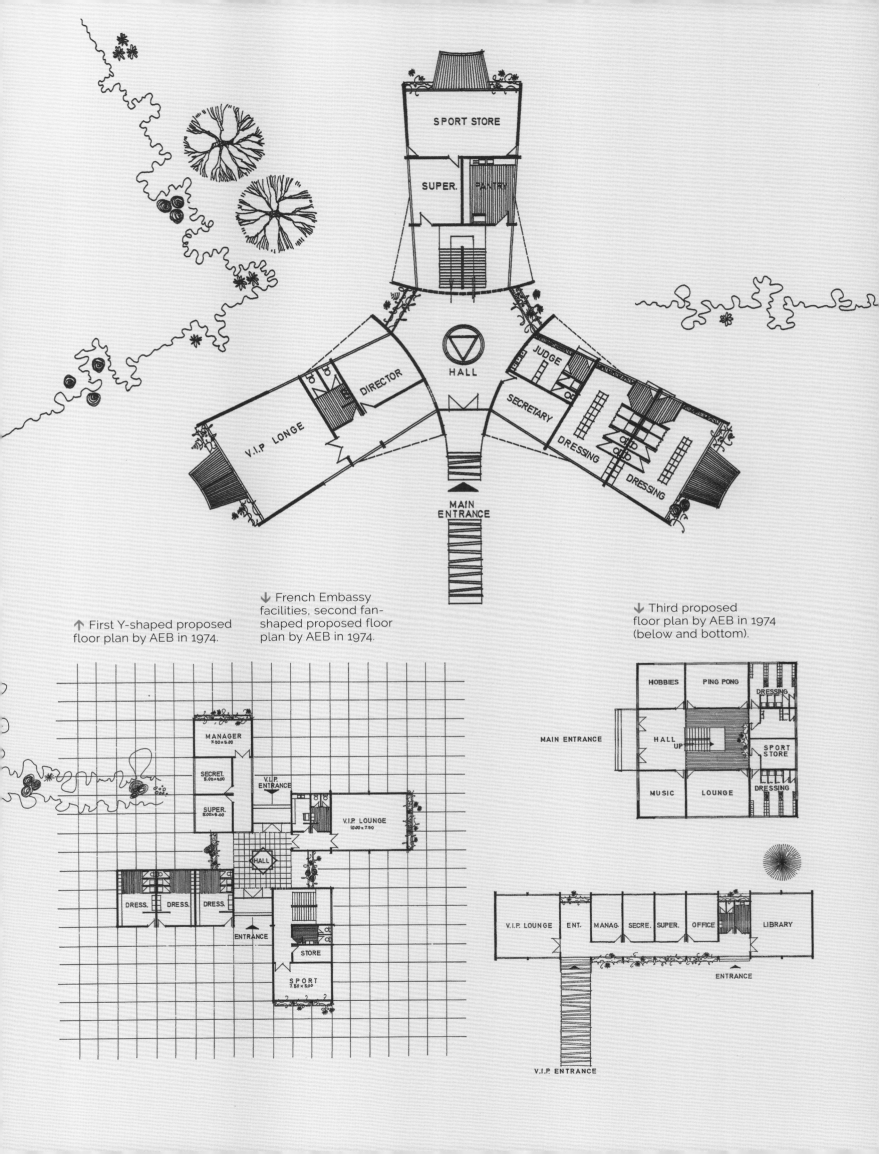

SPORT STORE

SUPER. PANTRY

HALL

DIRECTOR

V.I.P LONGE

JUDGE

SECRETARY

DRESSING

DRESSING

MAIN
ENTRANCE

↓ French Embassy
facilities, second fan-
shaped proposed floor
plan by AEB in 1974.

↑ First Y-shaped proposed
floor plan by AEB in 1974.

↓ Third proposed
floor plan by AEB in 1974
(below and bottom).

MANAGER
7.50 × 5.00

SECRET.
5.00 × 5.00

SUPER.
5.00 × 6.00

V.I.P
ENTRANCE

V.I.P LOUNGE
10.00 × 7.50

HALL

DRESS. DRESS. DRESS.

ENTRANCE

STORE

SPORT
7.50 × 5.00

HOBBIES PING PONG DRESSING

MAIN ENTRANCE

HALL
UP

SPORT
STORE

MUSIC LOUNGE DRESSING

V.I.P. LOUNGE ENT. MANAG. SECRE. SUPER. OFFICE LIBRARY

ENTRANCE

V.I.P. ENTRANCE

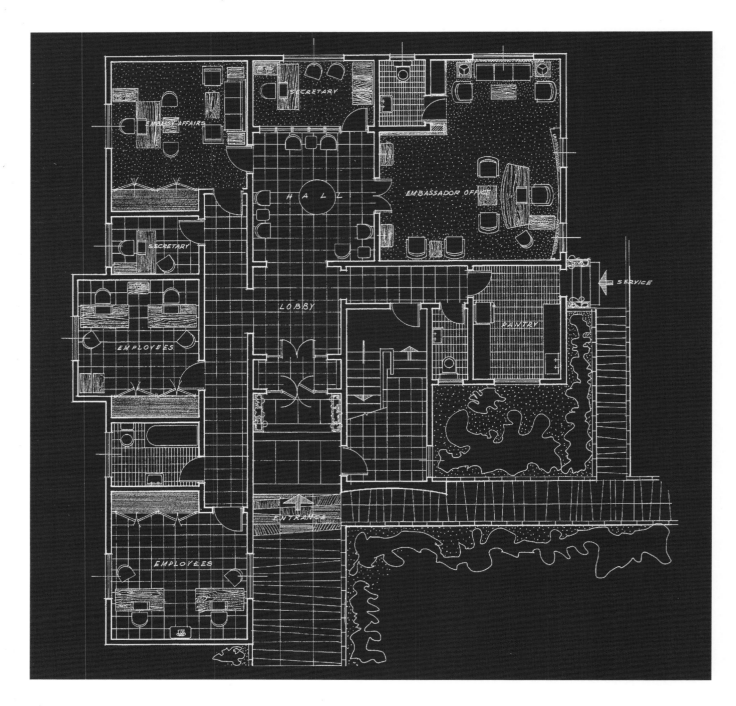

↑ MISR Embassy designed by
AEB in 1972, first-floor plan.

↓ Front elevation.

with the same floating, half-arches as the Ministry of Foreign
Affairs. The second proposal had a fan-like form, where
a central, square hall connected to the four annexes.
The third proposal had two buildings: one was a
cubic one wrapped by a columned veranda, while
the other building had a rectangular form. AEB also
designed the MISR Embassy and the Ambassador's Residence in 1972. The embassy showed a

↑ Ambassador of the Kingdom of Jordan's Residence, perspective view.

typical modern trend that could be seen in Egypt at that time, while the residence had a reflection of the layout for apartments in Cairo with a living room at the center and the rest of the rooms and spaces around it.

Another example designed by AEB in 1972 is the Ambassador of the Kingdom of Jordan's Residence, similarly with a fashionable, modern design inspired by the Levant cities, but this one is more geometrical. It has balconies that were also a common feature of that time in Doha.

↓ First-floor plan designed by AEB in 1972 (left) and second-floor plan (right).

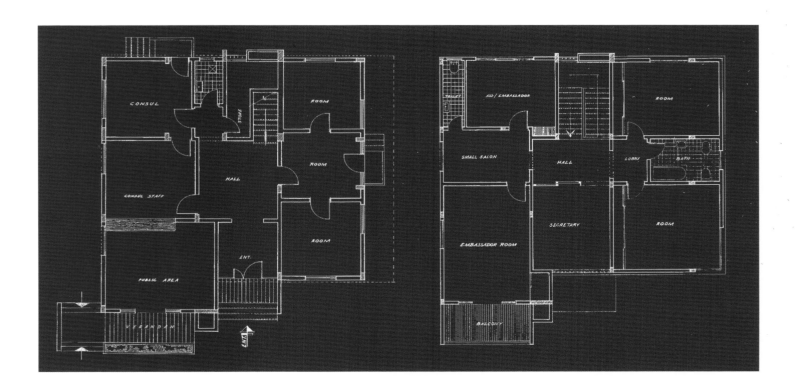

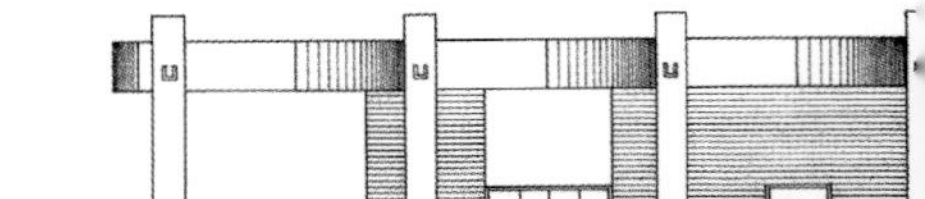

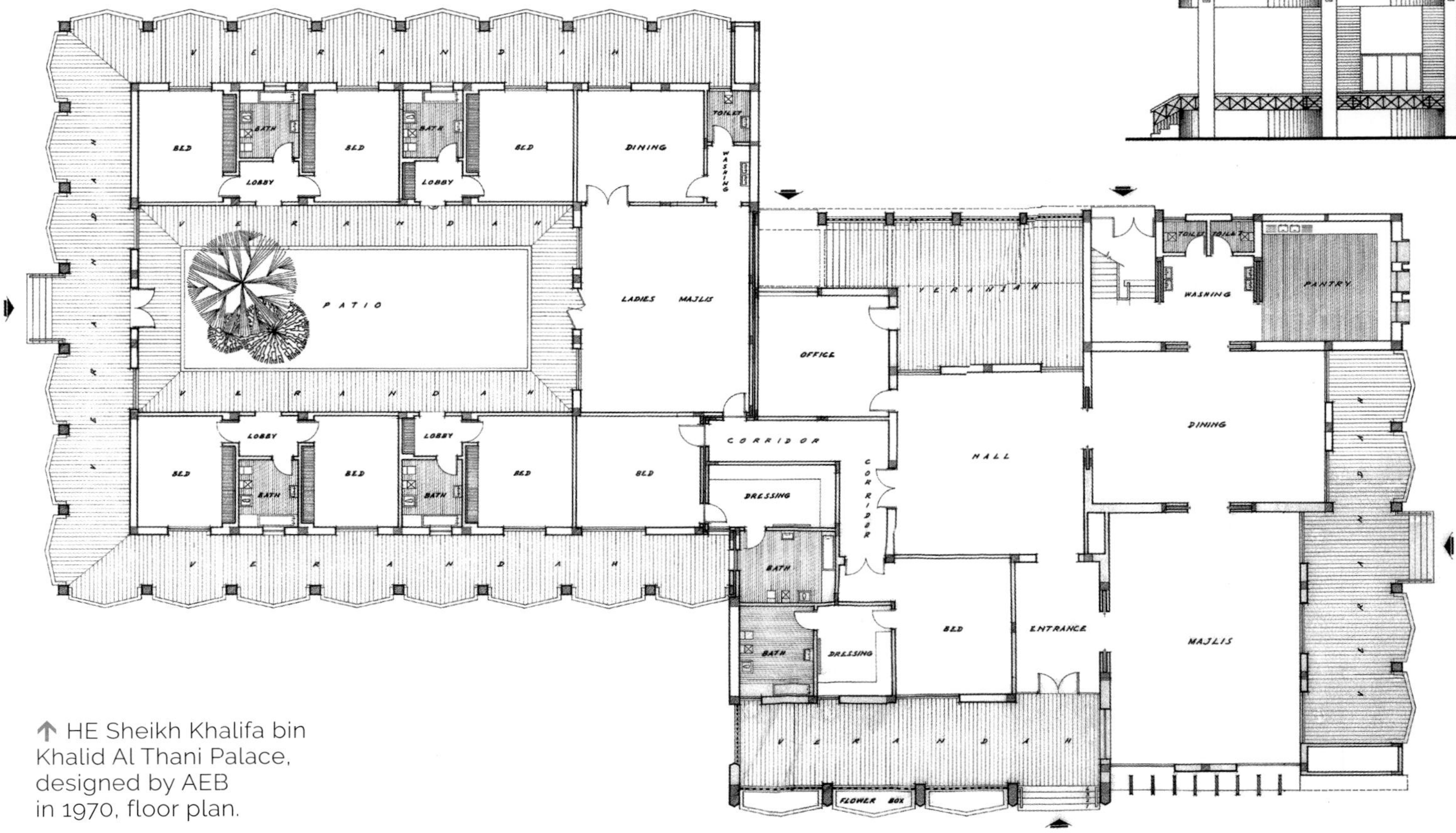

↑ HE Sheikh Khalifa bin
Khalid Al Thani Palace,
designed by AEB
in 1970, floor plan.

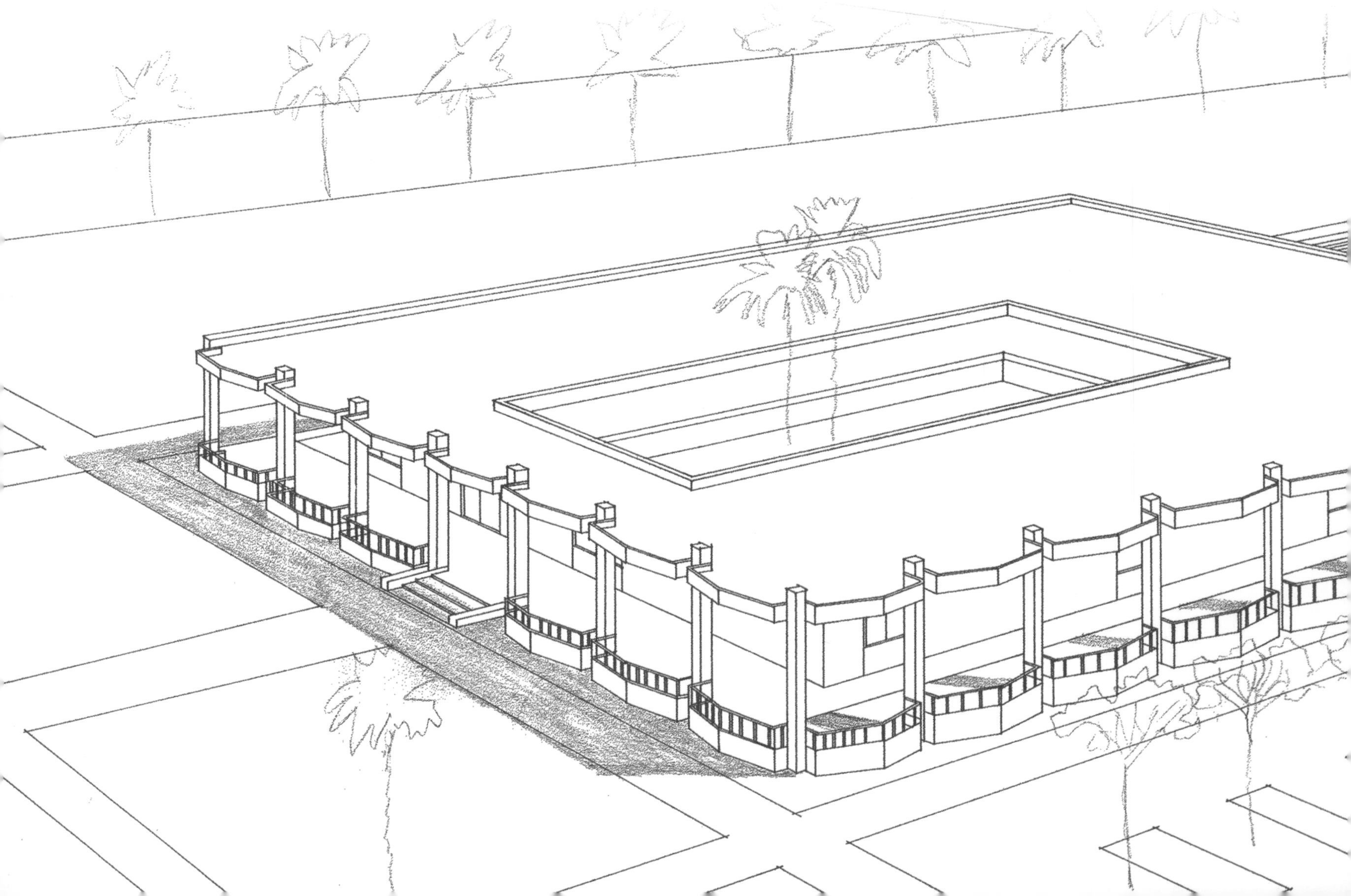

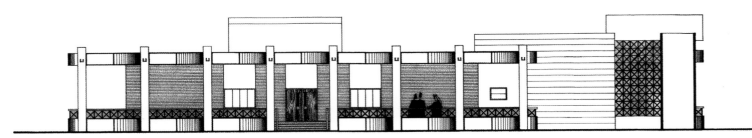

↑ Front elevation (top) and left-side elevation (above).

Palaces

The modern influence on architecture that was witnessed in many governmental and private sector projects in the 1970s also reached the newly planned palaces. AEB designed a palace in 1970 where the arches with the screening and pointed balconies replacing the *liwan* are the most unique features of the design.

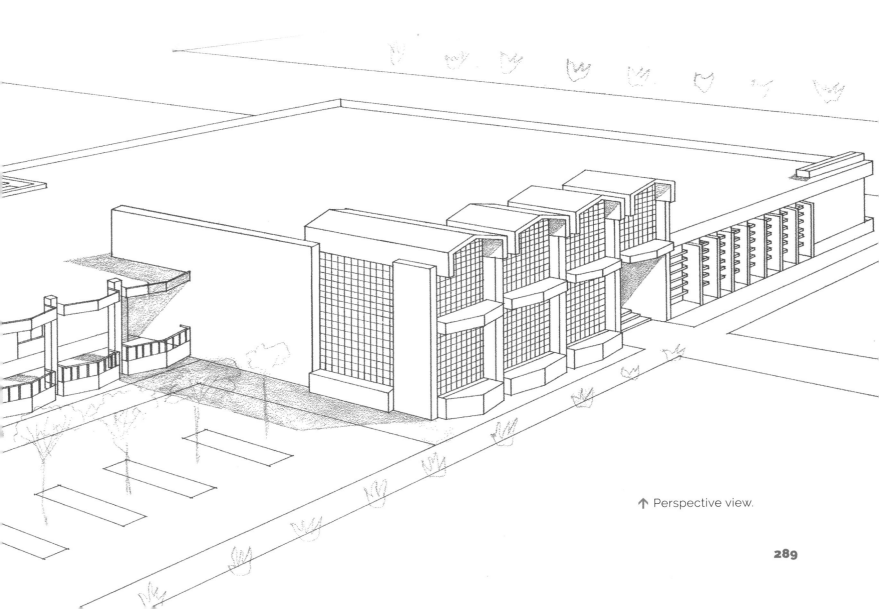

↑ Perspective view.

Another palace was also designed by AEB in 1971 for HE Sheikh Ahmed bin Mubarak Al Thani, which reflects the influence of popular designs brought back by the locals from travel destinations like Cairo, Baghdad, and Shiraz. The mosque in the corner is a sign of a trend of the time when palace owners would build a mosque on their property, adjacent to their palaces.

↓ Sheikh Ahmed bin Mubarak Al Thani Palace, perspective view.

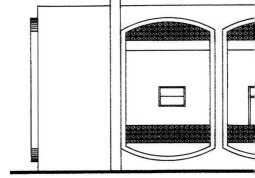

→ Front elevation.

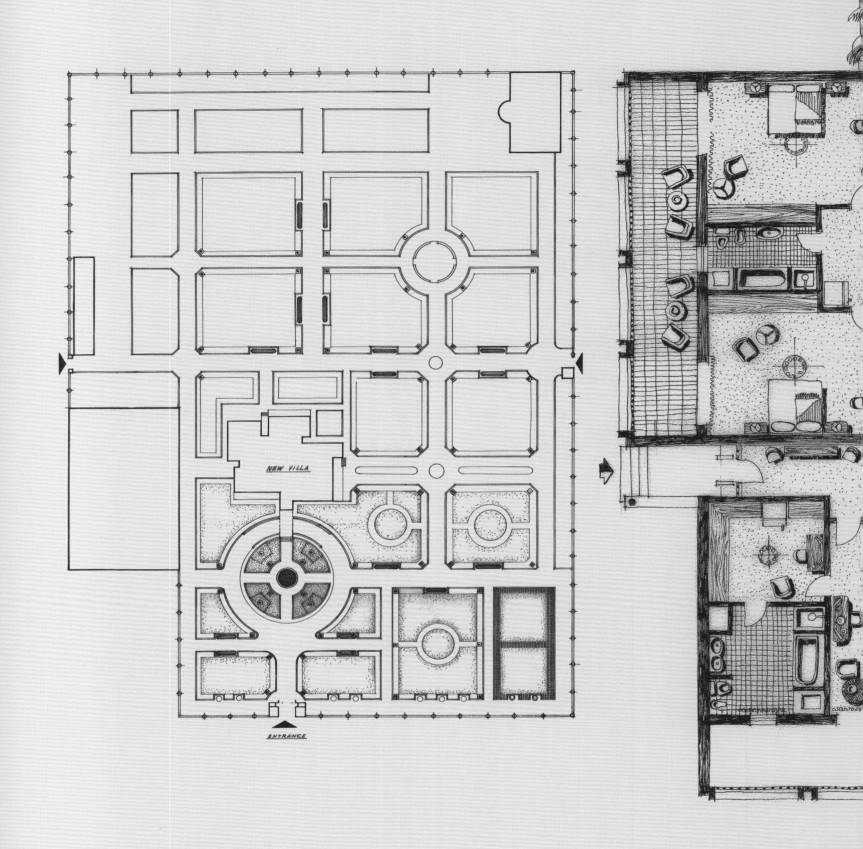

NEW VILLA

ENTRANCE

↑ Sheikh Ahmed bin
Mubarak Al Thani Palace,
site plan with landscape.

↑ First-floor plan.

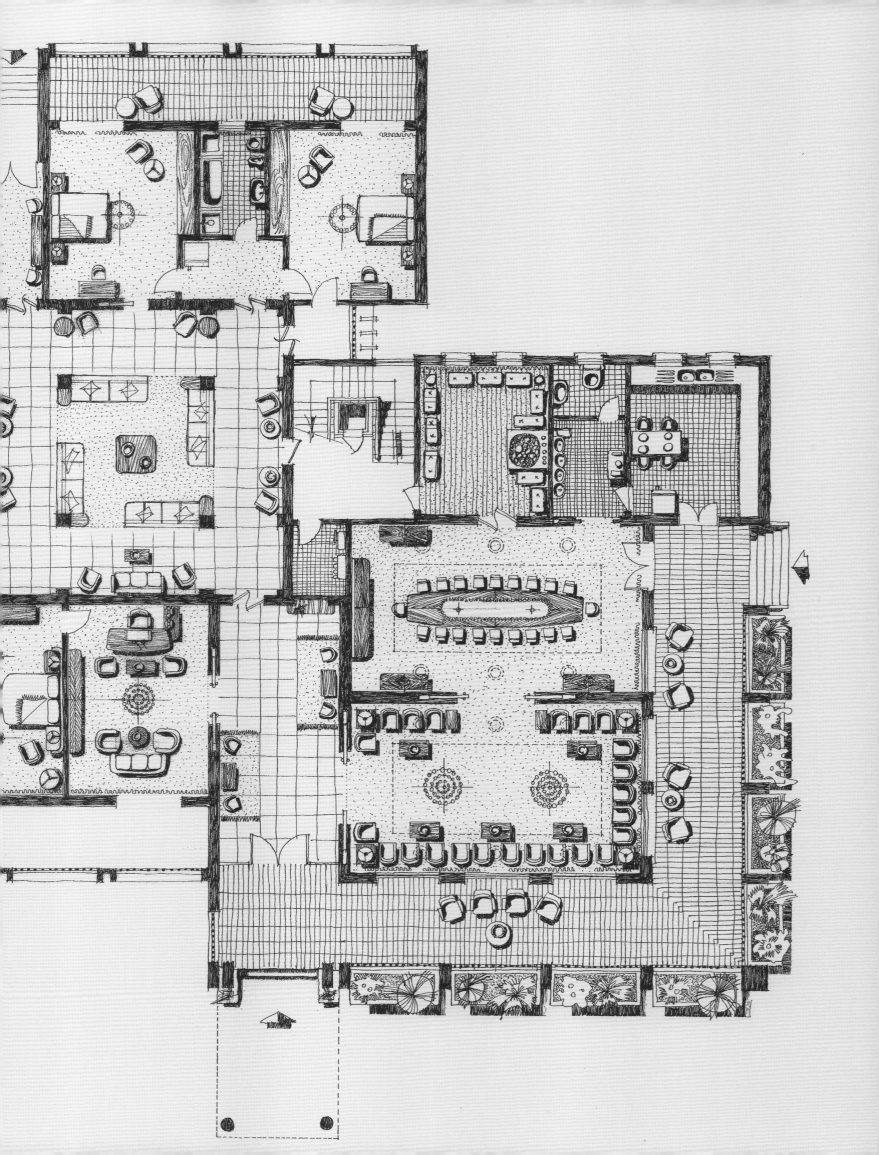

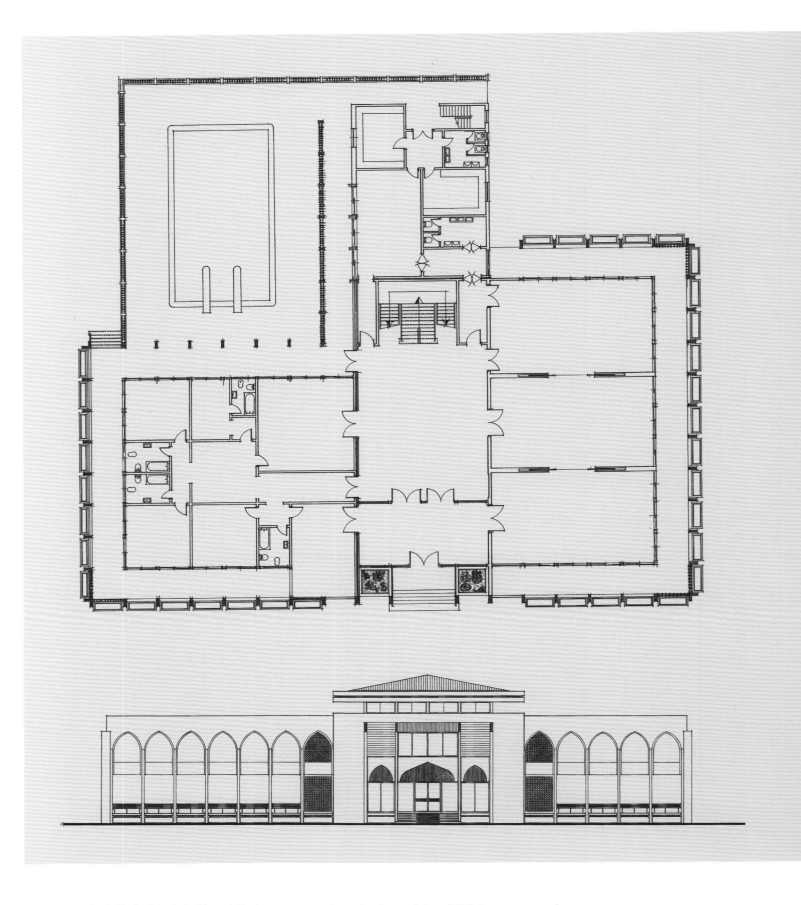

Abdullah Abdul Ghani Palace was also designed by AEB in 1973 and had the *liwan* concept extended to the upper floor where the arches with screening define the main entrance. AEB produced more palace designs in 1973, one of which was for Sheikh Khalid bin Hamad, where the trend at that

↑ Abdullah Abdul Ghani Palace, designed by AEB in 1973, first-floor plan (top) and front elevation (above).

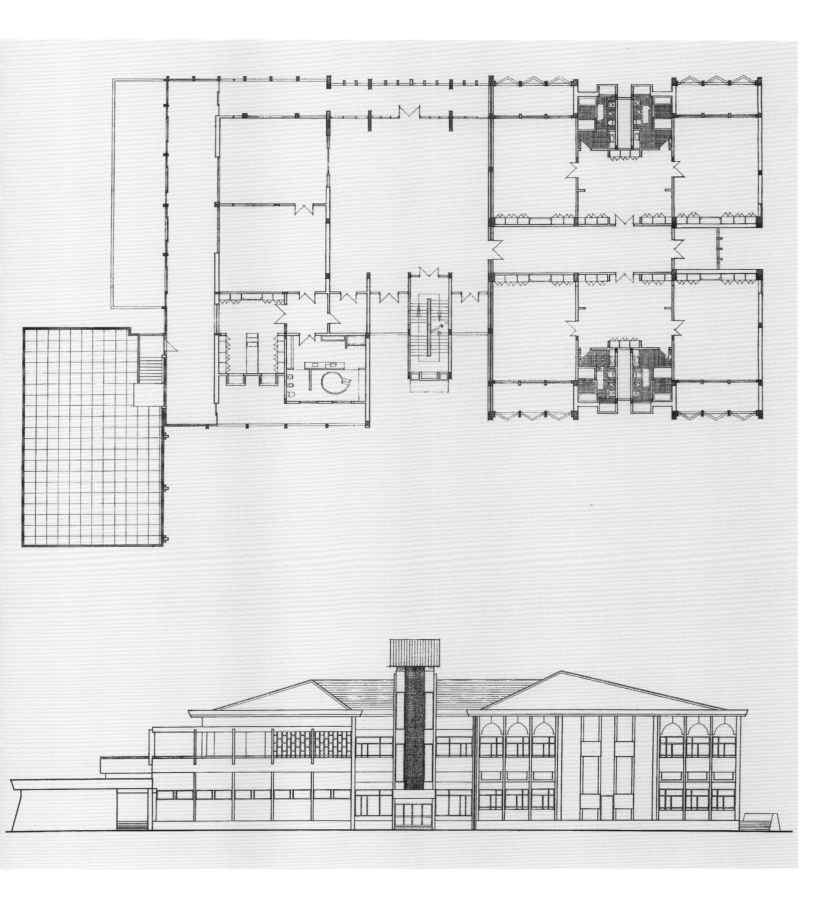

↑ Sheikh Khalid bin Hamad Palace, designed by AEB in 1973, first-floor plan (top) and front elevation (above).

time was more concentrated on the details of the veranda and balconies. AEB also designed a palace for Sheikh Ahmed bin Khaled in 1973 with flat, two-rounded and three-rounded arches that were inspired by the Ministry of Foreign Affairs.

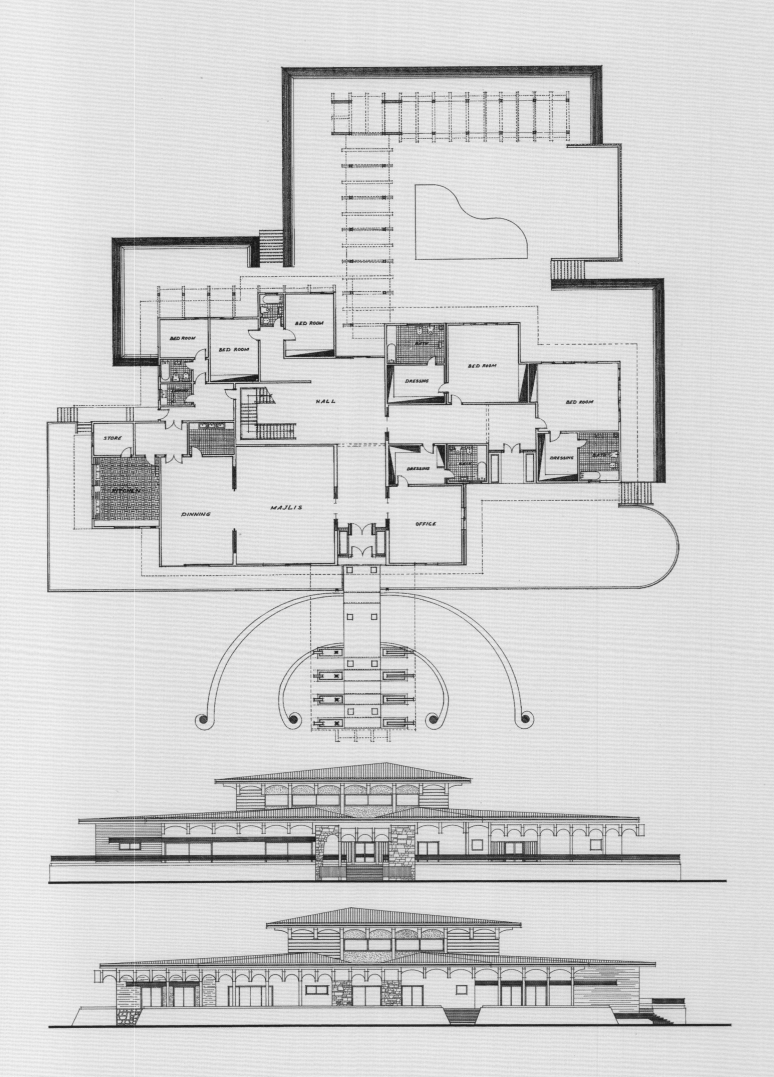

← Sheikh Ahmed bin Khaled Palace designed by AEB in 1973, first-floor plan (top), front elevation (middle), and back elevation (bottom).

Mixed-Use

The new master plan proposed by the western consultants for Doha in the 1970s contributed to defining plots for mixed-use buildings to accommodate the increase in population, especially in Bin Mahmoud, Al Najma, and Al Mansoura. AEB designed mixed-use buildings in Fereej Bin Mahmoud for Abdel Qadir Ahmed in 1972, where the design was flexible enough to take the form of the plot but at the same time remain symmetrical. The first floor was used as a commercial section while the upper floors were apartments. Another building was designed by AEB in 1972 for Sheikh Ali Bin Abdelaziz Al Thani, where the regular form breaks into smaller, stepped right angles to maximize the use of the plot. The commercial section on the first floor is presented with the modern sense of the veranda while the apartment units above are framed by balconies on both sides. AEB also designed mixed-use buildings for Sheikh Hamad bin Khalifa Al Thani in 1973, for a smaller plot where the first floor would have a showroom and an apartment on each floor of the upper levels.

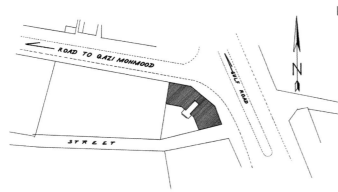

↑ Site plan of Abdel Qadir Ahmed's building designed by AEB in 1972.

→ Abdel Qadir Ahmed's building, typical floor plan.

↘ Perspective view.

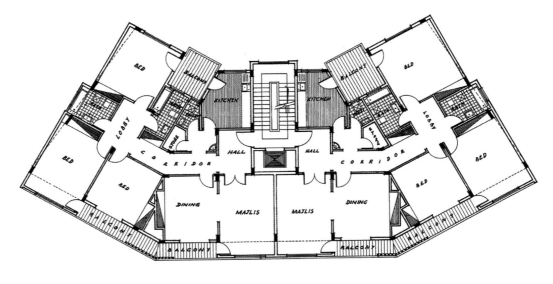

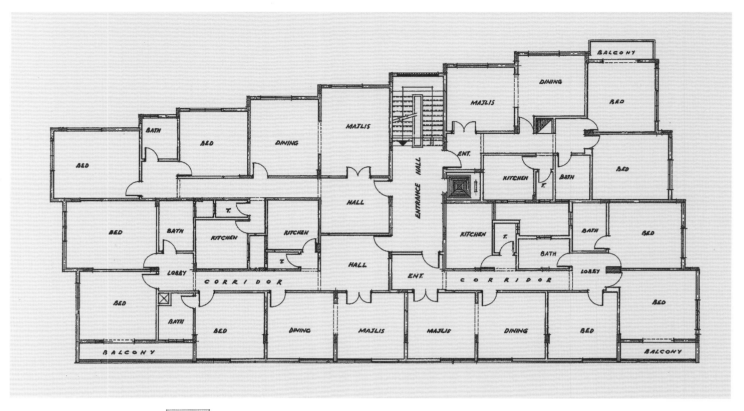

↑ Sheikh Ali Bin Abdelaziz Al Thani's building designed in 1972, typical floor plan.

← Front elevation.

↓ Perspective view.

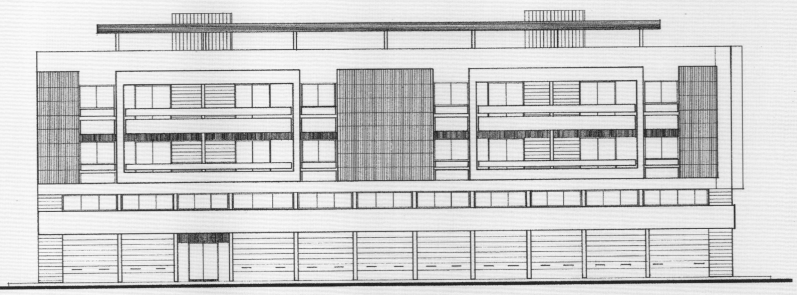

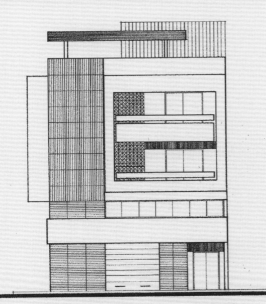

↓ Haider Sulaiman
Haider and Bros. building
designed by AEB in 1974,
first-floor plan (below) and
second-floor plan (bottom).

↑ Front elevation.

→ Side elevation.

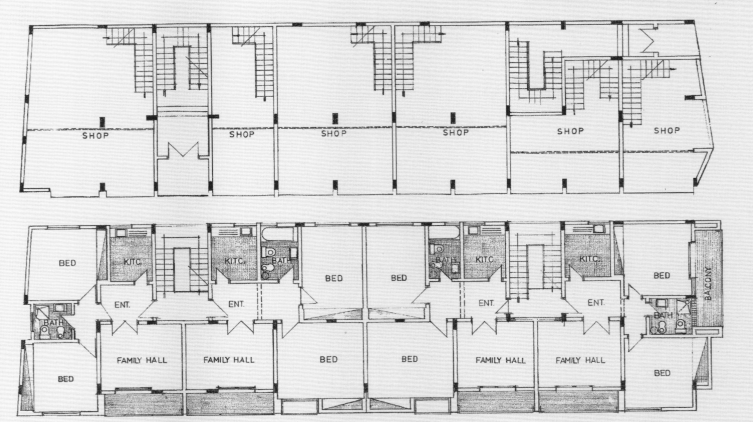

SHOP   SHOP   SHOP   SHOP   SHOP   SHOP

BED   KITC   KITC   BAT   BAT   KITC   BED
ENT.   ENT.   BED   BED   ENT.   ENT.
BATH   BATH
BED   FAMILY HALL   FAMILY HALL   BED   BED   FAMILY HALL   FAMILY HALL   BED
BALCONY

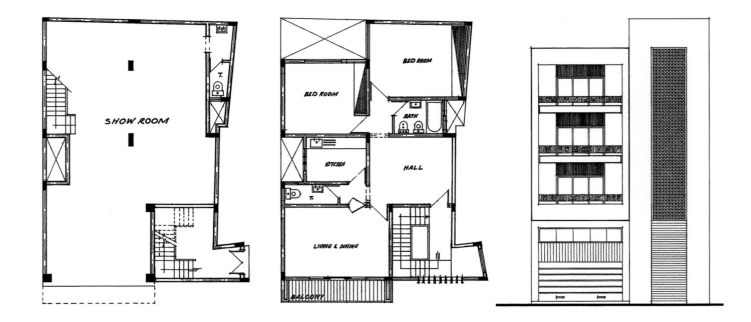

SHOW ROOM

BED ROOM

BED ROOM

BATH

KITCHEN

HALL

LIVING & DINING

BALCONY

The extending screen wall on one side of the elevation indicates the access and staircase, while the balconies, with their simple modern style, create the perfect balance for the whole facade. An interesting design produced by AEB in 1974 was a very contemporary mixed-use, low-rise building for Haider Sulaiman Haider and Bros., with framed balconies. This type of design was typically found in North Africa and the Levant and was brought to Qatar by expatriate architects from those regions.

High-Rise

The 1970s also witnessed the beginning of high-rise buildings as part of the proposed master plan by the western consultant to accommodate the population growth in Doha. AEB designed a high-rise building for HE Sheikh Khalifa bin Hamad Al Thani in 1974 where the first two floors took the free form of the plot while the ten upper floors have an interesting Y-shaped geometric form. The first two floors consist of the showroom, shops, reception, and parking area, while each upper floor has an apartment per annex, ending with a wide balcony. In 1976, AEB also designed some high-rise buildings that formed part of an urban development plan for HE Sheikh Jassim bin Ahmed. The building included ground level parking, seven typical apartment floors, and a penthouse at the top. The horizontal features clearly present the floors and balconies, while the penthouse is wrapped with RC blocks. Another high-rise building was designed by AEB in 1977 for HH Sheikh Nasser bin Hamad Al Thani. It was symmetrical with wide balconies, which were especially suitable for the expats as they came from places where people were used to such building design features.

↖ Sheikh Hamad bin Khalifa Al Thani's building designed by AEB in 1973, first-floor plan (left) and typical floor plan (middle).

↑ Front elevation.

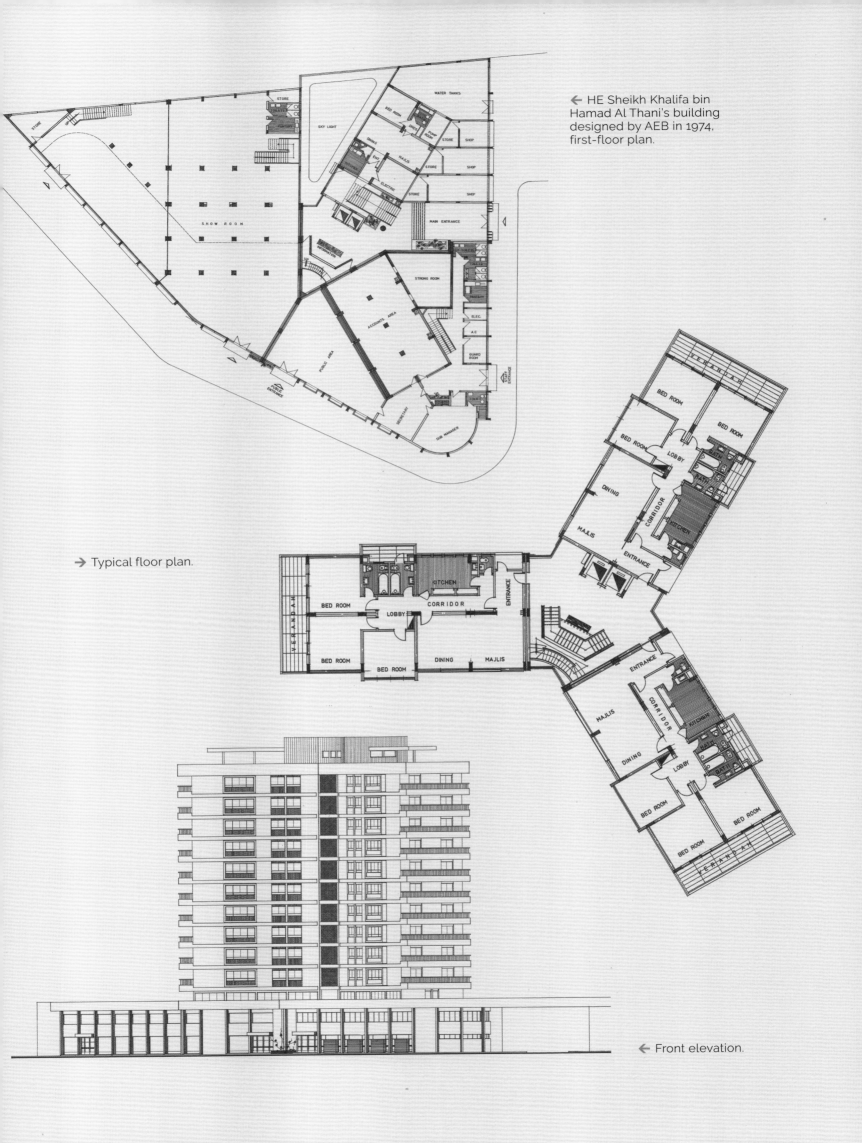

← HE Sheikh Khalifa bin Hamad Al Thani's building designed by AEB in 1974, first-floor plan.

→ Typical floor plan.

← Front elevation.

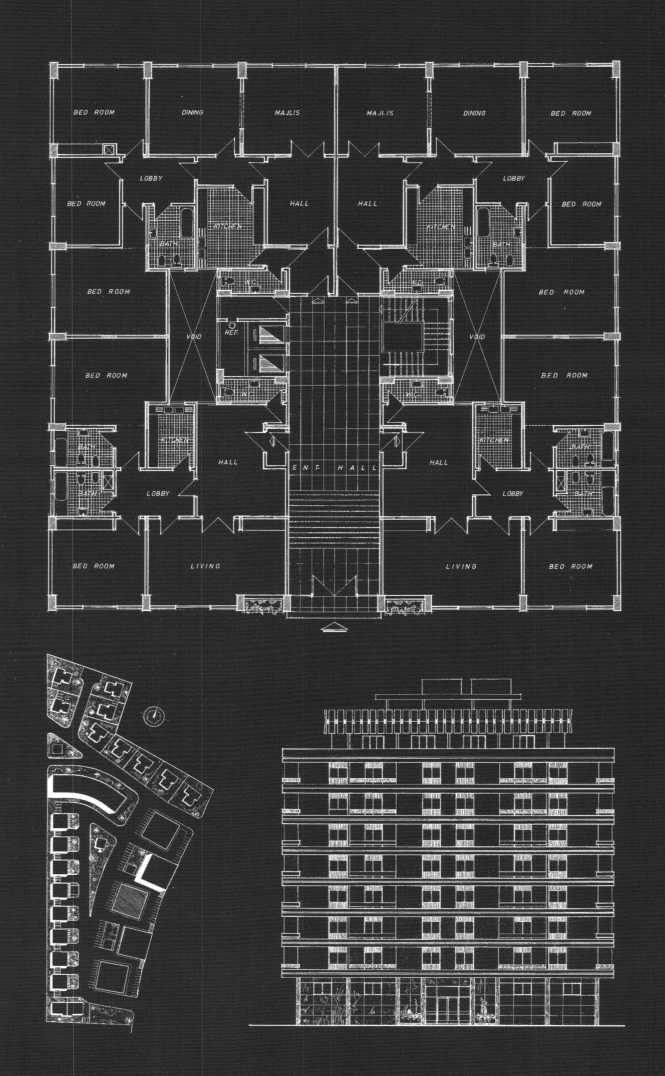

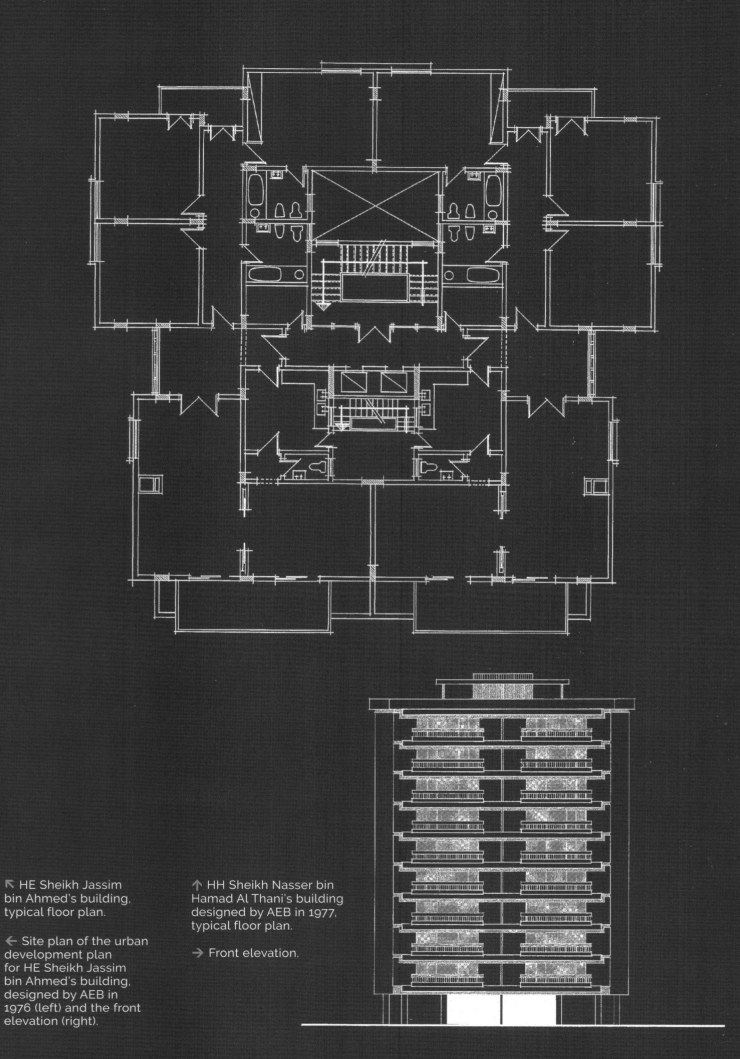

↖ HE Sheikh Jassim
bin Ahmed's building,
typical floor plan.

← Site plan of the urban
development plan
for HE Sheikh Jassim
bin Ahmed's building,
designed by AEB in
1976 (left) and the front
elevation (right).

↑ HH Sheikh Nasser bin
Hamad Al Thani's building
designed by AEB in 1977,
typical floor plan.

→ Front elevation.

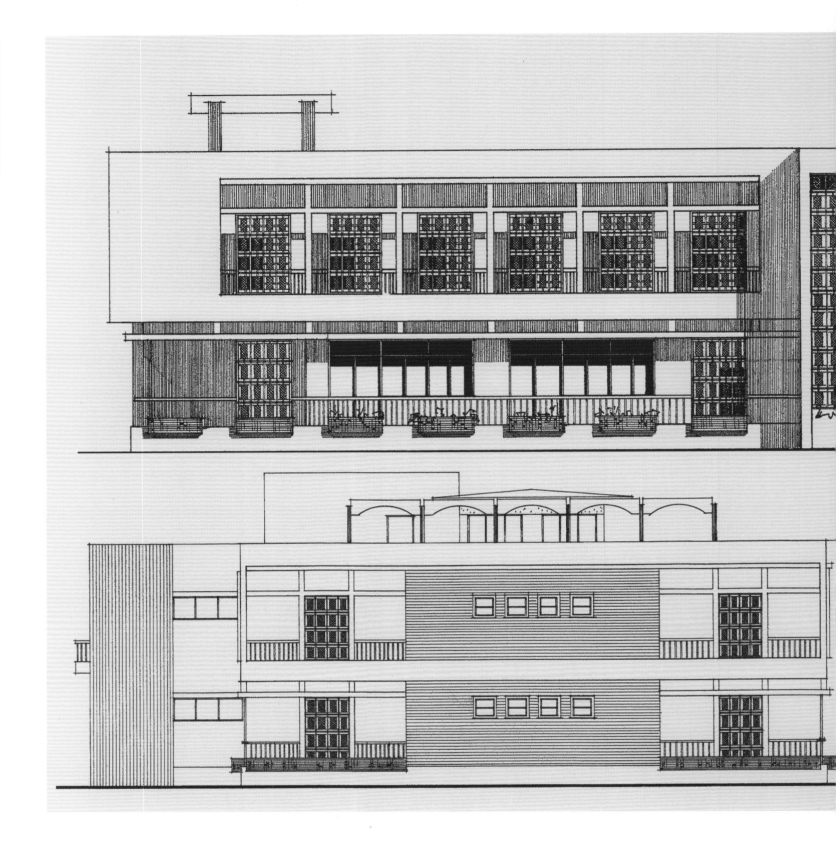

Villas

Doha experienced a massive construction of villas that corelated with the economic boom and agreed land-use for residential areas that was defined by the master plan. AEB produced many villa designs with modern architectural features that were trending in the 1970s. The trend that was common among some villas was the modern look of the veranda with rounded arches

↑ HE Sheikh Ahmed bin Khalid Al Thani's villa, designed by AEB in 1971, front elevation (top) and left elevation (above).

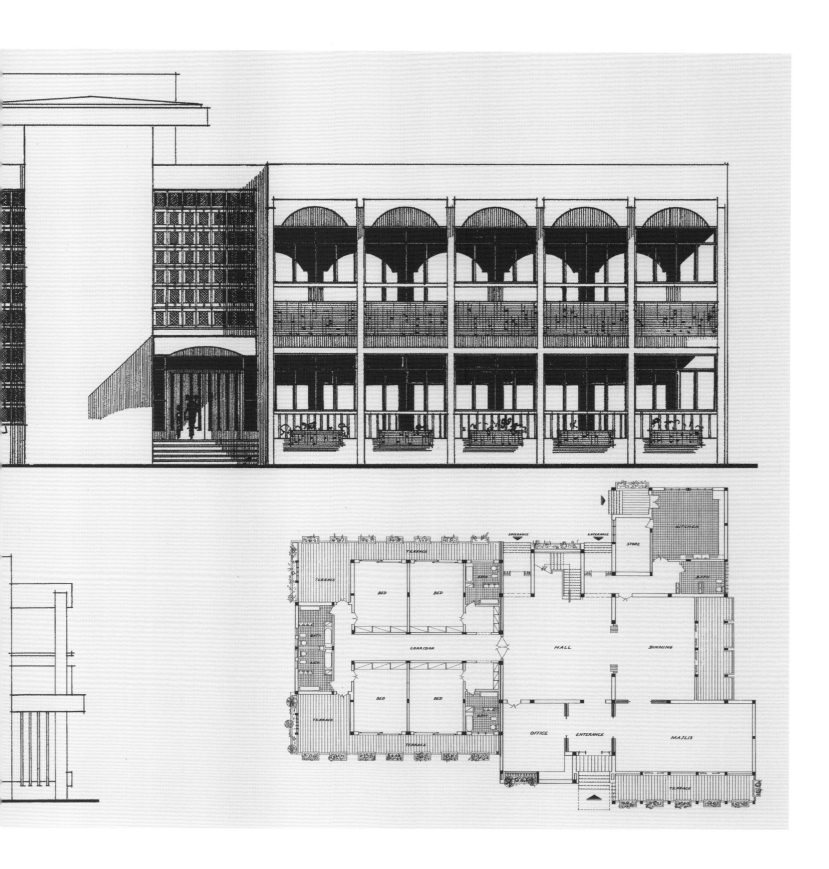

↗ First-floor plan.

at the top and flower beds by the railing. This is reflected in AEB's designs in 1971 for villas for HE Sheikh Ahmed bin Khalid Al Thani, Ahmed Al Maarfi, and Mohammed Mahdi. The elevations also featured two wall finishes, stone wall-cladding, and screen walls. Another group of villas designed by AEB with some common features were for Ahmed Al Badi in 1971, Ismail Ali Akbar Lari in 1971,

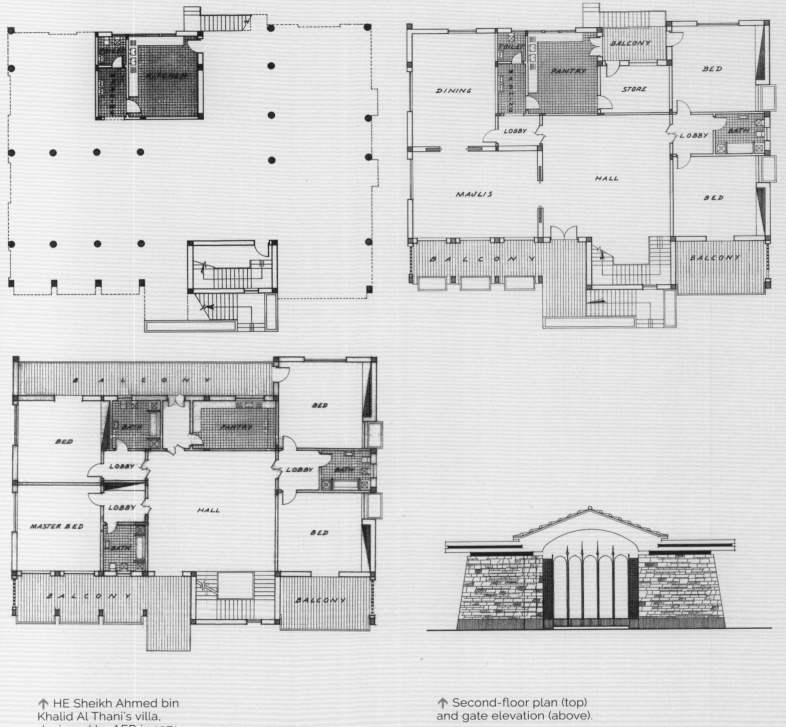

↑ HE Sheikh Ahmed bin Khalid Al Thani's villa, designed by AEB in 1971, first-floor plan (top) and third-floor plan (above).

↑ Second-floor plan (top) and gate elevation (above).

↙↓ Front elevation and left elevation.

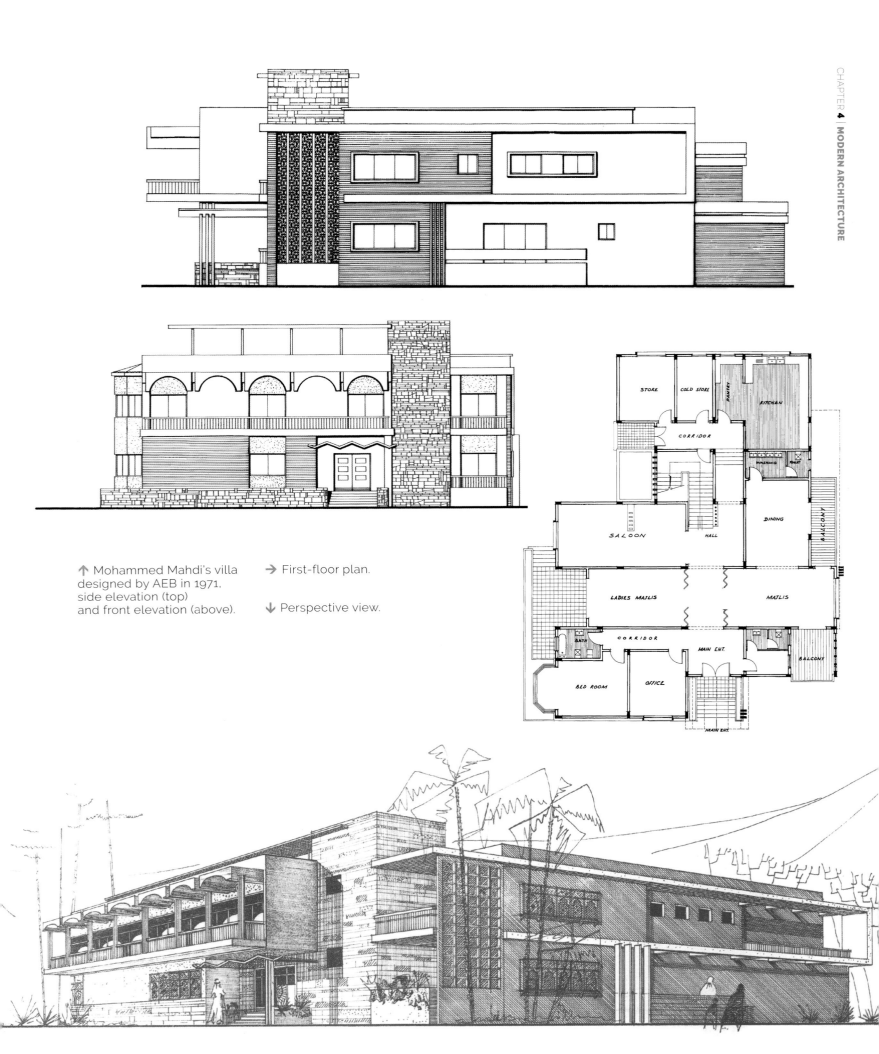

↑ Mohammed Mahdi's villa designed by AEB in 1971, side elevation (top) and front elevation (above).

→ First-floor plan.

↓ Perspective view.

STORE COLD STORE PANTRY KITCHEN

CORRIDOR

SALOON HALL DINING BALCONY

LADIES MAJLIS MAJLIS

BATH CORRIDOR MAIN ENT. BALCONY

BED ROOM OFFICE MAIN ENT.

MAIN ENT.

← Ahmed Al Maarfi's villa, designed by AEB in 1971, first-floor plan (left), and second-floor plan (right).

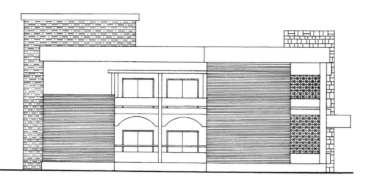

↑ Front elevation.

↗ Left elevation.

↓ Perspective view.

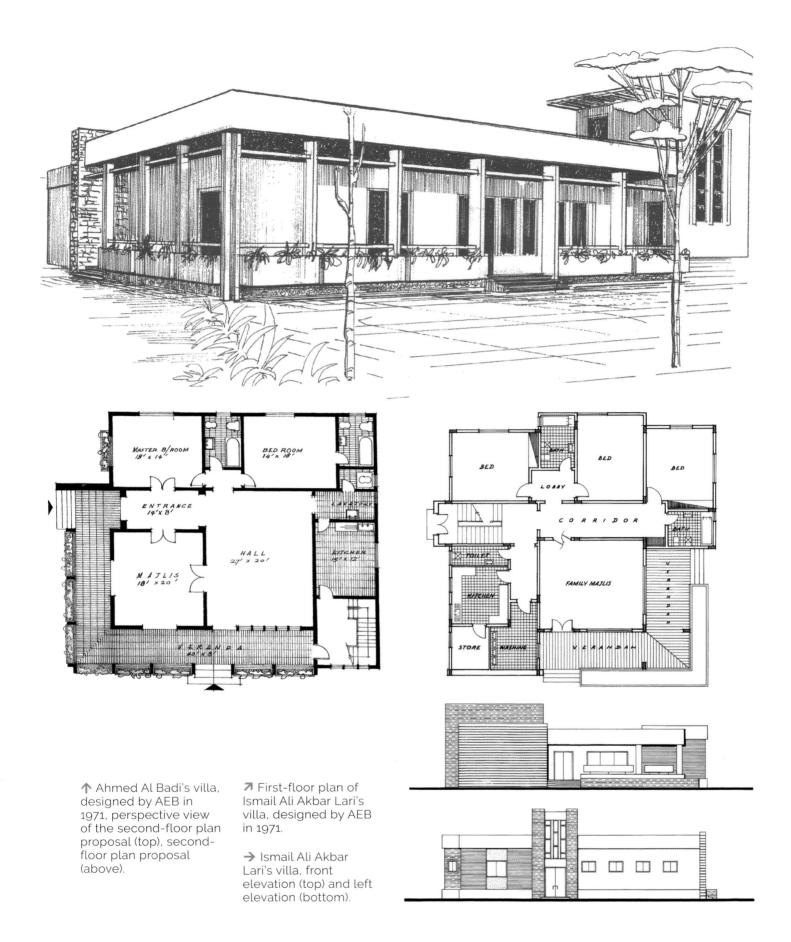

↑ Ahmed Al Badi's villa, designed by AEB in 1971, perspective view of the second-floor plan proposal (top), second-floor plan proposal (above).

↗ First-floor plan of Ismail Ali Akbar Lari's villa, designed by AEB in 1971.

→ Ismail Ali Akbar Lari's villa, front elevation (top) and left elevation (bottom).

Ali Al Khater in 1974, Sheikh Jasem bin Mohammed Al Ahmed in 1972, and for two unknown clients in 1972. They all featured vertical windows with protruding shading elements, a corner or courtyard veranda, wall cladding, and strong horizontal lines.

↓ Ali Al Khater's villa, designed by AEB in 1974, first-floor plan.

↑ Perspective view of Ali Al Khater's villa.

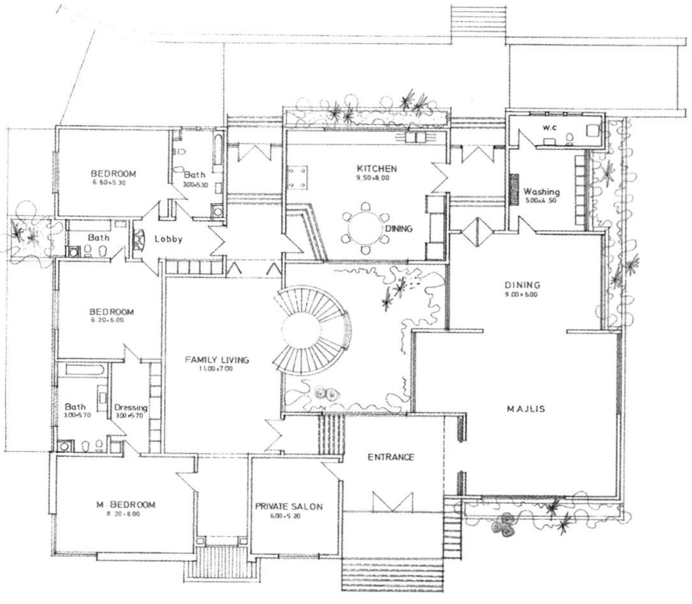

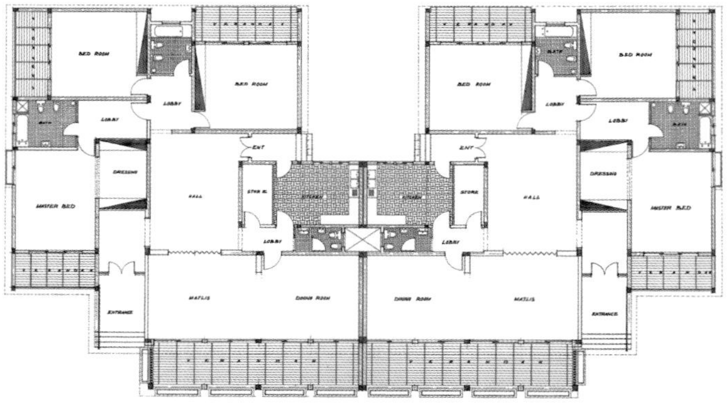

↑ Sheikh Jasem bin Mohammed Al Ahmed's villa designed by AEB in 1972, first-floor plan.

↓ Perspective view of Sheikh Jasem bin Mohammed Al Ahmed's villa.

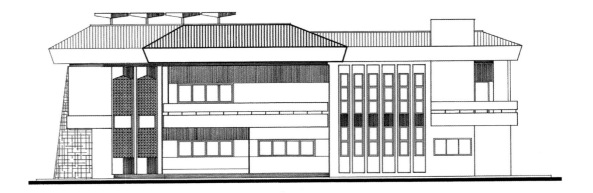

← Jaber bin Ahmed
Al Sulaiti's villa, designed
by AEB in 1974, right-side
elevation.

→ Front elevation (left)
and first-floor plan (right).

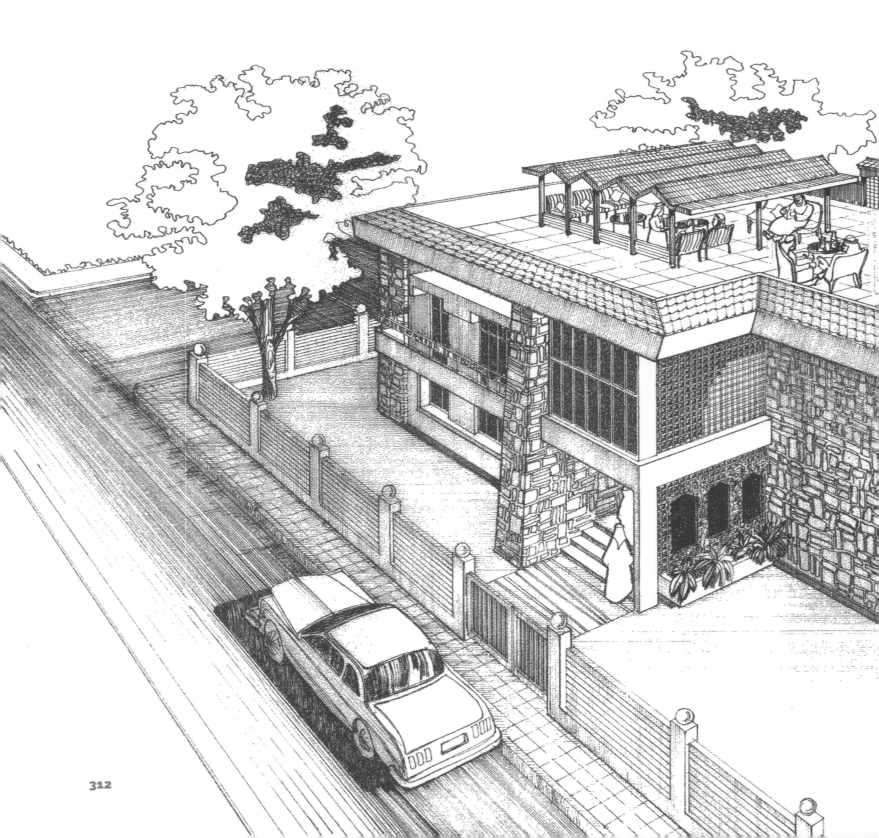

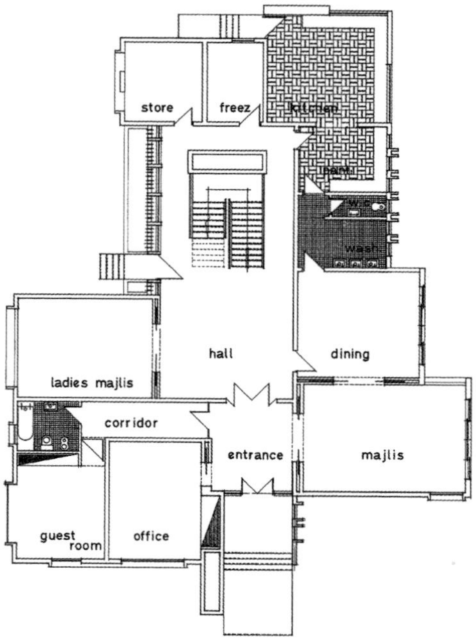

store   freez   kitchen

store

ladies majlis

hall   dining

corridor

entrance   majlis

guest room   office

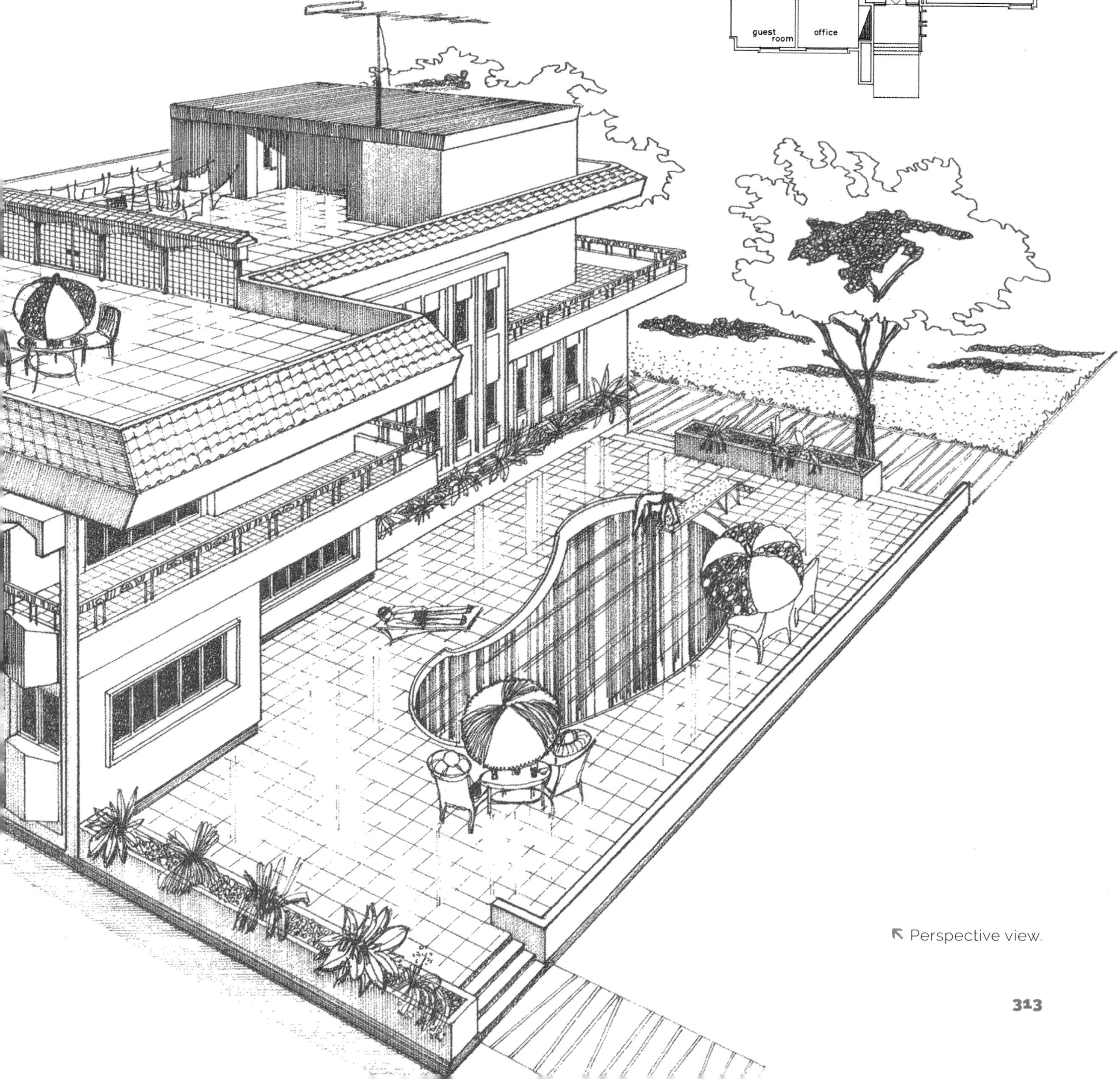

↖ Perspective view.

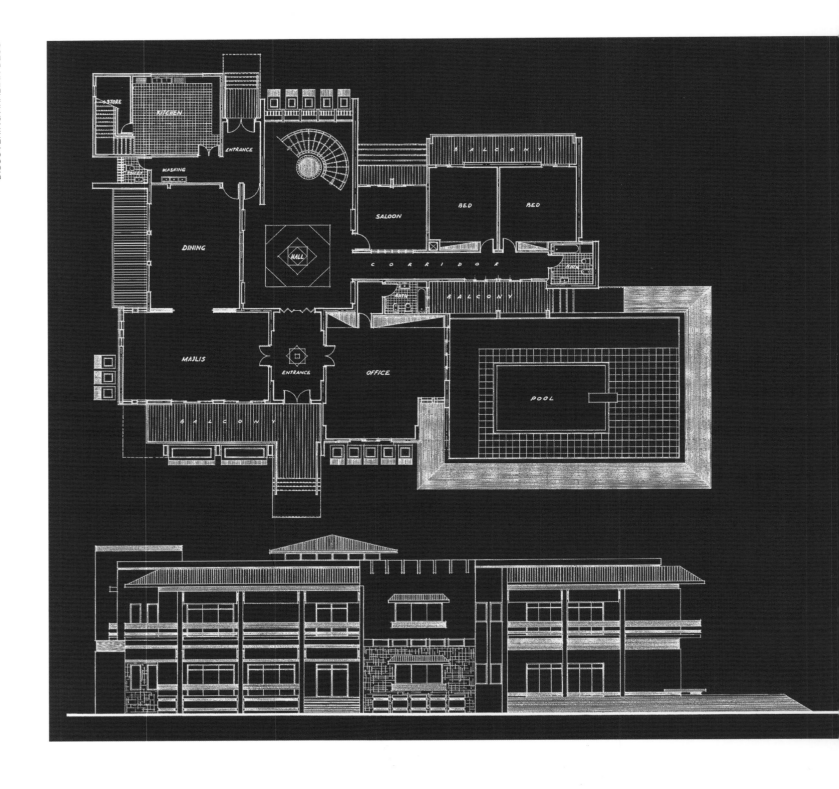

↑ Sheikh Nasser bin Hamad Al Thani's villa designed by AEB in 1972, first-floor plan (top) and front elevation (above).

↗ Second-floor (top) and left elevation (bottom).

→ Saad Abdel Latif Al Mana's villa designed by AEB in 1972, first-floor plan (left) and front elevation (right).

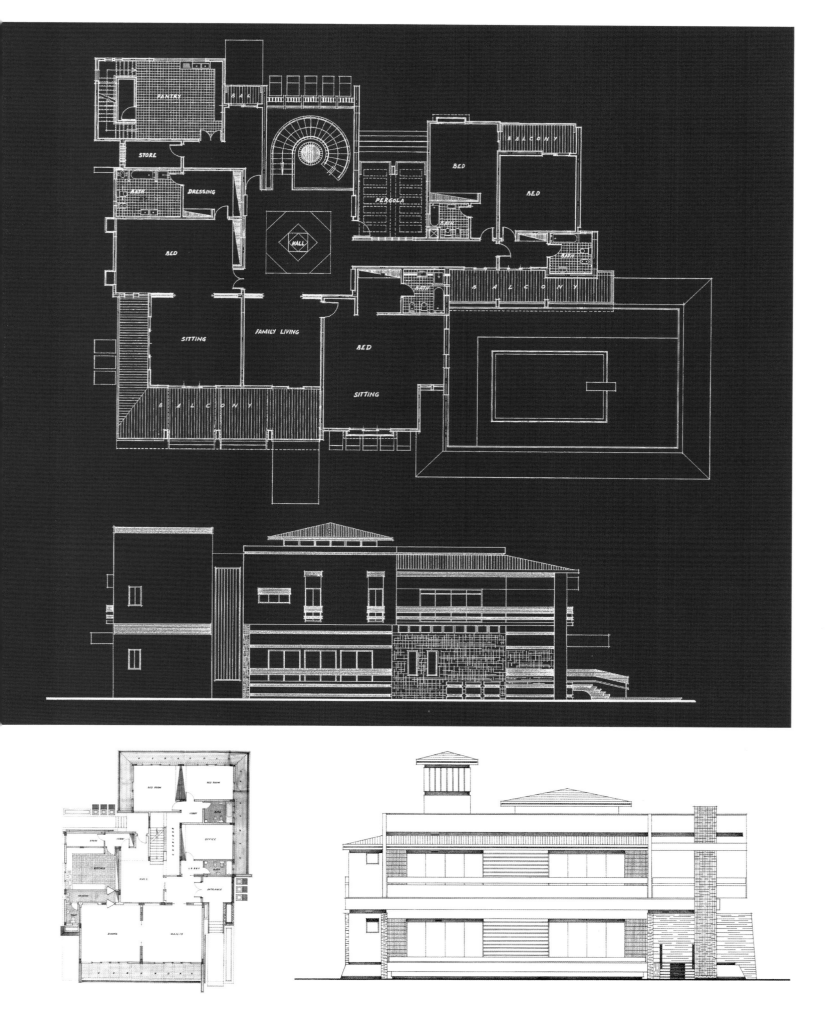

→ Perspective view for a villa designed by AEB in 1972 for an unknown client.

↓ First-floor plan for the unknown client's 1972 villa.

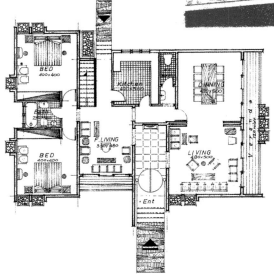

↖↑ Floor plans of a villa designed by AEB for another unknown client in 1972.

← Perspective view of the other unknown client's villa designed in 1972.

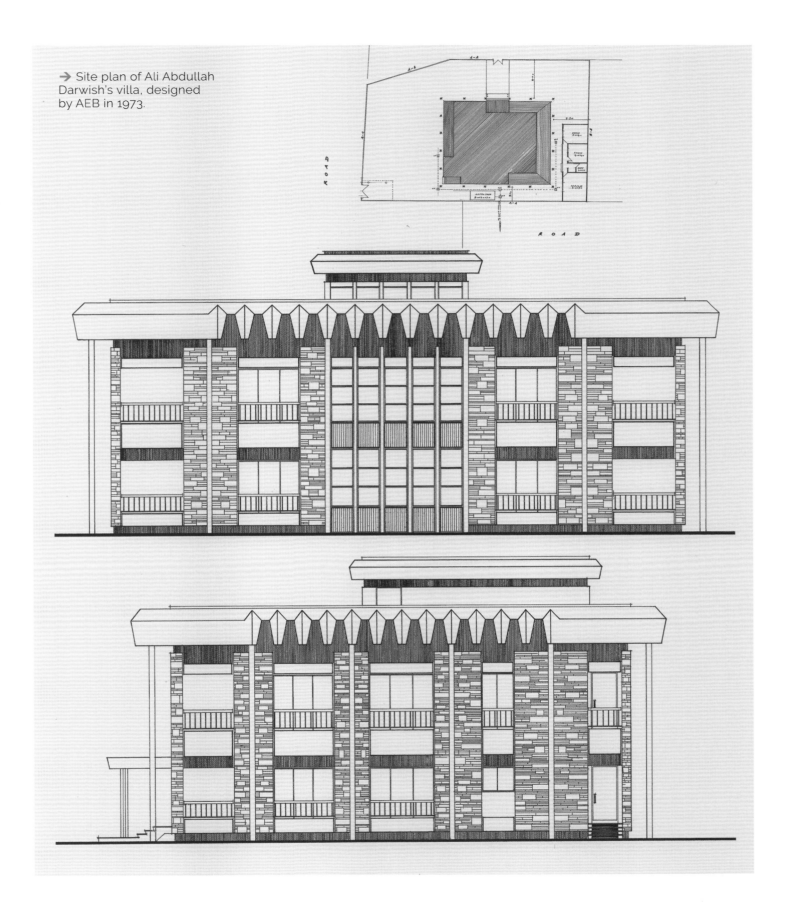

→ Site plan of Ali Abdullah Darwish's villa, designed by AEB in 1973.

↑ Ali Abdullah Darwish's villa, back elevation (middle) and right elevation (above).

Other villas were designed by AEB for Jaber bin Ahmed Al Sulaiti in 1974, Saad Abdel Latif Al Mana in 1972, Sheikh Nasser bin Hamad Al Thani in 1972, and Ali Abdullah Darwish in 1973. They all exhibit vertical features, pointed and rounded arches, chamfered parapets, and horizontal skylights.

317

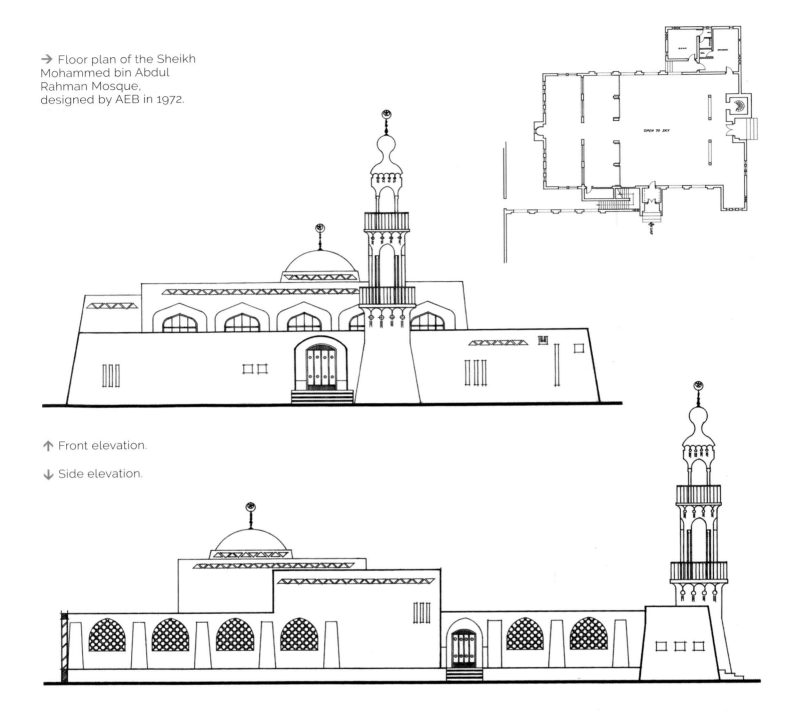

→ Floor plan of the Sheikh
Mohammed bin Abdul
Rahman Mosque,
designed by AEB in 1972.

↑ Front elevation.

↓ Side elevation.

Mosques

The early 1970s witnessed an increase in the number of mosques, different in
scales and styles, designed by AEB: the Sheikh Mohammed bin Abdul Rahman Mosque in 1972, the Sheikh Jasim bin Mohammed Al Thani Mosque in
1973, and the Sheikh Sohem bin Hamad Al Thani Mosque in 1975. AEB proposed three designs for three mosques that presented Nubian architecture, which was influenced by Hassan Fathy. These were mainly characterized by the balanced mass ratio and geometrical relation, the pointed arches,
the screen walls, and the simple decorative band at the top. Another four
mosques were designed by AEB for Sheikh Sohem bin Hamad Al Thani in 1975,

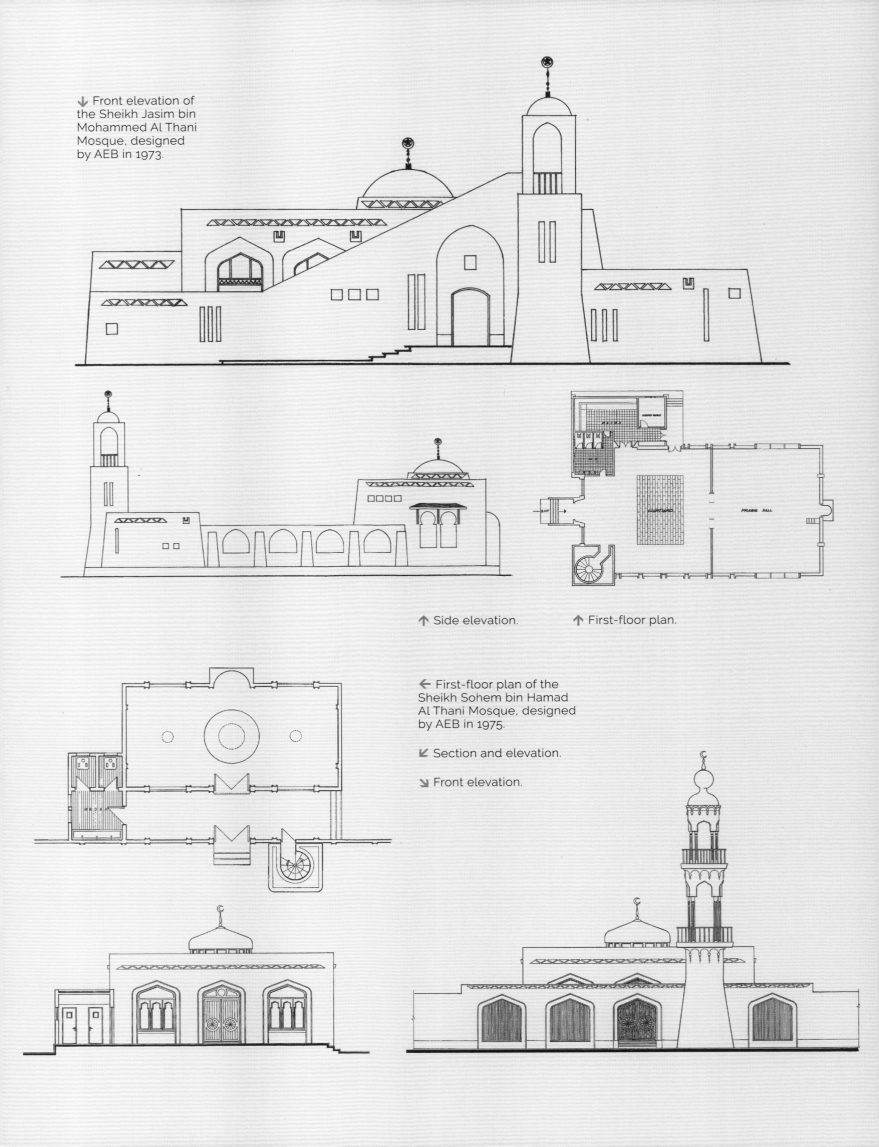

↓ Front elevation of the Sheikh Jasim bin Mohammed Al Thani Mosque, designed by AEB in 1973.

↑ Side elevation.

↑ First-floor plan.

← First-floor plan of the Sheikh Sohem bin Hamad Al Thani Mosque, designed by AEB in 1975.

↙ Section and elevation.

↘ Front elevation.

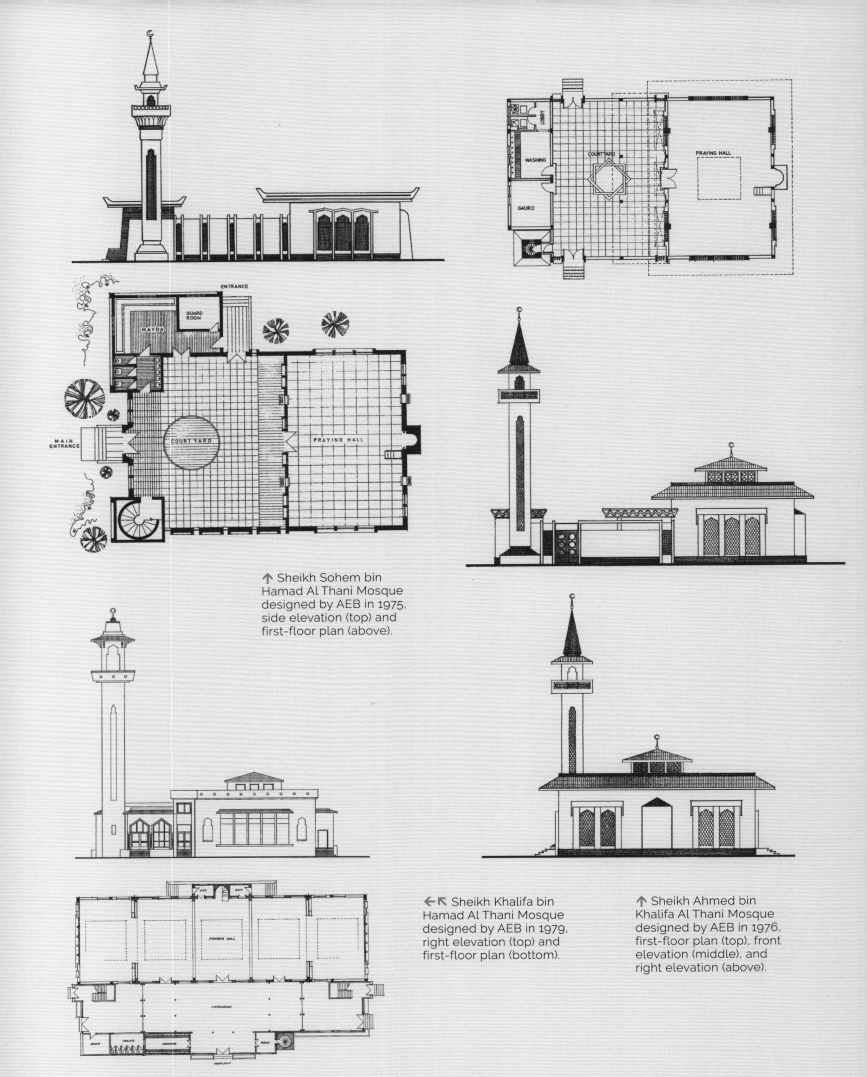

↑ Sheikh Sohem bin Hamad Al Thani Mosque designed by AEB in 1975, side elevation (top) and first-floor plan (above).

←↖ Sheikh Khalifa bin Hamad Al Thani Mosque designed by AEB in 1979, right elevation (top) and first-floor plan (bottom).

↑ Sheikh Ahmed bin Khalifa Al Thani Mosque designed by AEB in 1976, first-floor plan (top), front elevation (middle), and right elevation (above).

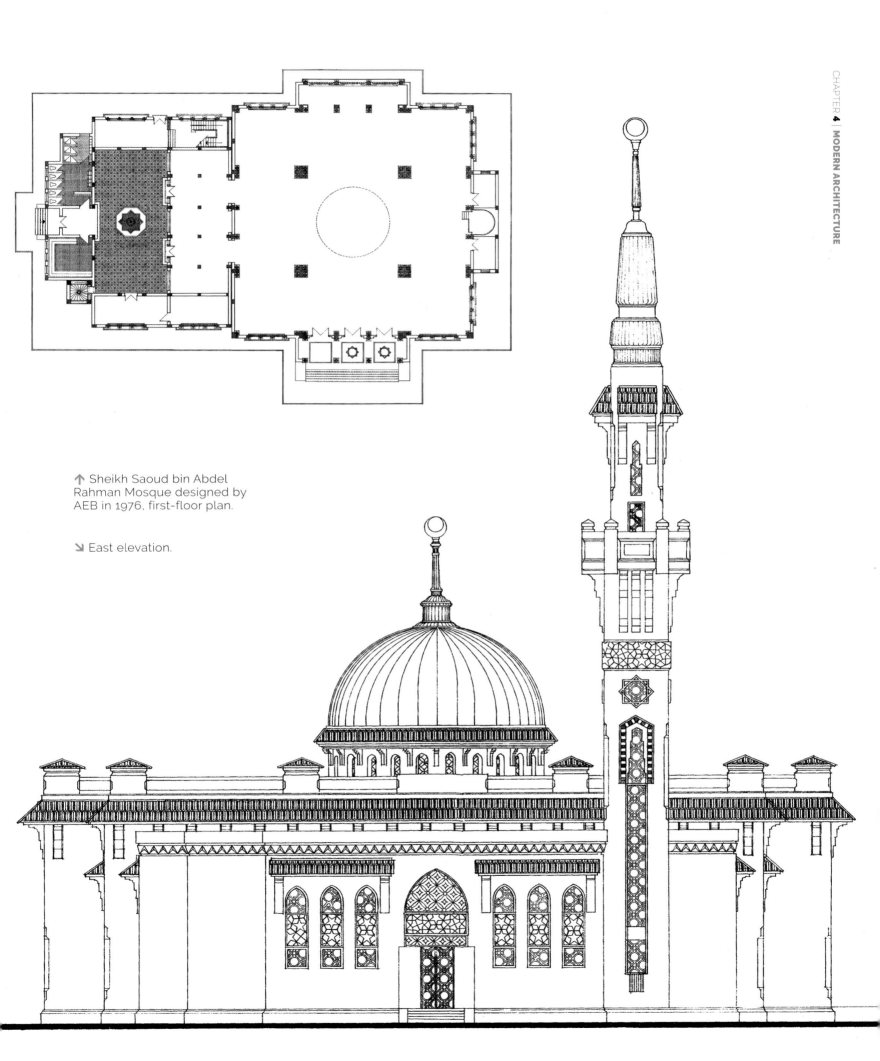

↑ Sheikh Saoud bin Abdel
Rahman Mosque designed by
AEB in 1976, first-floor plan.

↘ East elevation.

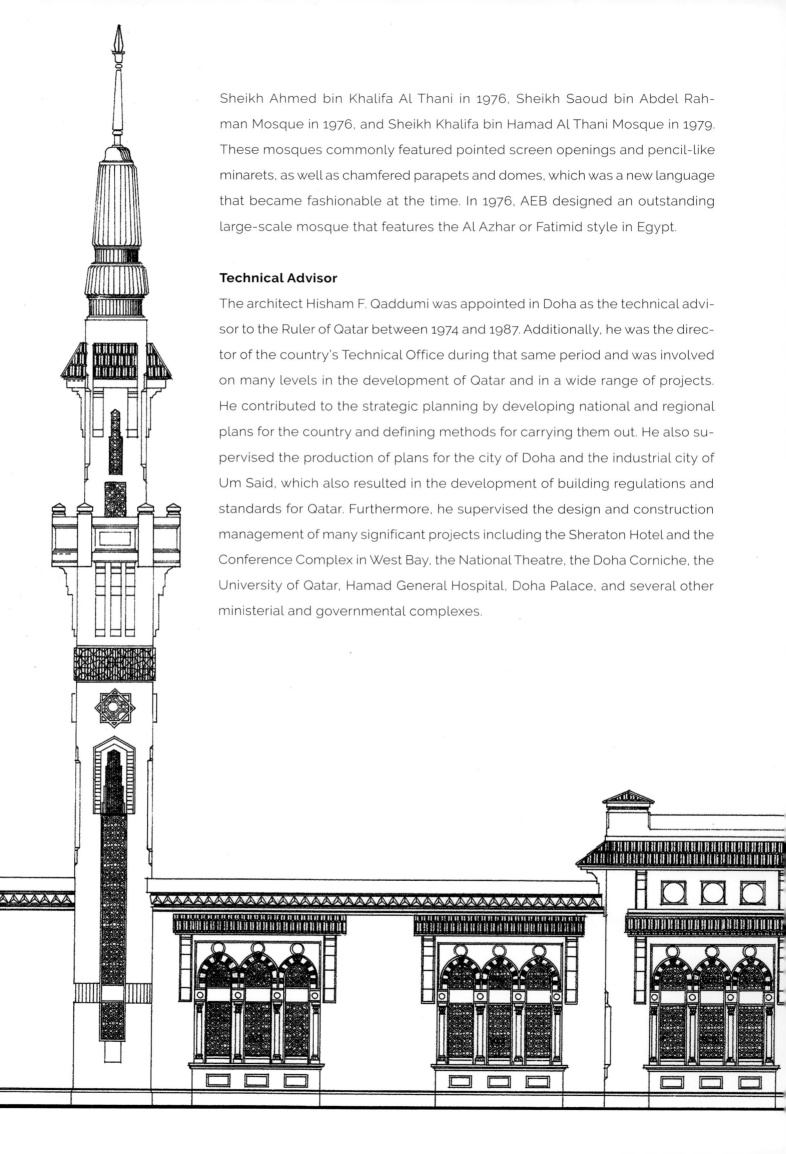

Sheikh Ahmed bin Khalifa Al Thani in 1976, Sheikh Saoud bin Abdel Rahman Mosque in 1976, and Sheikh Khalifa bin Hamad Al Thani Mosque in 1979. These mosques commonly featured pointed screen openings and pencil-like minarets, as well as chamfered parapets and domes, which was a new language that became fashionable at the time. In 1976, AEB designed an outstanding large-scale mosque that features the Al Azhar or Fatimid style in Egypt.

Technical Advisor

The architect Hisham F. Qaddumi was appointed in Doha as the technical advisor to the Ruler of Qatar between 1974 and 1987. Additionally, he was the director of the country's Technical Office during that same period and was involved on many levels in the development of Qatar and in a wide range of projects. He contributed to the strategic planning by developing national and regional plans for the country and defining methods for carrying them out. He also supervised the production of plans for the city of Doha and the industrial city of Um Said, which also resulted in the development of building regulations and standards for Qatar. Furthermore, he supervised the design and construction management of many significant projects including the Sheraton Hotel and the Conference Complex in West Bay, the National Theatre, the Doha Corniche, the University of Qatar, Hamad General Hospital, Doha Palace, and several other ministerial and governmental complexes.

Conclusion

The significance of the 1970s when compared to the 1950s and 1960s was not only due to the new efficient government, or the financial boom, or the quality of buildings produced, or magnitude of construction, but also globalization. The new Qatari Government started attracting international experts by commissioning western planning consultants for master planning, and local consultants to ensure cultural continuity. This was considered the first proper survey and planning carried out for the existing and future urban development of Doha. It was also considered the first time for setting protocols for land-use, building regulations, construction, services, and road networks. The landscaped roundabouts with monuments added a new modern feature to its road system and urban development. The newly designed and constructed ministries introduced early modern architectural features, which became a trend that could be found in other projects at that time. New types of buildings like sports clubs, shopping malls, and movie theaters also introduced new, modern architectural features that characterized the decade. The early modern style was also featured in the new palaces, villas, high-rise buildings, mixed-use buildings, and mosques. Some of these early modern buildings are still present today, marking that style in the city's urban fabric and architectural image.

↙ North elevation of the Sheikh Saoud bin Abdel Rahman Mosque.

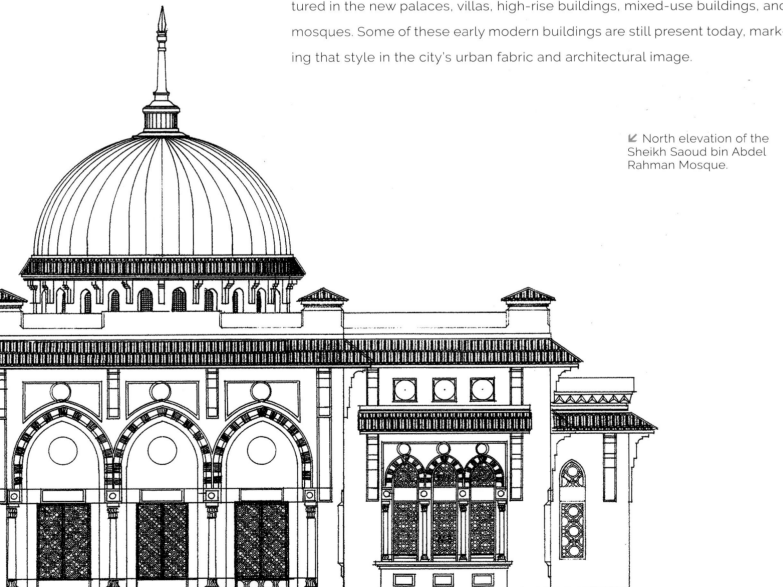

Biography

IBRAHIM MOHAMED JAIDAH

Born and raised in Qatar, Ibrahim M. Jaidah grew up with a passion for photography and art that taught him to appreciate the uniqueness of the past and present of his home country, Qatar, and inspired his career in architecture. As a result, he ranks today as a pioneer of a new architectural movement that combines the influences of local traditions with contemporary style to create memorable landmarks.

Ibrahim M. Jaidah is the Group CEO & Chief Architect of Arab Engineering Bureau, which he acquired in 1991. Since then, his firm has completed more than one thousand projects that he has overseen personally. In each project, Jaidah attempts to retain the identity of his culture while embracing the modern. His focus on vernacular architecture has brought a new dimension to this field within the region.

Jaidah has won numerous awards including the Organization of Islamic Capitals and Cities Award, Arab Town Organization Awards, and he has been nominated three times for the Agha Khan Award. In 2005, Jaidah was honored with the State of Qatar Encouragement Award.

His passion for vernacular architecture resulted in the publication of *The History of Qatari Architecture 1800-1950* (2009), which has become a reference work in many educational institutions in Qatar and the region. Since then, Ibrahim has authored *99 Domes Masjid of Imam Muhammad ibn Abdul Wahhab* (2015), initiated and published in collaboration with Qatar Museums, and *Qatari Style* (2019), which showcases the architectural identity in Qatar and celebrates the hospitality of the Middle East. He is also a frequent lecturer at local and international universities, and regularly participates as a speaker at international events relevant to the construction industry and architectural design.

Jaidah's projects reflect the cultural, historical, and environmental context in which they are situated. He is also a dedicated advocate for sustainability, and is a co-founder of the Qatar Green Building Council.

Bibliography

Arabic

Al-Jaber, M. S. "Qatar: Human Geography." Unpublished Master thesis submitted to Cairo University, 1977.

Al-Jaber, M. S. *The Economic and Social Development in Qatar (1930-1973)*. Doha: The Centre for Records and Humanities, 2002.

Al-Kuwari, F. M. "State of Qatar, a Study in Land Use, an Economic Geography." Unpublished PhD thesis, Department of Geography, University of Ain Shams, Cairo, 1987.

Al-Kuwari, N. Y. M. "City of Doha: a Study in Urban Geography." Unpublished PhD Thesis, Department of Geography, Cairo University, Cairo, 1994.

Al Obideli, S. A. *Wooden Doors in the Qatari Vernacular Architecture*. Doha: Katara Publishing House, 2019.

Al-Othman, N. M. *Dark Forearms: The story of Oil in Qatar*. Doha: 1980.

Al Shimlan, S. M. "Al bi'thah, newsletter of the Kuwaiti cultural delegations." 1952, issue 8, 405.

Ghazal, Z. R. *The Journey of Radio Qatar 1968-2018*. Doha: 2018.

Hassan, A. H. *Planning Cities in The State of Qatar*. Doha: Qatar University, 1994.

School Buildings Research Section. *The Development of School Buildings in the State of Qatar*. Doha: The School Building Administration Department, 1987.

English

Adham, K. "*Rediscovering the island: Doha's urbanity from pearls to spectacle.*" The Evolving Arab City: Tradition, Modernity and Urban Development, Elsheshtawy, Y., ed. Abingdon, UK, and New York: Routledge, 2008, 218–57.

Al Buainain, F. "Urbanisation in Qatar: A Study of the Residential and Commercial Land Development in Doha City, 1970–1997." PhD thesis, University of Salford, 1999.

Al-Kholaifi, M. J. *The Traditional Architecture in Qatar*. Doha: National Council for Culture, Arts and Heritage, Museum and Antiquities Department: 2006.

Al-Kuwari, M. K. "The Development of Doha and a Future Urban Strategy for Qatar." Unpublished PhD thesis, Department of Geography, University College of Swansea, Wales, 1992.

Al Mulla, M. B. *The Development of the First Qatar National Museum*. In "Cultural Heritage in the Arabian Peninsula: Debates, Discourses and Practices," edited by Exell, K. and T. Rico. Ashgate Publishing, 2014, 117–25.

Alraouf, A. A. "Constructing future utopias: a new paradigm of knowledge-based urban development in Doha". *Traditional Dwellings and Settlements Review* 22:1 (2010): 46–47.

Alraouf, A. A. "A tale of two suqs: the paradox of gulf urban diversity". *Open House Int.* 37:2 (2012): 72–81.

Alraouf, A. A. *A Paradigm Shift from Resources Economy to Knowledge Economy: The Case of Urban Development in Qatar*. In "Proceedings of ISOCARP Conference Cities We Have vs. Cities We Need." Durban, South Africa: 12-16 September 2016, 248–65.

Alraouf, A. A. *The Knowledge Urbanity in Qatar: An Alternative Dynamic*. In Alraouf, Ali A. "Knowledge-Based Urban Development in the Middle East." PA, USA: IGI Global, 2018, 60-79.

Alraouf, A. A. *The Value of Less and Small: Transforming Metropolitan Doha into Connected, Human and Resilient Urban Settlements*. In "Proceedings of 55th International Society of City and Regional Planners (ISOCARP) World Planning Congress." Jakarta-Bogor, Indonesia: 2019, 58-77.

Al Thani, H. A., Taha, M. Y., and A. Peterson. *Forts, Strongholds and Towers: A Documentary Study of Historical and Heritage Sites in Qatar*. Doha: Katara Publishing House, 2016.

Beguin-Billecocq, X. *Le Qatar et les français*. Paris: Collection Relations Internationales & Culture, 2003.

Boussaa, D. "Al Asmakh historic district in Doha, Qatar: from an urban slum to living heritage." *J. Architect. Conserv.* 20(1): (2014a), 2–15.

Boussaa, D. "Rehabilitation as a catalyst of sustaining a living heritage: the case of Souk Waqif in Doha, Qatar." *Art Des. Rev.* 2: (2014b), 62–71.

British Library Partnership Team. "Country Profile: Qatar." Qatar Digital Library, https://www.qdl.qa/en/country-profile-qatar. Accessed April 11, 2021.

Carter, R. *Sea of Pearls: Seven Thousand Years of the Industry that Shaped the Gulf*. Arabian Publishing, 2010.

Carter, R., Eddisford, D. "Origins of Doha—season 1 archive report," 2013. Doha: UCL-Qatar, http://www.academia.edu/attachments/32352254/download_file. Accessed October 2020.

Carter, R., Eddisford, D. "Origins of Doha Project, season 2: joint QM-UCL Qatar Old Doha rescue excavations 2013–2014," forthcoming. Doha: UCL-Qatar.

"Doha (Al Bida) Harbour," British Library: India Office Records and Private Papers, IOR/L/PS/12/2160B, f 53. In Qatar Digital Library, https://www.qdl.qa/archive/81055/vdc_100042760282.0x00000e. Accessed April 11, 2021.

Eddisford, D., Roberts, K. *Origins of Doha Project, Season 2: Historic Building Survey Report*, 2014. Doha: UCL-Qatar. https://originsofdoha.files.wordpress.com/2015/03/origins-of-doha-and-qatar-season-2-building-survey-report.pdf, Accessed October 2020.

Eddisford, D., Carter, R. "The vernacular architecture of Doha, Qatar." *Post-Medieval Archaeology*, 51(1): (2017), 81-107. doi:10.1080/00794236.2017.1320918

Exell, K., Rico, T. "There is no heritage in Qatar: Orientalism, colonialism and other problematic histories." *World Archaeology* 45(4): (2013), 670–85. doi:10.1080/00438243.2013.852069

Fletcher, R., Carter, R. "Mapping the Growth of an Arabian Gulf Town: The Case of Doha, Qatar." *Journal of the Economic and Social History of the Orient* 60: (2017), 42–87. 10.1163/15685209-12341432.

Garba, S. B., Boussaa, D., Ghada, F., Al-Yafei, A. M., Al-Hassan, A. A., Aldarwish, A., and H. Bakhit. "Heritage Documentation and National Identity in Qatar; Case of the Al-Zaman House." *International Journal of Heritage Architecture*, WIT Press, 1(3): (2016). http://www.witpress.com/journals/ha.

"Gazetteer of the Persian Gulf. Vol. II. Geographical and Statistical. J. G. Lorimer. 1908." British Library: India Office Records and Private Papers, IOR/L/PS/20/C91/4. In Qatar Digital Library. https://www.qdl.qa/node/506. Accessed April 11, 2021.

Gotting, F. J. "History of medicine in Qatar." PhD thesis, University of Glasgow, 1995.

Hobbs, M. "George Barnes Brucks and the First English Survey of the Gulf." Qatar Digital Library, https://www.qdl.qa/en/george-barnes-brucks-and-first-english-survey-gulf. Accessed April 11, 2021.

Hobbs, M. "Qatari History: Pivotal Moments Revealed in India Office Records." Qatar Digital Library, https://www.qdl.qa/en/qatari-history-pivotal-moments-revealed-india-office-records. Accessed April 11, 2021.

Jaidah, I. M., Bourennane, M. *The History of Qatari Architecture from 1800 to 1950*. Milan: Skira Editore, 2009.

Jaidah, I. M. *99 Domes: Masjid of Muhammed Ibn Abdul Wahhab*. Milan: Skira Editore, 2015.

Jaidah, I. M. *AEB 1966–2016: Fifty years of architectural design in Qatar*. Milan: Skira Editore, 2016.

Khalil, R., Khaled. S. *Rebuilding Old Downtowns: The Case of Doha, Qatar*. 2012. 10.13140/2.1.3296.1600.

Kobaisi, A. J. "The Development of Education in Qatar, 1950–1977 With an Analysis of Some Educational Problems." Durham theses, Durham University, 1979. Available at Durham E-Theses Online: http://etheses.dur.ac.uk/1856/

Lorimer, J. G. *Gazetteer of the Persian Gulf, Oman and Central Arabia*. Calcutta: Superintendent Government Printing, 1908.

Othman, N. *With Their Bare Hands: The Story of the Oil Industry in Qatar*. London: Longman Publishing Group, 1984.

Palgrave, W. G. *Personal Narrative of a Year's Journey through Central and Eastern Arabia 1862–63*. London: Macmillan, 1866.

"Persian Gulf Gazetteer. Part 1. Historical and political materials. Précis of Katar [Qatar] affairs, 1873-1904." British Library: India Office Records and Private Papers, IOR/L/PS/20/C243. In Qatar Digital Library, https://www.qdl.qa/annos/search/81055/vdc_100000000884.0x0001c9. Accessed April 11, 2021.

"Persian Gulf Gazetteer. Part 2. Geographical and Descriptive Materials. Section II Western Side of the Gulf." British Library: India Office Records and Private Papers, IOR/R/15/1/727. In Qatar Digital Library, https://www.qdl.qa/archive/81055/vdc_100000000193.0x0002bd. Accessed April 11, 2021.

Photograph No. 3, "Dohah (Central) Looking NW." British Library: India Office Records and Private Papers, IOR/L/PS/12/1956, f 10. In Qatar Digital Library <https://www.qdl.qa/archive/81055/vdc_100040870685.0x000004. Accessed April 11, 2021.

Photograph No. 4, "Dohah (West) Looking South." British Library: India Office Records and Private Papers, IOR/L/PS/12/1956, f 11. In Qatar Digital Library, https://www.qdl.qa/archive/81055/vdc_100040870685.0x000005. Accessed April 11, 2021.

Pollalis, S. N., Ardalan, N. *Gulf Sustainable Urbanism: The Past* (1st ed., Vol. 1). Hamad Bin Khalifa University Press: 2019. ISBN 9789927118951.

Pollalis, S. N., Ardalan, N. *Gulf Sustainable Urbanism: The Past* (1st ed., Vol. 2). Hamad Bin Khalifa University Press: 2019. ISBN 9789927118968.

Radoine, H. *Souq Waqif: Onsite Technical Review Report*. Geneva: Aga Khan Award for Architecture, 2010.

"Rough Map of the Katar Peninsula." British Library: India Office Records and Private Papers, IOR/R/15/1/370, f 164. In Qatar Digital Library, https://www.qdl.qa/archive/81055/vdc_100023556313.0x000001. Accessed April 11, 2021.

Scharfenort, N. T*he Masheireb Project in Doha: The Heritage of New Urban Design in Doha*. In "Cultural Heritage in the Arabian Peninsula: Debates, Discourses and Practices," edited by Exell, K. and T. Rico. Ashgate Publishing, 2014, 189–204.

Shandas, V., Makido, Y., and S. Ferwati. "Rapid Urban Growth and Land Use Patterns in Doha, Qatar: Opportunities for Sustainability?" *European Journal of Sustainable Development Research* 1(2) 11: (2017). doi: 10.20897/ejosdr.201711.

"Trigonometrical Plan of the Harbour of El Biddah on the Arabian Side of the Persian Gulf." By Lieuts. J. M. Guy and G. B. Brucks, H. C. Marine. Drawn by Lieut. M. Houghton. British Library: Map Collections, IOR/X/3694. In Qatar Digital Library, https://www.qdl.qa/archive/81055/vdc_100000010848.0x000001. Accessed April 11, 2021.

Wiedmann, F., Salama, A. M. *Demystifying Doha: On Architecture and Urbanism in an Emerging City*. Ashgate Publishing, 2013.

Wiedmann, F., Salama, A. M. "From pre-oil settlement to post-oil hub: The urban transformation of Doha." *Int. J. Archit. Res.* 7(2): (2013), 146–59.

Glossary

Al Askar: the military.

Al Banaa: a mason or master builder.

Al Hukumah: the government.

Al Kutub: single noun *kitab* (book), plural *kutub* (books).

Al Qadeem: referring to anything old.

Al Qubib: single noun *qubba* (dome), plural *qibab* and *qubeib* (small domes).

Al Shuyukh: single *sheikh*, and it is used for the head of an Arab family or of a clan or tribe. It can also mean the chief of an Arab village or district or a religious official.

Amiri Diwan: the governmental headquarters of the State of Qatar.

Badgheer: a rectangular opening designed to let the air in and keep the dust out.

Bait: a house.

Baraha: big open space surrounded by buildings like a plaza and defined by local names.

Basgill: bamboo lain over *danshal* wood beams in traditional roof construction.

Courtyard: an open courtyard is the place around which the spaces are organized. The courtyard is usually an area with shade and a source of water to provide humidity.

Dakkah: Qatari name for a bench by the wall (also *dacha*).

Danshal: a tree that grows in Zanzibar (now part of Tanzania). Its wood was imported and used in the construction of traditional Qatari buildings.

Dar: the house of.

Farij: a neighborhood (sometimes the word *freedj* is used).

Furdha: Qatari name for port.

Qalaat: a fort.

Iwan: a vaulted hall that opens onto a courtyard on one side.

Juss: a white powder used as a mortar and paint after mixing with water.

Khokha: a small door inside a bigger door to allow entry without opening the big doors.

Libn: earth and chaff mixture for building.

Liwan: the space under the arcade.

Ma'arif: single noun *ma'rifa* (knowledge or education).

Madrasah: the word madrasah (also madrasa) is Arabic for school and is commonly used throughout the Arab and Islamic world to refer to any learning place. It also refers to Koranic schools.

Manara: the minaret of the mosque.

Majlis: a formal room for receiving guests (also known as *diwaniya*).

Manghrour: a mat of woven cane or palm tree branches.

Mihrab: a niche in the wall of a mosque that faces toward Mecca (see *qibla*): it indicates the direction of prayer. Muslims around the world face the direction of Mecca when they pray.

Mashrabiya: an architectural element, a type of projecting oriel window enclosed with carved wood latticework, located on the upper floor of a building, characteristic of traditional architecture in the Islamic world.

Masjid: the place of worship and prayer (also called mosque).

Riwaq: an open porch or balcony overlooking an interior courtyard, where people would sit during the hot season because it provides more shade than the open courtyard.

Sikka: an alleyway.

Souq: a traditional Arab market.

Tendail: a mason or master builder.

Ustad: a mason or master builder.

Wadi: the bed or valley of a stream that is usually dry except during the rainy season.

Design & Copy Editing
Break Point S.a.s.

© 2022 Mondadori Libri S.p.A.
Distributed in English throughout the World
by Rizzoli International Publications Inc.
300 Park Avenue South
New York, NY 10010, USA

ISBN: 978-8-8918-3486-7

2022 2023 2024 2025 / 10 9 8 7 6 5 4 3 2 1

First edition: December 2022

This volume was printed at Errestampa S.r.l.
Via Portico 27, Orio al Serio, Bergamo
Printed in Italy

Visit us online:
Facebook.com/RizzoliNewYork
Twitter: @Rizzoli_Books
Instagram.com/RizzoliBooks
Pinterest.com/RizzoliBooks
Youtube.com/user/RizzoliNY
Issuu.com/Rizzoli